Reclaiming Diné History

Reclaiming Diné History

The Legacies of Navajo Chief Manuelito and Juanita

Jennifer Nez Denetdale

The University of Arizona Press   Tucson

The University of Arizona Press

Library of Congress Cataloging-in-Publication Data
Denetdale, Jennifer.
Reclaiming Diné history : the legacies of Navajo Chief Manuelito
and Juanita / Jennifer Nez Denetdale.
p. cm.
Includes bibliographical references and index.
ISBN 978-0-8165-2420-4 (hardcover : alk. paper) —
ISBN 978-0-8165-2660-4 (pbk. : alk. paper)
1. Manuelito, Navajo chief, 1818–1893. 2. Juanita, ca. 1845–
1910. 3. Navajo Indians—Biography. 4. Navajo Indians—Public
opinion. 5. Navajo Indians—History. 6. Southwest, New—History.
I. Title.
E99.N3.M367 2007
979.004'97260092—dc22 [B]   2006039812

Publication of this book is made possible in part by the proceeds of a permanent endowment created with the assistance of a Challenge Grant from
the National Endowment for the Humanities, a federal agency.

An earlier version of chapter 4 was previously published as "'One of the
Queenliest Women in Dignity, Grace, and Character I Have Ever Met':
Photography and Navajo Women—Portraits of Juanita, 1868–1910," *New
Mexico Historical Review* 79 (Summer 2004): 289–318; copyright © Univer-
sity of New Mexico Board of Regents, all rights reserved. An earlier version
of chapter 5 was published as "Remembering Our Grandmothers: Navajo
Women and the Power of Oral Tradition," in *Indigenous Peoples' Wisdom
and Power: Affirming Our Knowledge through Narratives*, ed. Nomalungelo I.
Goduka and Julian E. Kunnie (Aldershot: Ashgate Publishing, 2006).

Manufactured in the United States of America on acid-free, archival-
quality paper.

Dedicated to Rose and Frank Nez

ˈAhéheeˈ, Shimá dóó shizheˈé

Contents

Figures

Acknowledgments

This study began as a dissertation at Northern Arizona University, where I had the opportunity to work with Susan Deeds, Karen Powers, and George Lubick. Their belief in my ability to be a historian bolstered my determination to become the first Diné with a Ph.D. in history. NAU remains my second home. I spend many wonderful hours in the company of my friends and colleagues Sanjam Ahulwalia (shopping trips), Sanjay Joshi, Loma Ishii, Leilah Danielson, Eric Meeks, Ann Cummins, Jeffrey Berglund, and Monica Brown.

Thanks to Patti Hartmann and Alan M. Schroder at the University of Arizona Press for all of their hard work. I am especially grateful for Patti's patience and her commitment bringing this study to fruition.

A Katrin H. Lamon Fellowship (2003) from the School of American Research (SAR) afforded me the luxury of thinking more deeply about how to develop and craft my study. SAR fellows, including Lynn Meskell, read drafts and helped move the study toward completion. At the University of New Mexico, our Indigenous Scholars Group— Elizabeth Archuleta, Lloyd Lee, Glenabah Martinez, Tiffany Lee, Eric Tippeconnic, Ann Calhoun, and Leola Tsinniginnie—willingly read drafts of various chapters. In addition to the Indigenous Scholars Group, Native Studies faculty and staff provided camaraderie. These included Greg Cajete, Tiffany Lee, Beverly Singer, Maria Williams, Mary Bowannie, and Delia Halona. I always found friendship in the home of Delia Halona and Jeremy Vicente. I am very appreciative for the fabulous support and encouragement of Andrea Smith,

J. Kehaulani Kauanui, Angela Gonzalez, Audra Simpson, James Riding In, Susan Miller, and Estevan Rael-Gálvez. Their work in Indigenous Studies and history has inspired me to formulate my own Diné history and continue my work to develop critical Navajo studies.

Many thanks to Kathy M'Closkey, James Faris, Andrea Smith, Liz Archuleta, Barbara Reyes, Virginia Scharff, and Larry Emerson for graciously agreeing to read chapters. Their insightful criticism has improved my work tremendously. I also thank the anonymous reviewers for their time and suggestions—their critical and thoughtful comments could only make for a better manuscript. In addition, I thank many UNM colleagues who have provided a supportive atmosphere: Barbara Reyes, Sam Truett, Pat Risso, Jane Slaughter, Durwood Ball, Margaret Connell-Szasz, Paul Hutton, Cynthia Radding, Virginia Scharff, Alyosha Goldstein, Carmen Nocentelli, Gail Houston, among many others. David Brugge, Peter Iverson, Martha Blue, Charlotte Frisbie, Marsha Weisiger, Winona Begay, and Tracy Goode supported me in all sorts of ways, from taking me out to lunch, to sharing references with me, to sending notes of encouragement my way. I thank Dave Brugge for sharing his knowledge on existing studies of Navajos. Thanks to Roseann Willink and Marilyn Help-Hood for help with Diné spellings and translations, and to the Judy Giesberg and Ed Fierros gang, who always welcomed me into their home, where we spent many hours talking about our craft. I am also grateful for the assistance of Cate Gilles (1956–2001), who took many of the family photographs for this project. I miss her dearly. Thanks also to Gwen Saul and Carl Bennett, who assisted with the photographs. Thanks to Jenny Nez and Cherie Lee Bytheway for making sense out of the genealogy and creating a fabulous chart. My genealogy outline developed out of sources from land claims papers and consultations with Rose Nez, Joan Kinsel, Charles Manuelito, Faye Yazzie, Art Holyan, Nancy Allison, Ira Burbank, Larson Manuelito, Herman Morris, and Peter Sage. Their interest in my book project served as a source of inspiration for me. As I worked many hours revising this manuscript, I listened to the music of Radmilla Cody and Joe Tohonnie Jr. Thank you both for such beautiful music!

This study began as an idea that I presented to *shi cheii* (maternal grandfather) Charles Manuelito, who enthusiastically embraced it. Charles shared newspaper clippings and letters from his private collection with me. Sadly, Charles died in January 2003, before he could see the published history of his great-grandparents, Manuelito and Juanita. Other grandparents, Joan Kinsel, Mike Allison Sr., Art Holyan, Helena Bitsilly, Faye Yazzie, and Robert Manuelito expressed support and enthusiasm for this project. Matrilineally, we are all descended from our grandmother, Juanita, and have taken on her clan, the Tł'ógi—which means Zia, or Weaver in English. On occasion, shi cheii Art Holyan calls me to pass on information about other Navajos who are interested in my study and often claim lineage to Manuelito. Shi cheii Mike Allison Sr. died in 2004 at the age of one hundred four. His wife Anna Allison (*Shi másáni*) had died two years earlier. Mike Sr. and Anna invited my mother and me into their home, where we spent wonderful summer afternoons listening to stories. The Allison clan—Mike Sr. and Anna's children and their families—were wonderful and invited my family to celebrate the anniversaries and birthdays of Mike Sr. and Anna. In particular, Nancy Allison, the youngest of the Allison family and the only daughter of Mike and Anna's ten children, graciously supplied information and photographs for this project. In previous works, talks, and publications, I had referenced "Mike Sr." as "Michael Sr." Nancy Allison kindly corrected me, telling me that her father's name was Mike.

My many Tł'ógi relatives—almost the entire clan—never failed to ask me how my study was going and when it would be finished. When my article on the photographs of Juanita was published in the *New Mexico Historical Review*, I was obligated to pass it out to them. Thanks to Herman and Pat Morris, Peterson Yazzie, Priscilla Duncan, Jodee Dennison, Charleen Benally, Stella Shirley, LaVerne Cinniginnie (1944–2005), Rex Morris Jr., Richard Morris, Sherman and Alice Manuelito, Ernest and Sarah Manuelito, Donna and Andrienne Dennison, and Larinda Dennison and all of their families for their encouragement and faith in my ability to complete this study.

My mother, Rose, and my father, Frank, were sources of inspiration to me throughout the years I worked through personal traumas and strove to recover my spirit. They never failed to stand with me as I struggled through my years of education. My father, a healer and roadman, sustained me with prayers of protection, healing, and blessings. Thank you for the beautiful prayers, stories, and songs. My children, Nathaniel and his wife, Billie Jean; Nicholas and his son, Tyler Frank Denetdale; and Melissa and her son Terry Douglas Begay, were understanding and supportive of their ceaselessly working mother.

Although we have gone through hard times, we have managed to stay close to each other. My sister, Jenny Nez, and her sons, Brian and Eric Bowman, were faithful companions throughout this study. My sister, Wanda Orr; her husband, Colin; and their children, Kelly and Heather Orr, Camilla, Ammon, Nathan, and Hillary, saw me through some of the hardest times in my life. Many hours on the phone with Wanda helped me keep my sanity. We shared our many triumphs and misfortunes with each other. My sister, Victoria Denetdale; her husband, Herman, and their children, Miranda and Aaron, were encouraging and often came to the Native American Church prayer meetings that my father sponsored for me. My brother, Alexander (the youngest of us), displaying his superb wit, provided all of us with much laughter. I'm proud to be a part of the Frank Nez family, all of whom supported this project with prayers, money, food, coffee, love, and laughter. And of course, I have to acknowledge my infamous pug, who is simply known as The PUG. Pug is a faithful companion who keeps watch over all of us at the Dibé bitó (Sheep Springs).

A number of scholarships and fellowships made this study possible: the Office of Navajo Nation Scholarship and Financial Assistance, the NAU Frances McAllister Scholarship, the NAU History Department, the Ford Foundation, the Smithsonian Institution, the Museum of Northern Arizona, the Katrin H. Lamon Fellowship from the School of American Research, and the UNM Department of History. During my research trips to archives in Washington, D.C., Chris O'Brien of the Ford Foundation generously opened her home to me.

Any proceeds from this book will go to the Office of Navajo Nation Scholarship and Financial Assistance. The Navajo scholarship staff has been generous. By donating any proceeds to their scholarship fund, I begin to give back to my community.

As I traveled to archives, I met so many librarians and archivists who gave their time. Thanks to staff at the NAU Cline Library's Special Collections, the Library of Congress, the National Archives, the Navajo Nation Museum and Library, the Autry National Center, and the Southwest Museum. Thanks also to Irving Nelson, program manager at the Navajo Nation Library, and his staff for being so helpful with the Land Claims Papers and library materials.

I am truly fortunate to have such splendid family, friends, and colleagues.

Reclaiming Diné History

1/Introduction

In March 1998, I found myself navigating Los Angeles traffic as I made my way to the Southwest Museum, in Pasadena, California. In George Wharton James's *Indian Blankets and Their Makers*, I had come across a photograph of Juanita, one of the wives of the nineteenth-century Diné leader, Manuelito (see fig. 12).[1] I didn't know that photographs of Juanita, who was my great-great-great-grandmother, existed. In the photograph, Juanita sits against an adobe wall. The hem of her woven dress, called a *biil* in Navajo, reaches almost to her ankles, and she stares back at the camera's eye.[2] She is elderly, a grandmother. Her stern gaze hints at her strength.

An investigation revealed that a series of photographs of Juanita and her family—her daughters, sons-in-law, and grandchildren—rested in the Southwest Museum's American Indian Collection (figs. 9–12). I also discovered that Juanita's dress and the rug she had woven, ostensibly for George Wharton James, were part of the museum's collection. The archivist made arrangements for me to see the dress. Kathleen Whitaker, the curator, was processing a collection of Indian weavings for preservation treatment. Juanita's dress (fig. 21) was included in the array of weavings to be sent out. If I went to Whitaker's work place that day, I would get a chance to see Juanita's dress and rug. Considered rare, the dress was one of a very few that has survived from the early reservation period, 1868–75.[3] Made of black wool with panels of bayeta red at the top and the hem, the dress showed extreme wear.[4] The fibers at the waist were loose. Perhaps it had been caused by the overlay of a woven red sash, and, on top of that, the silver belt that Navajo women wore to cinch their dresses. Turning the dress around to its backside, I noted Juanita's handiwork as a seamstress. She had patched portions of the lower half of the dress with calico and black cotton fabrics. White thread looped the border of each patch. A look at the inside of the dress revealed extensive patching.

That dress had once belonged to Juanita. According to George Wharton James, Juanita had treasured the dress and had kept it stored away as a memento. During one of his sojourns into the Southwest, probably in 1902, James had appropriated Juanita's dress. He claimed that Juanita had been initially reluctant to part with the dress, but that she had eventually relented and presented it to him in a spirit of friendship.[5] James was one of those white men who had promoted the Southwest as a place of splendor and exotica. In his efforts to promote and commodify the Southwest, he was not above tricking the Natives into having a photograph taken. He went to great lengths to procure their valuable things. Once he had appropriated their rugs, dresses, blankets, pottery, and baskets, he offered them for sale as rare and authentic Indian objects. These "objects" often had significant meanings for their Native owners. What had the dress meant to Juanita? Juanita had lived through one of the most traumatic periods in Navajo history. She had lost some of her children to slave traders. She possibly might have been sold as a slave herself. She had seen her family members die during the Navajo wars. What kinds of memories had the dress held for her?

That afternoon, as I held my great-great-great-grandmother's dress, in a place far from Navajo Land, I thought about the journeys the Diné have undergone. In many ways, the fate of the dress reminded me about how the Navajo past has been constructed by non-Navajo writers and of my efforts to recover a past that highlights what we deem important, which includes valuing our traditional beliefs and values. The dress, like the history of Navajos, has been appropriated, classified, and defined by non-Navajos. It lay in a foreign place, a museum, its Diné meaning obscured. Yet it is valued because it had once belonged to the wife of a war chief, because it was one of a kind, rare. The dress is made rare by the ongoing conquest of the Navajos, which seeks to destroy all facets of difference and yet at the same time romanticizes and yearns for what it has destroyed.

What I knew about Juanita and Manuelito was no different from what most other Diné—or non-Indians, for that matter—knew (see figs. 3 and 7). In the American histories about Navajos, Manuelito plays an important part in resisting American expansion, whereas Navajo women like Juanita are virtually invisible. In my search to find out more about Juanita and Manuelito, I undertook many journeys. I read many books that narrate the Navajo past. I traveled across Navajo Land to interview the descendants of Juanita and Manuelito and to archives and libraries across the United States. According to standard Navajo histories, Manuelito was the most vocal warrior to resist the Mexican and American invasions in the nineteenth century. With the military defeat of the Diné after 1868, Manuelito remained an important leader during the early reservation period. American-produced narratives of Manuelito mostly reflect white Americans' notions about Navajos either as cultural borrowers or as aggressive and warlike people, whereas accounts generated by Navajos reflect Navajos' continuing appreciation for their leader.[6] For many Navajos, Manuelito strove to keep Navajo land and believed that we should remain a sovereign people.

Although Manuelito looms large in American narratives, Juanita is visible mostly in pictures taken by frontier photographers. Few references are made to her in written documents. Significantly, I discovered some stories about Juanita, or Asdzáá Tł'ógi—Lady Weaver, as some Navajos knew her—still remembered by her maternal clanspeople. The condition of Juanita's dress, patched with calico, was not unlike the state in which I found the stories of Juanita. My interviews with the great-grandchildren of Manuelito and Juanita, who are my maternal grandparents, revealed bits and pieces of stories, fragments, images, and genealogy. Naïvely, I had hoped to recover full life histories of my great-great-great-grandparents.

The contrast between how Manuelito is depicted in American histories and how Juanita is remembered in Navajo oral histories demarcates the boundaries between non-Navajo and Navajo-produced narratives about the Navajo past and demonstrates that history is constructed and shaped by cultural beliefs and values. Anthropologies and histories about Navajos have been researched, written, and published by non-Indian scholars, and, as such, are embedded in systems of power and authority that privilege certain kinds of knowledge about Navajos.[7]

During the civil rights era of the 1960s, Navajos claimed the authority to write their own past and produced oral histories and other texts that were acts of defining and affirming Navajoness against colonial rule. Interestingly, many Navajo narratives took shape in a colonial context, thereby privileging male agency and showing how Navajos have negotiated meanings by selectively appropriating parts and incorporating them into their own narrative about the past. Significantly, the knowledge recovered by land claims researchers in the 1950s and 1960s, along with anthropological reports, became the basis for articulating a Navajo past, especially a Navajo national past. There remain unwritten Navajo narratives told within communities and matrilineal clans that privilege women's roles and indicate their places in the conveyance of tradition and its persistence in our society.

Objectives and Research Procedures

As a Diné woman, teacher, and scholar, I have always questioned the ways in which Navajos are represented. Written Navajo histories that rely on written documents generated by the Spaniards, Mexicans, and Americans, have frequently skewed Navajo historiography. Although many scholars have attempted to correct the historical picture by incorporating Navajo oral histories into their work and collaborating with Navajos, a dichotomy remains between Navajo and non-Navajo perspectives on the Navajo past. With few exceptions, non-Navajo perspectives about Navajos have been shaped by several generations of observers who have reduced Navajos to stereotypes.[8] Even though Navajo teachers and scholars have been instrumental in conveying traditional teachings at community-based schools and at the tribally owned Diné College, non-Navajo scholars still dominate the arena of research and publication. As long as this is the case, Navajos will continue to be understood within Western categories of meaning that sustain colonialist discourses and serve to perpetuate ideas of dominance, hierarchy, and asymmetry.

To interrogate the ways in which Navajo history has been constructed, I focus on Manuelito and Juanita. I draw from the critical studies of scholars like Haunani-Kay Trask, Linda Tuhiwai Smith, Waziyayawin Angela Wilson, Winona Stevenson Wheeler, Julie Cruikshank, Andrea Smith, and Edward Said, among many others, who have illuminated Western studies of indigenous peoples as primarily imperialist projects that purport to represent the indigenous world to the West. These scholars have also proposed Native histories that position oral traditions as vehicles to create histories that better reflect Native people's perspectives on the past.[9] Ironically, Western documents that have been used to name, classify, and catalogue indigenous cultures and lands are now resources that indigenous people use to reclaim identities and recover their respective histories.

Like other indigenous peoples, Navajos understand and talk about the past in very different ways than those presented within Western narratives by American historians. Drawing upon a body of studies that interrogates the relationship between "oral tradition" and "history," I propose that traditional Navajo perspectives on the past are grounded in the creation narratives that contain within them Diné beliefs and values. The creation narratives are a vital part of our oral tradition and are the foundation in which Navajo historical perspectives are embedded. For many Diné, they remain the authoritative explanations for the cultural and social transformations in our communities.

This study has two major objectives. I intend to examine existing histories that focus on Manuelito and pay little attention to Juanita in order to demonstrate that much of what has been written about Navajos by non-Navajos reflects American biases about Navajos, including American beliefs about the successful assimilation of Navajos into American society and the nature of gender construction and social organization. Historian Erika Bsumek has mapped the genesis and prevalence of the idea of Navajos as cultural borrowers, which began among ethnologists and anthropologists around 1900. This concept of Navajos as cultural borrowers has retained its power and is still widely used by numerous scholars and writers.[10] One favorite tenet of the cultural borrower theme includes Navajos as late arrivals in the Southwest, just in time to greet the Spaniards. Such formulations of the Navajo past do not reflect how we see ourselves as a people, and, significantly, have led many people to see Navajo claims to land as less valid than those of other tribal people in the region and somehow "less traditional" than other Natives.

Second, to demonstrate that Navajos perceive their own past differently, I will examine how Navajo narratives have served as vehicles to convey Navajo beliefs and values on several levels. As I have discovered, multiple perspectives on the Navajo past are shaped within a colonial space where Navajos interrogate existing histories and create new histories that often combine Western sources with Navajo ones in the ongoing move toward sovereignty. In much the same way that Andean indigenous people have taken age-old cultural symbols and meanings and redeployed them to meet the concerns of the present, so, too, have the Diné.[11]

Significantly, Navajos have looked to Manuelito's words and image to convey messages about Navajo values and tradition. At the same time, narratives about the past are conveyed at the local community level and within clans. These narratives include stories kept by matrilineal clans, such as those about Juanita. They reflect themes present in the creation narratives, and because they circulate within a matrilineal clan, they emphasize women's roles in the persistence of Navajo beliefs and values. An examination of the remaining stories of Juanita adds further evidence to the earliest non-Indian observations that Navajo women wielded a significant amount of autonomy and authority in their society.

The Great-Grandchildren of Manuelito and Juanita

Manuelito and Juanita are my great-great-great-grandparents. Like Juanita, my matrilineal clan is the Tł'ógi of Tohatchi, New Mexico. I am born for 'Áshiihí (Salt People). Manuelito was Bit'ahnii (Within His Cover or Folded Arms People) and born for the Tsi'naajinii (Black Streak Wood People).[12] My maternal grandparents trace their lineage to Juanita through two of her daughters, who are also Tł'ógi. The oldest daughter who was married to Dághá Chíí (Red Mustache) and is listed as Dághá Chíí be Asdzáá (Red Mustache's wife) in available census rolls. In letters written by Indian agents stationed at Fort Defiance, she is named as "Shizie," the meaning of which remains obscure (see figs. 8, 10, and 11). The younger daughter of Manuelito and Juanita was known as Ałk'iníbaa (spelled Ahkinbah in available documents). Her husband was Dághá Chíí Bik'is (see figs. 8, 9, and 12).

Although a number of my maternal grandparents are descended from two daughters of Juanita and Manuelito, I chose to interview only those with whom my mother keeps in communication. These grandparents, who are her aunts and uncles, are relatives that can count on her to assist them during ceremonies such as the N'da'(Enemy Way) or the Kinaaldá (women's puberty rite) and who invite our family to their birthdays, graduations, weddings, and other social occasions.

Descended matrilineally from either of the daughters, the great-grandchildren express interest in affirming clan kinship ties and conveying the importance of relationships that began with Juanita and her daughters to the following generations.

The great-grandchildren of Manuelito and Juanita regard each other as brothers and sisters. Their mothers were the children of one of Juanita and Manuelito's two daughters. The first person to whom I expressed my desire to write a book about our ancestors was my grandfather, Charles Manuelito (fig. 18). Charles, who died in January 2002, was descended from Juanita's older daughter and was my mother's uncle. He always expressed a special fondness for his *ma'yázhí* (little mother), my mother, Rose. Early on, he expressed interest in my project, brought out carefully saved newspaper and magazine articles, and allowed me to use letters that had once belonged to Juanita and her oldest daughter, Dághá Chíí be Asdzáá. The fact that my grandfather had saved these written accounts impressed upon me Navajo concerns to create continuity with the past. Others to whom I spoke include my grandmother, Joan Kinsel, Charles's older sister (fig. 19), who gave to my mother a necklace that had belonged to Dághá Chíí be Asdzáá. Due to Charles's death in January 2002, Joan is the sole surviving grandmother from our side of the clan, that is, from Juanita and Manuelito's oldest daughter, Dághá Chíí be Asdzáá. Descendants from the younger daughter of Manuelito and Juanita whom I interviewed include Mike Allison Sr., Faye Yazzie, Arthur Holyan, Isaac Allison, Helena Bitsilly, and Robert Manuelito, who died in 2001 (see figs. 17, 20, 22, and 23).

Beyond this generation of descendants, few others of my clan relatives knew much about their great-great-grandparents, although some know that they are descended from Manuelito and Juanita. Clan members expressed disappointment and concern that we were forgetting clan ties that had been important to the daughters of Manuelito and Juanita. As Raymond Morris, whose grandmother was Ałk'iníbaa, stated, "Our grandmothers said long ago that we should not forget the ties that connect us as kin." Today, those ties that link the two daughters to their mother, Juanita, are being revived through stories that work to recreate reconnections among clan members. Recognition of the value and place of oral traditions in understanding how Navajos perceive their past, how narratives are used to shape their perceptions of the past and their own experiences, and how they convey beliefs and values from ancestors enlarges the historical scope to include those people conventional Western history has ignored and excluded.

In his discussion of how literary forms such as travel writing and novels have served imperial projects of domination, Edward Said notes, "stories are at the heart of what explorers and novelists say about strange regions of the world; they also become the method colonized people use to assert their own identity and the existence of their history."[13] So it is that Navajos in the very telling and retelling of their own stories, their experiences under colonialism, have resisted Americans' representations of Navajos. As a Diné scholar, I follow in the paths of other Native scholars who have begun the process of remapping and reclaiming our territory, geographical and cultural.

Navajo Culture and History

We call ourselves the Diné or The People. We also name ourselves Náhookah Diné (Earth Surface People) and Bilá 'ashdla' (Five-Fingered Ones). In this study, I alternate between the name Diné, Navajo, and The People. Our homeland, called Dinétah or Diné Bikéyah, means Navajo Land or Navajo Country and is bounded by the four sacred mountains: Sisnaajiní in the east; Tsoodził in the south; Dook'o'osłííd in the west; and Dibé nitsaa in the north.[14] We Diné trace our origins into Dinétah by a journey from the First World into this present one. The Holy People created the world as we know it today. From the Holy People, the Diné received knowledge, material gifts, and rituals and ceremonies for a proper life. The Holy People also provided knowledge on proper relationships between the world and all beings.[15]

Our journey and emergence into the present world can be best understood as a movement from chaos to order, which is also reflected in the phrase, "Sạ' ah naagháí bik'eh hózhóón," which Diné poet Rex Lee Jim translates as "May I be everlasting and beautiful living." Jim explains that the phrase encapsulates a declaration to live a healthy and wealthy lifestyle and the practice of applying its teachings to life.[16] This term embodies a Navajo way of life that has served as a template for our ancestors from time immemorial. Not only is Sạ' ah naagháí bik'eh hózhóón the means by which we should live, but it has also been the foundation for renewal and survival into the twenty-first century. Navajo traditional narratives are embedded in this philosophy and continue to inform our perspectives on our origins and our place in the world, past and present.

For more than three hundred years the Diné have been known as a pastoral people who also practiced agriculture. Prior to the eighteenth century, as the creation narratives also note, our Navajo forebears were simple people who hunted and gathered.[17] In the 1700s, the Diné saw vast cultural and economic transformations, including the incorporation of livestock, the intermixing with Pueblo people, Navajo population increase, and Navajo territorial expansion. The adoption of the horse transformed the Navajos into a military force that ably resisted and counteracted Spanish and then Mexican invasions.[18]

Tension, conflict, and peace marked the colonial period as Navajo relationships with Pueblo peoples, the Spaniards, the Mexicans, and then the Americans, shifted along a continuum of kinship and peace to conflict and war.[19] Spanish reports noted that Navajos traded at various Pueblos and that they were not particularly interested in Spanish civilization.[20] The cycles of peace and conflict that characterized much of the colonial Southwest were directly related to the slave trade, of which Navajo women and children were the primary targets. Spanish treatment of the Pueblo peoples, who resented their colonizers, eventually led to an open rebellion in 1680 as the Pueblos united and successfully drove out the enemy. However, thirteen years later, the Spaniards returned with even more determination to bend the Native peoples to their will.

The arrival of the Americans in 1846 resulted in an escalation of conflict among Native peoples, New Mexicans, and the Americans. Navajos saw the Americans in much the same light as they had the Spaniards and the Mexicans: they saw little differences between the colonizers. The slave trade remained a vital component of the colonial economy and was the prime reason for an increase of violence between Navajos and New Mexicans.[21] American thirst for natural resources and a desire to open a route to California also fueled hostilities with Navajos. When Americans built a fort in the heart of Navajo land in 1851 at present-day Fort Defiance, Arizona, tensions increased.

In 1863, the Americans instigated an all-out war against Navajos. Under James Carleton, the Indian fighter Kit Carson literally scorched Navajo country, forcing Navajo surrender.[22] As prisoners of the U.S. military, in 1863, Navajos were exiled to Fort Sumner, New Mexico, where they were imprisoned from 1864 to 1868.[23] This period, known as the Long Walk, is a watershed in Navajo history and a point of departure for stories that Navajos tell within their clans and families.[24] In 1868, the Navajos signed a treaty with the Americans, Manuelito being one of the Navajo leaders. Along with other Navajos, Manuelito and Juanita returned to Navajo Country, where life was reestablished on a reservation carved out of a portion of their former homeland. Manuelito remained a respected leader among his people and American officials sought his assistance in many matters on the reservation. After the death of Manuelito in 1894, his widow moved closer to the present-day Tohatchi community with her two daughters and their families. There she and her eldest daughter continued to convey messages of Manuelito urging retention of Navajo lands and acquisition of an American education for Navajo children.

Diné Today

In two recent interviews, Spokane/Coeur d'Alene author Sherman Alexie characterized Indian reservations as "ghettos," saying, "I left the reservation. And I encourage everyone to leave." Alexie goes on to criticize some Native scholars who argue that, as scholars and writers, they must be responsible to their Native communities. Alexie calls these scholars "cultural cheerleaders" because they romanticize Indian cultures and the reservation.[25] Alexie's written descriptions of reservation life paint bleak pictures of poverty, chronic unemployment, inadequate housing, high homicide and suicide rates, and violence, all against the backdrop of seemingly barren land. In many ways, the Navajo nation could be characterized in much the same way. I am familiar with Alexie's portrayal of reservations and Indian life. I experience the contradictions that romanticize and condemn the reservation—a love/hate relationship—and I know well the inclination to flee if one has the resources. And yet, like many Diné, I find valuable and worthy our traditions and values. In them lie the possibilities of better lives and places to rear the coming generations.

I grew up in Navajo Country, where I attended a two-room schoolhouse near Ganado, Arizona, until I was eleven years old. My father, who was employed by El Paso Natural Gas, was then transferred to Tohatchi, New Mexico, where I attended the public school until I graduated from high school. Although my education on the Navajo Nation certainly did not prepare me for college, I was fortunate to have parents who insisted that my siblings and I attend school on a daily basis. Even though my parents struggled financially to raise their family of five children, somehow my father found the means to purchase encyclopedias, dictionaries, and books. A voracious reader, I devoured everything that was printed: James Thurber's short stories, Leo Tolstoy's novels, *True Romance* magazines, and cereal box sides. My ability to read well was the one skill that assisted me on my journey of education.

According to the 2000 Census, the Navajo population is now at a record 298,200. Navajos also claim one of the largest populations of indigenous peoples who listed only a Navajo heritage, as opposed to a mixed-heritage background.[26] Navajos have kept culturally distinct traditions and values, including the retention of our own language. Throughout the late-nineteenth century and into the early twentieth century, lands were added to the original reservation so that today Navajo Land includes approximately 17.3 million acres that span the states of Arizona, New Mexico, and Utah. Three land bases sit outside of Navajo Land: the Ramah community, south of Gallup, New Mexico; Alamo, in southern New Mexico; and To'hajiili, near Albuquerque, New Mexico.

More than half of the Navajo population is urban, scattered in major cities like Los Angeles, Phoenix, and Albuquerque, although many continue to travel home and retain kin ties. The other half lives on lands formerly inhabited by their ancestors, often upon lands passed through maternal clans, although tract housing, mostly homes built under the Navajo Housing Authority, has sprung up in communities all over the reservation. Because of the lack of jobs on Navajo Land, many travel to nearby border towns like Gallup, Farmington, and Flagstaff to work, whereas others travel further to work in and around urban areas. The forced relocation of more than twelve thousand Navajos from lands awarded to Hopis in 1974 also resulted in forced migration into urban America.[27] Diné poet Luci Tapahonso captures very well our sentiments when we have to return to the places where we make our homes because of our jobs and commitment to education. In her poem, "The Weekend Is Over," the narrator, a Navajo woman, gathers her reluctant children to return to Kansas. We are left with images of grandparents saying their good-byes and giving hugs, memories of loving family, and the taste of grilled mutton ribs, roasted green chiles, and sweet Navajo cake.[28]

On any weekend and through the summer and winter months, Navajo families conduct a variety of ceremonies and rituals calculated to bring family members back into harmony and balance. On Friday or Saturday mornings, men are erecting Plains-style teepees for peyote meetings of the Native American Church. On any given American holiday, Navajo prepare for the festivities in much the same way as other Americans. Along with American holidays and celebrations, they also celebrate a baby's first laugh with a feast and their daughter's coming into womanhood with the Kinaaldá. Sunday evening, those who live in cities make their rounds of good-byes until the next time they return home.

The Navajo nation shares the concerns of other indigenous nations about the loss of language and the erosion of tribal traditions even as we continue to look to our own traditions for answers to issues and problems. We experience some of this country's highest rates of unemployment, violence toward women and children, alcoholism, and poverty. Nevertheless, Navajos exhibit resilience and determination to retain traditional beliefs and values. In many sectors of our society, Navajo parents, teachers, scholars, counselors, Navajo Nation employees, and others are committed to conveying our traditions to the next generation. This study emphasizes an examination of how Navajo histories as Western cultural constructions have served to keep structures of inequalities and injustices entrenched and, at the same time, offers an approach to resee the Navajo past on Navajo terms.

In chapter 2, I map the evolving discussion about the relationships between oral tradition and history by providing a critical overview of Navajo Studies. Initially, oral traditions and history were studied as dichotomous cultural interpretations of the past. Although much of Navajo Studies still relies on and perpetuates stereotypes about Navajos, there is exciting and innovative scholarship that is not only slowly moving toward recognition of the colonial nature of scholarship, but also recognizes the validity of oral traditions to create a more accurate reconstruction of the Navajo past.[29] I propose a similar approach to writing Navajo history. By comparing oral traditions, including some of the earliest ones collected by ethnologists, with narratives related by the descendants of Manuelito and Juanita, it becomes possible to ascertain how the past—an evolving past—is continuously used to explain the present. Furthermore, as Dakota historian Waziyatawin Angela Wilson notes, tribally based histories that privilege indigenous oral traditions are intended to interrogate the colonizing forces that have damaged our communities and to reaffirm and revitalize traditional ways that have served our ancestors well.[30]

In chapter 3, I analyze primary and secondary sources that refer to Manuelito, including biographies, American and Navajo histories, primary documents, and Navajo oral histories, in order to explore American and Navajo views about the meaning of Manuelito's role in America's conquest of and claims to the Southwest. A close reading reveals that Manuelito's story has been inserted into existing American history narratives wherein indigenous leaders are presented along a continuum from noble savages to subjugated warriors who inevitably succumb to defeat by a superior civilization.[31] Although Manuelito met a fate common for indigenous people, where alcoholism and/or diseases often led to impoverishment and death, his own people do not pay much attention to how he died. Such portrayals justify their inhumane treatment, confirm belief in the inevitability of vanishing natives, and deny their dispossession. Rather, Navajo stories and portrayals of their leader highlight his commitment to his people's survival, and his lifelong passion that Navajos retain their land for future generations.

Chapter 4 examines twelve photographs of Juanita and Manuelito and employs gender as a category of analysis. Looking closely at how Navajos were expected to conform to Western ideals about proper gender roles gives an indication of how roles for men and women were transformed after 1868. Specifically, photographs of Navajos played a significant role in conveying messages about how Navajo men and women had conformed to American family practices.[32] In this chapter, I raise questions about the photographic portrayal of Navajo men and women by examining extant photographs of Juanita and Manuelito that span several decades, from 1868 to 1902 (figs. 1–12). Although thousands of photographs of Navajo women are deposited in archives all over the country, only two Navajo women are consistently named: Juanita and Elle of Ganado. More than half the photographs of Navajo women depict them as weavers, thus entrenching that image in the American popular mind. Although Juanita is not named or referred to specifically as a weaver in those Western accounts, some of the photographs of her as a weaver foreshadow the popular portrayal of Navajo women in that role.

In chapter 5, I examine narratives about Juanita, which are relayed in her matrilineal clan, the Tł'ógi, many of whose members reside in and around Tohatchi, New Mexico. Today, oral traditions in the form of autobiography, biography, and creation and other traditional stories, including ritual and ceremony, circulate within matrilineal clans as they have for generations. As historian Angela Wilson notes, oral tradition includes oral history within its definition and refers to the "way in which information is passed on rather than the length of time something has been told." Furthermore, "Personal experiences, pieces of information, events, incidents, etc., can become part of the oral tradition at the moment it happens or the moment it is told, as long as the person adopting the memory is part of an oral tradition."[33] Juanita's matrilineal clan is Tł'ógi, suggesting a kin affiliation with Zia Pueblo. Although her family name has been forgotten, Juanita was known as Asdzáá Tł'ógi in the public realm. Moreover, during my perusal of notes left by the anthropologists who conducted the research for the Navajo land claims in the 1950s, I discovered a note in a margin next to Juanita's name: "her grandmother was from Zia Pueblo." Juanita lived to be sixty-five to seventy years old, living from around 1845 to 1910.[34] The Tł'ógi stories about Juanita reveal the centrality of women's roles in Navajo society and illustrate how oral tradition is used to organize social units, connect Navajos to the land, and interpret life experiences and the past.

Chapter 6 continues my exploration of the stories about Juanita that circulate among members of her maternal clan in order to delineate how storytelling structures contemporary Navajo uses of the past. Stories about Juanita and her daughters serve as the vehicle that connect her descendants to the land, reaffirm clan/kin relationships, and act as a link to land use privileges. This last chapter is also a personal reflection of the author's own search for her past. My experiences are similar to those of many other Native people who were not allowed access to their own histories in schools. Although I grew up in Navajo Land and am familiar with our own traditions and stories, I have found that studying and critiquing Navajo history is part of an ongoing process—which includes the recovery and revitalization of our community, family, language, and traditions—in which many Native scholars are presently engaged. As a personal narrative, this chapter also offers Navajos and other native people an opportunity to share my journey of reclaiming the Navajo past on multiple levels that span the personal to the national.

2/Recovering Diné Intellectual Traditions

At the Intersection of History and Oral Tradition;
Or, "It's Hard Work Traipsing Around in Indian Country"

One of the many journeys that I embarked upon was one of recovering my own intellectual traditions and using them to shape a Navajo-centered history. Haitian historian Michel-Rolph Trouillot makes the observation that the project of recovering history for those "previously without history" requires a commonality of assumptions of historical narratives and that writing about "Third World countries" is based in and has been shaped by Western conventions and procedures. He notes, "First, the writing and reading of Haitian historiography implies literacy and formal access to a Western—primarily French—language and culture, two prerequisites that already exclude the majority of Haitians from direct participation in its production," and "Second, regardless of their training and the degree to which they may be considered members of a guild, Haitian and foreign narrators aim to conform to guild practice." He goes on to note that in addition to holding preconceived notions shaped by European thought, historians also make assumptions about their audience and are limited in the kinds of narratives they can tell. He writes, "To contribute to new knowledge and to add new significance, the narrator must both acknowledge and contradict the power embedded in previous understandings."[1]

Given that writing history has been mostly a Western tradition that requires mastery of Euro-American intellectual practices, those who live outside of Western societies find themselves excluded in the writing of their own histories.[2] This chapter is a discussion of my own endeavor to recover Diné intellectual traditions, first, by examining how Navajo history has been constructed, and, second, by proposing yet another way to write a Navajo history. Writing about the Navajo past requires sifting through my own education processes, identifying standard history conventions that have created portrayals of Navajos that perpetuate colonialist frameworks, and then articulating a history model that better reflects Diné understandings of the past. Furthermore, as many Native scholars have declared, our intellectual endeavors should support Native sovereignty. In articulating a model of Navajo perspectives on the past, I draw on previous studies that have examined the relationships between oral tradition and history. As scholars have demonstrated, placing oral traditions at the center of our histories illuminates how Native peoples experience history differently. Amazingly, oral traditions have stood the test of time and examining how they inform Native histories attests to their vitality and persistence. In my own study, I provide a critique of Diné studies in order to illuminate how these studies have been projects of imperialism wherein Navajos could be controlled through discursive practices, and I offer a Navajo perspective on that past, one that places Diné philosophy at the center.[3] In writing a Navajo history, I also outline a methodology that better fits the needs of the Navajo community. For too long, research about Native peoples has neither reflected how we perceive the past nor benefited our own communities.

It is not my intention to examine every single publication in Navajo Studies. Rather, I have selected a number that reflect major movements and transitions in intellectual output. In my examinations of these publications, I have come to several conclusions. First, initial studies in anthropology and history have created portrayals of Navajos that contrast: anthropology, with its focus on culture, created a portrait of Navajos as cultural borrowers and late arrivals in the Southwest, whereas historians, with their privileging of written documents, have presented Navajos as aggressive nomadic people who required subjugation by the Americans so the region could be stabilized. These persistent images of Navajos have been used in various ways to justify the historical treatment of them by a host of federal officials, missionaries, health officials, scholars, educators, traders, and so forth, and to confirm Euro-American understandings of Navajos.

Second, I found that scholars are moving toward the recognition that many of the existing studies have served to reinculcate the existing structures of inequality and injustices in which the Diné continue to live. Moreover, scholars across disciplines have turned to further examinations of our oral traditions, bringing about fresh interpretations on Navajo origins and presence in the Southwest and the meaning of the Navajo past. Unfortunately, however, Navajos continue to be understood within Western frameworks, thereby contributing to the ongoing distortion of the realities of Native lives, cultures, and histories.

Although a few non-Indians like Paul Zolbrod, Klara Kelley, Charlotte Frisbie, and Peter Iverson have collaborated with Navajo scholars and community members, most students of Navajos continue to rely on non-Navajo sources to create their studies and to regard Navajos as their "informants." Their professional careers have benefited enormously, while few Navajos have received any tangible benefits from these studies and publications.[4] Indeed, fairly recently, a writer known as Nasdijj turned out to be a non-Indian, Timothy Patrick Barrus, who, in his previous life, had written gay pornographic fiction. Posing as a Navajo, Barrus won national acclaim and book prizes (many meant for Native writers) for his memoirs. This particular case indicates not only that non-Indians prefer their own constructions of what and who is Native, but also that "playing Indian" is still very much a popular American pastime.[5] Moreover, Barrus/Nasdijj's portrayals of Navajos cast them as bizarre, sadistic, and sexually aberrant, causing untold damage to how Navajo are perceived in the public eye.

Perspectives on Navajos Across Disciplines

Historian William Lyons notes that prior to 1848 non-Indians knew very little about the ancestors of the present-day Diné. Spanish and Mexican reports portrayed the Diné primarily as traders, raiders, and the weavers of fine textiles.[6] Initially, American expansionists made favorable observations of Navajos, calling them industrious and freedom loving and even went so far as to suggest that their attacks on New Mexican settlements were justified as they were defending themselves against encroaching raiders who stole women and children for the slave trade. However, as historian Carol Douglas Sparks argues, these favorable reports quickly turned negative when Americans gained control of the Southwest and discovered that Navajos did not consider the Americans their superiors. Americans quickly came to view Navajos as savages who attacked their settlements and required either extermination or relocation to a place where they would not be a threat.[7]

Several processes with roots in Euro-American intellectual traditions have shaped Diné historiography. These intellectual traditions created the portrayals of Navajos that still inform our understanding of Navajos and have two main branches, anthropology and history. Within these two disciplines, two predominate images emerged: Navajos as hunter-gatherers who migrated to the Southwest sometime between A.D. 900 and 1500 with little or no cultural material and ceremonial knowledge of their own; and as Navajos who, having borrowed most cultural items by which they are today characterized, became one of the most aggressive and warlike indigenous peoples. These dichotomous images of Navajos as primarily cultural borrowers who were nomadic and aggressive, needless to say, do not adequately reflect how we see ourselves.

The genealogy of anthropology among the Navajos is yet to be fully examined, but from the late-nineteenth century into the 1930s, 1950s, and the present, anthropologists visited Navajo Country. Just as it is true for the relationships between late-nineteenth-century anthropologists and other Native peoples, Navajos were defined within an evolutionary schema associated with Lewis Henry Morgan.[8] According to Morgan's classification, Navajos were closer to the "savage" end of the scale based on their cultural and physical attributes.

Such views of Navajos began to change when army surgeon-turned-ethnologist Washington Matthews announced that the Navajos had a culture worthy of study. Working in Navajo country from 1880 to 1884 and 1890 to 1894, Matthews published a version of the creation stories and descriptions of ceremonies like the Nightway. In 1997, coeditors Katherine Spencer Halpern and Susan Brown McGreevy published a set of essays devoted to Washington Matthew's studies among Native peoples, with an emphasis on his Navajo studies.[9] The essays indicate that Matthews's contributions were vast, spanning several disciplines, from folklore to literary studies to anthropology. According to several of the contributors, Matthews set the standard for thorough and exact ethnographic observation. For his time, he was an extraordinary observer who exhibited sensitivity and a respect for his subjects. However, contributor James Faris reminds us that, although it may indeed be true that Matthews was a man ahead of his time, he was with the occupation army and that, as a man of science, Matthews did not accept Navajo medicine and healing on its own terms.[10] Rather, as many observers (even Navajos) still assert, Navajo medicine and healing methods work primarily through psychology. Faris notes that Matthews was working within standard anthropological assumptions of his day, which meant that Navajos had derived almost all of their ceremonial knowledge and practices from surrounding tribal peoples like the Pueblos.[11] As a man of his time who believed in the evolutionary scale as a mode to ascertain civilization, Matthews also completed physical anthropological studies on Navajos.[12]

In the epilogue to the essays on Washington Matthews, Diné educator and artist Gloria Emerson offers a Diné perspective, saying that we often have contradictory feelings about studies such as Matthews's. On the one hand, we have objected to the predatory ways in which studies have been conducted and how they have been used; on the other hand, as we continue to experience the consequences of colonialism, including language loss and knowledge of cultural ways, especially as a result of Western education, we have turned to studies such as those of Matthews to recover traditional knowledge.[13] Subsequent researchers have relied heavily on Matthews's work as reference for their own studies and have expanded upon it. For example, Father Berard Haile's extensive notes and translations of ceremonies, prayers, and rituals provide valuable ethnographic data on Navajo life, as well as their ceremonies.[14] Today, Haile's papers are housed in Special Collections at the University of Arizona.

The 1930s marked a new era in Native-white relationships in which the federal government shifted from a determination to eradicate Native traditional lifeways, ceremonies, and language to a policy of tolerance, to promote the preservation of traditional practices and Native languages. This shift was also reflected in scholarship associated with anthropologist Franz Boas, who preached cultural relativism. In the 1930s, the Diné, who were struggling to reclaim their self-sufficiency by reviving their livestock herds, were once again subjected to federal government force when they were ordered to reduce their livestock. Citing environmental damage as the major reason for livestock reduction, range management experts attempted to educate Navajos about superior Western science-based agricultural and range management practices. The contingent of experts who descended upon Diné Bikéyah included anthropologists who used their expertise to influence the Navajo Service, which provided education, health, and employment programs for the Navajos. From the 1930s into the 1950s, Diné Békeyah became a prime study area for anthropologists like Clyde Kluckhohn, Alexander and Dorothy Leighton, Ruth Underhill, Mary Shepardson, and Gladys Reichard, among others. Their studies remain the foundation from which budding scholars of Navajos begin their research.

Anthropologist Gladys Reichard remains an important scholar whose ethnographies have become the touchstone for the current interest in Navajo weavings. A student of Franz Boas, Reichard was the first anthropologist to live with a Navajo family, the women sharing their weaving knowledge and techniques with her.[15] Conducting studies of ceremonies, Reichard attempted to create a nomenclature of Navajo religion, proving that it was difficult, if not impossible, to categorize Navajo culture, history, and religion separately, for it is difficult to find parallel definitions across languages for ideas and thoughts that appear similar.[16] More recently, feminist scholars like Louise Lamphere have claimed Reichard as the first feminist ethnographer who brought innovation to anthropology, including the use of participant-observation techniques, the use of the personal voice and experiences in studies, and the centering of women's experiences. Significantly, in a period when white women were discouraged from leaving their domestic spaces, Reichard carved out a career in the only professional field that allowed women to participate. Her work heralded transitions in gender roles in the early twentieth century.[17]

Other feminist scholars like Kathy M'Closkey have raised questions about how feminists like Reichard and those who valorize her scholarship have ignored how Reichard's classification of Navajo women's knowledge as secular (as opposed to sacred) has contributed to a devaluation of women's knowledge and labor.[18] This devaluation is made visible as M'Closkey examines current dialogues among textile scholars, curators, and art dealers who have refused to acknowledge the historic relationship between colonialism and the appropriation of colonized people's resources, labor, knowledge, and traditions for the colonizers' own uses and benefits. Scholars' categorization of weaving within Western paradigms has also served to reaffirm non-Navajo naming of Navajos as primarily cultural borrowers who arrived late in the Southwest, a claim that contradicts Navajo understandings of their own past and origins. Indeed, over the span of several years, I have heard textile scholars dispute Roseann Willink and Paul Zolbrod's thesis that weavers' textiles have ceremonial and spiritual significance, thereby demonstrating that women possess sacred knowledge, something that many anthropologists usually associated with Navajo men. Rather, the preferred thesis is that Navajo weavers learned the skill from Pueblo weavers.[19] As M'Closkey and anthropologist Lessie Joe Frasier point out, present-day attitudes and practices sustain colonial practices.[20]

In the 1940s, 1950s, and 1960s, anthropologists continued to wear a path to Navajo Land. They came from any number of disciplines, including folklore, education, linguistics, psychology, and medicine. For example, folklorist Maude Oakes transcribed Jeff King's version of how the Hero Twins went in search of their father, the Sun. The text is illustrated beautifully with sand paintings that accompany the narrative and the ceremony, which is still in practice today.[21] Oakes's text is accompanied with commentary by Joseph Campbell, who is widely known for his work on mythology. Campbell explicates the significance of the story by comparing it to similar narratives from other cultures and by describing how the process of going through the ceremony transforms an individual's consciousness, thereby moving him or her to another level of understanding. Another set of transcribed Diné creation narratives is folklorist Aileen O'Bryan's *Navaho Indian Myths*, which was initially published by the Bureau of American Ethnology, Smithsonian Institution, in 1956.[22] Certainly a reflection of the times is how non-Navajos labeled our creation narratives "myths" and how Navajo educator Ethelou Yazzie published a version of the narratives and titled her publication *Navajo History*. Although many non-Indians who specialize in Navajo Studies no longer call our narratives "myths," because the word suggests the stories are "imaginary" or "fiction," at the 2004 Navajo Studies Conference keynote speaker New Mexico senator Leonard Tsosie had to chastise one non-Navajo presenter who called our creation narratives "myths."

In the 1970s and 1980s, English professor Paul Zolbrod journeyed west to learn more about Native people who still kept oral traditions. Zolbrod then embarked on a mission to include them as an important and often-overlooked component of the American literary tradition. Coming across Washington Matthews's rendition of the Navajo creation narratives, Zolbrod built upon them and returned elements that the army surgeon had deleted because of white sensibilities of the time. Zolbrod subsequently published his formulation as *Diné Bahane': The Navajo Creation Stories.*[23] As in other studies he made of Navajo oral tradition, Zolbrod claims in this book that our stories are as valuable and sophisticated as European intellectual traditions. Zolbrod's work mirrors the work of literary critics like Arnold Krupat and Brian Swann, who also sought to claim a place for Native oral and literary traditions in the broader American literary and poetic circles.[24]

In addition to revising Matthews's version of the Diné creation narratives to include a sense of Navajo poetics, Zolbrod's *Diné Bahane'* also returns the element of sexuality to them, which is so crucial to understanding cultural values. Concepts of sexuality are important for understanding the Navajo worldview, in which duality and complementarity organize the world. In the Navajo perspective, the world is largely divided into male and female, and it is through the capacity to procreate, through the sexual act, that new life is brought forth. There are also stories of dire consequences when people do not recognize the importance of females and males. Zolbrod delineated for a non-Navajo audience the ways in which traditional stories serve as a template for how Navajos should live and how they should relate to the rest of the world, including the natural world. He noted a number of differences between oral and literary traditions and how these differences reflect contrasting worldviews between Navajos and whites:

> In my research I encountered a direct relationship between the elements of Navajo poetic tradition and the way Navajos conduct their daily lives. The separateness of art that marks our own culture simply does not apply in Navajo culture, and Navajo poetry in particular cannot be isolated from its social context or its moorings in the broader frame of life. . . .
>
> To this day, then, the Navajo creation story gives individual Navajos . . . an important ethnic identity. It defines meaningful relationships among members of the community and between the community and the entire cosmos.[25]

The centrality of oral narratives to Navajo identity, to Navajo well-being, and to the ability to cope with the stresses of life, especially the effects of colonialism, is well-known. In particular, Zolbrod realized that oral traditions cannot be adequately captured in text and that narrations vary from region to region, from storyteller to storyteller, from telling to telling. Interestingly, although *Diné Bahane'* remains a significant contribution to the mountainous literature in Navajo Studies, oral traditions written down cannot began to convey fully the continuing vitality that oral traditions have for Navajos. However, Zolbrod's collaborative project with Diné linguist Roseann Willink gives an indication of how oral tradition still permeates Navajo communities.

Paul Zolbrod and Roseann Willink also engaged with weavers from Crownpoint, New Mexico, to examine historic textiles housed at the Museum of New Mexico, and they published their findings in *Weaving a World: Textiles and the Navajo Way of Seeing.*[26] Expanding on Zolbrod's ideas about the poetic traditions of indigenous cultures, Zolbrod and Willink document how Diné women have woven their worldview into their weavings so that "reading" a textile could offer historical and cultural information. For example, weavers commented on how one textile incorporated their surroundings, showing how shifts in colors reflect light changing as a new day dawned in the east and ended with the sun in the west. Other textiles reflect history, depicting the Navajo people's traumatic experiences at Bosque Redondo in the mid-1860s. Still others tell stories about the creation and were used for protection by warriors.

As Willinks and Zolbrod reveal, textiles are important "texts" that reflect weavers' knowledge of sacred materials, including the creation narratives, ceremonies, and prayers. Importantly, women's knowledge is rooted in the sacred, and upon closer look delineates cultural values wherein concepts of *K'e*, kinship, are expressed. Willink and Zolbrod brilliantly demonstrate that Navajo weavers produce original and creative works, and they challenge the notion that Navajos are primarily "cultural borrowers."[27] Zolbrod continues his examinations of Diné oral traditions with his recently published article, "Squirrel Reddens His Cheeks: Cognition, Recognition, and Poetic Production in the Ancient Navajo Stories."[28]

Works by Zolbrod, Willink, and M'Closkey have been followed by still more studies of Navajos that demonstrate the importance of investigating oral traditions to understand the Navajo past, and how they inform contemporary issues. For example, archaeological reexaminations such as Ronald Towner's *Defending the Dinétah*, Klara Kelley and Harris Francis's "Abalone Shell Buffalo People: Navajo Narrated Routes and the Pre-Columbian Archaeological Sites," and

Richard Begay's "Tsé Bíyah 'Anii'ahí: Chaco Canyon and Its Place in
Navajo history," raise questions about the origins of Navajos and their
relations with neighboring Native people. According to oral tradition,
Diné ancestors had relationships with the ancient ones who lived at
Chaco Canyon. Such stories move the focus away from preoccupation
with Diné appearance in the Southwest and raise questions about the
nature of Diné relations with other early peoples and the source of
their knowledge, ceremonies, and clanships.[29] Taking oral tradition
seriously has meant taking Navajo views seriously.[30]

Before the 1960s, historian Frank Reeves was the first to write
Navajo history. His extensive number of articles, most of which were
published in the *New Mexico Historical Review*, followed a few historical publications by anthropologists Ruth Underhill and Richard Van
Valkenburgh. Underhill's *The Navajos* was first published in 1956. Her
foreword gives an indication of transition in American intellectual
thought and its link to federal Indian policy. Of her study, Underhill wrote, "These pages describe as faithfully as possible the experiences of the Navajos, as an American Indian tribe, as they changed
from food-collecting nomads to gardeners and pastoralists to, finally,
modern wage earners."[31] Her approach to Navajo history was shaped
by American assumptions about progress and development; that is,
Navajos as cultural borrowers have been successful in making transitions into modern American society but there were still many problems and issues that needed to be addressed for them to make a fully
successful transition. Publications like Underhill's were designed to
inform the American public and the increasing number of scholars going to the Southwest to study Indian tribes. Historian Colleen
O'Neill, in a synthesis of paradigms used to write Native histories,
notes that development theorists wondered how Natives could successfully move into modern American society, especially as their traditions were vanishing.[32] Underhill's study reflects how advocates of
development disseminated their messages through a variety of venues, including scholarly publications.[33]

Frank Reeve's histories were published as a series of articles in the
New Mexico Historical Review from 1937 to 1971. Relying exclusively on
archival sources, he outlined Navajo relations with Spaniards, Mexicans, and Americans. Reeve discovered a period of peace during the
era of Navajo-Spanish relations, whereas the prevailing view held that
a constant state of warfare existed during the colonial period until the

mid-1860s, when Americans finally subjugated the Navajos. His writings illustrate assumptions about the Navajos that continue into the present, primarily that as warlike, aggressive tribal peoples, Navajos warranted being warred upon and eventually defeated, thereby continuing the justification for American invasion and conquest in the Southwest.

In 1997, historian Don Fixico published a collection of essays written by prominent historians of Native peoples who reviewed the changing field of Indian history, noted trends, and described how the field had changed in response to New Western history's aims.[34] Inspired by New Western historians who argued that in the American West people have faced cycles of conquest and responded according to their cultural dictates, historian William Hagen explained that New Indian historians revised portrayals of the Indian past by showing responses to colonialism and resistance and resilience among Native peoples. New Indian historians have also aimed to counter the ethnocentric biases of white historians by presenting more balanced and sympathetic views of American Indians.[35] Certainly, the turn in Indian history has also been a response to Lakota scholar Vine Deloria Jr.'s scathing criticism of federal Indian policy and the ways in which Native peoples have been depicted in white scholarship.[36] More recently, Angela Wilson has remarked on the present state of Native history, in which white historians remain in control. "Very few [historians] have attempted to find out how Native people would interpret, analyze, or question the documents they confront," she writes, "nor have they asked if the Native people they are studying have their own versions or stories of their past. As long as history continues to be studied and written in this manner," she asserts, "the field should more appropriately be called non-Indian perceptions of American Indian history."[37] A number of Navajo histories reflect the goals of New Indian historians, including Garrick Bailey and Roberta Glenn Bailey, authors of the *History of the Navajo: The Reservation Years.*[38] Explaining Diné growth, territorial expansion, and seeming success at meeting the demands of modernity, the Baileys have examined Diné life within the framework of continuity and change in which Navajos have kept traditional practices alive while responding to the consequences of colonialism. As historian Kerwin Klein writes, "Driven partly by American Indian scholars like Vine Deloria Jr., a new story emerged in which Native American cultures heroically survived and even overcame Euro-American oppression."[39]

Frank McNitt's *Navajo Wars: Military Campaigns, Slave Raids, and Reprisals* also reflects the objectives of New Indian history. McNitt has examined the reasons for Navajo warfare against the Spanish, Mexicans, and Americans from the middle of the seventeenth century to 1864. Whereas the major initial cause of war between American Indians and Europeans and Americans lay in colonists' thirst for indigenous lands, Navajo reprisals were directly related to the slave trade in which Navajos were primary targets. Relying almost exclusively on Spanish, Mexican, and American archival sources, McNitt places the Navajo within a standard historical framework in which they responded to the cycles of conquest. Typical of Western historians, McNitt presents the West as a place of violence and unrest until the Americans arrive with their freedom and democracy.

Frank McNitt's finding that Navajos reacted to the colonizers largely as a result of the slave trade, in which Navajo women and children were targets, has become a major research interest for several scholars. David Brugge, part of a team of researchers who assembled a Navajo archive, conducted research for the Navajo land claims in the late 1950s and made the first sustained examination of Navajos and the southwest slave trade when he examined New Mexico Catholic Church records from 1694 to 1875.[40] Brugge's perusal yielded a wealth of information that confirmed McNitt's argument that the slave trade directed at Navajos heightened conflict during the cycles of conquest in the Southwest. Historian James Brooks contextualizes the nature of the slave trade by centering women's experiences as slaves. The violence of being captured as a slave and then incorporated into a host society defined many women and children's experiences.[41] During his examination of interviews taken as part of the Federal Writers Project in the 1930s, New Mexico State historian Estevan Rael-Gálvez discovered the invisible presence of captive Native women and children in northern New Mexican households.[42] These studies of captives and the slave trade are changing the ways in which we have thought about race, culture, and identity. For example, although Navajos acknowledge intermixing with non-Navajos through clans, such as the Mexican clan, created when a non-Navajo woman was brought into a Navajo family, they did not specify blood quantum for the children born of such cross-cultural intimate relationships. However, today, no new clans have been established and Navajos of mixed parentage often state their blood quantum. Navajos still deem clan membership central, and historically they have often adopted non-Navajos into their families and clan groups. Children born of Navajo mothers and non-Indian fathers are still identified with their mother's clans.

Raymond Friday Locke's *Book of the Navajo* remained one of the most popular Navajo histories until the publication of Peter Iverson's history in 2003.[43] Locke presents a sympathetic portrayal of Navajos. He devotes a significant portion of his narrative to creation stories, thereby suggesting that Navajos see these stories as their history. His sympathy is particularly evident when he retells the story of the Diné leader Narbona's willingness to coexist peacefully with the United States. In 1846, during the course of a meeting between the Navajos and the Americans at Red Copper Pass, New Mexico, tensions between the two parties surfaced. A New Mexican with the army claimed that he had spied one of his horses among the Navajos. In an exchange of gunfire that followed, Narbona was murdered and scalped. Locke's empathy with the Navajos is evident throughout his description of this historical moment.

Although sympathetic, histories like Locke's do not counter or refute assumptions that, as a warlike and aggressive people, Navajos required subjugation by the U.S. military. An investigation of Native American history demonstrates that Native peoples throughout North America were forced to relinquish their lands to the white invaders. If they refused, they were warred upon, defeated, and relocated to lands that white settlers did not initially desire. It did not matter whether Native peoples were seen primarily as peaceful and friendly, like Nez Perce leader Chief Joseph and his band. Nor did it matter whether they were considered civilized, like the Cherokee of Georgia, some of whom adopted white manners of living in order to retain their lands and cultural practices, or the "most bloodthirsty" of the tribal peoples, like the Apaches. If white settlers desired indigenous lands, Native peoples were removed under threats of extermination. Navajo histories have not challenged or overturned the colonial framework that denies the larger picture in which Native people's land, resources, and lives were stolen and they were reduced to the state of dependency. As Angela Wilson declares, many historians "are guilty of focusing solely on the resiliency of Indigenous people while refusing to offer an honest and critical indictment of state and federal governments, leaders, and all the citizens of America who have been complicit in our bodily extermination, cultural eradication, and assaults on our lands and resources. Most historians," she writes, "have been accomplices in a great conspiracy to ensure Indigenous subordination."[44] By the 1980s, scholars had begun to overturn the "defeated and vanishing Indian" paradigm, first, by delineating how global and regional economic forces had reduced Natives to states of dependency in which they were forced to rely on the U.S. government for their very basic needs, and, second, by centering Natives as active agents determined to retain their own lifeways. Dependency paradigms sought to counter development theories wherein it was recognized that Natives had not improved their conditions under development projects; rather, Natives were still struggling to claim self-sufficiency. For example, Thomas Hall, in *Social Change in the Southwest, 1350–1880*, presents a broad sweep of more than five hundred years and delineates historical changes in the Southwest under the impact of capitalism and industrialization. Spain and the United States rose to domination in a process enhanced by their relationships to nonstate societies. Although Natives were subjected to hegemonic forces that sought both to exterminate and/or to assimilate them into the dominant society, they relied upon a number of strategies to maintain themselves as separate and distinct peoples.

Hall assesses the degree of incorporation of Southwestern peoples by examining not only the relative strength of the nation-states but also the nature of sociopolitical organization in each nonstate society. Spaniards had more success in dominating the tightly knit hierarchical Pueblo villages, whereas Athapaskan groups such as the Navajo and Apache remained on the periphery of the Spanish empire and effectively resisted its overtures. Relationships between the indigenous societies shifted with Spanish presence and, in turn, influenced their ability to resist European intrusion. Many other factors affected the incorporation process, including Native peoples' access to goods from other imperial sources such as the French and their geographical location in relation to the conquerors. The relationships between imperial powers also influenced interactions with and among Indian peoples. The introduction of guns and horses increased the chances of survival for many Native groups.

Dependency theories explained the process of how Navajos were rendered into a state of dependency after their military defeat in 1864. One chapter in Nancy Parezo and Thomas Sheridan's *Paths of Life: American Indians of the Southwest and Northern Mexico* historicized

Navajo culture by describing Navajos' efforts to maintain cultural integrity in the face of internal and external change and emphasizing the ways in which cultural values have shaped and provided direction for the Navajo communities. Parezo and Sheridan elaborate anthropologist Edward Spicer's concept of enduring cultures by examining how Native peoples retained a separate cultural identity that did not necessarily hinge upon a common language, homeland, or racial identity; rather, they have persevered under the harshest conditions of colonial invasions.[45] One of the features of Southwest Native nations has been their ability to endure by employing symbols, rituals, and words. For the Navajos, the continuing significance of clan relationships, a sense of community with the land, and the importance of pastoralism are connected through a philosophy that stresses the continual search for *hózhó*, the path to harmony and Old Age.

Navajo histories of the twentieth century such as Richard White's *Roots of Dependency: Subsistence, Environmental and Social Change among the Choctaws, Pawnees, and Navajos* employ a dependency framework. White's examination of the livestock reductions of the 1930s and 1940s paved the way to understand the Navajo past within a broader global framework and highlighted the larger colonial forces that created Navajo dependence on outside economic forces. From the 1860s into the early twentieth century, their flock and livestock saw a dramatic increase. According to Indian agents' hazy guesses, Navajos held between fifteen and twenty thousand head of sheep in 1869. Although the severe winters of 1873–74 and 1882–83 reduced the herds, by the mid-1880s, Navajos owned almost one million head of sheep and goats. Their horse herds had also substantially increased.[46] By the 1930s, herd levels had multiplied to well over the one million count. Navajo subsistence was in danger due to a number of factors, including a shortage of available grazing lands as non-Indians contested Navajo use of the public domain.[47] Richard White challenges conventional explanations for forced livestock reduction, including assumptions about Navajo misuse of grazing ranges and lack of understanding about basic livestock management. Rather, larger U.S. capitalistic interests, including concerns that soil erosion was creating silt buildup behind Hoover Dam, destroyed Navajo subsistence patterns while Indian service agents introduced a number of Western scientifically based technologies slated to improve Navajo land and livestock. For Navajos, livestock had been so thoroughly integrated into their lives that sheep meant literally and figuratively "life." Their way of valuing sheep brought them into collision with whites, who believed that scientific technology and know-how would bring about a solution to environmental degradation. More recently, historian Marsha Weisiger brings about a much-needed corrective to the study of the livestock era through her examination of Diné women during the implementation of the federal government's livestock reduction policy. Not only does Weisiger demonstrate the difficulty of understanding women's place during this crucial time in Navajo history, she also shows that women were important to economic production and that their influence ultimately shaped the direction that Navajos took in response to forced livestock reduction.[48]

Studies of Navajo life and culture have also addressed contemporary issues, such as the so-called "Navajo-Hopi land dispute." Rooted in the history of federal Indian policy, the dispute has its origins in President Chester Arthur's arbitrary decision to create a land base for Hopis where Navajos also lived. In 1958, the Hopi and Navajo tribes agreed to resolve their claims through the U.S. court system. The court's decision in 1962, *Healing v. Jones*, called for an equal division of the land, which resulted in the Navajos losing a substantial amount of territory to their Hopi neighbors. Whereas about three hundred Hopis were ordered to move off land awarded to Navajos, more than nine thousand Navajos were affected.

One of several accounts about the Navajo-Hopi land dispute is David Brugge's personalized narrative of the events leading up to the court decision, its impact on Navajos and Hopis, and ongoing resistance from Navajos. Brugge gives evidence of how indigenous people continue to be affected by colonial practices that keep them dependent on outside social, political, and economic forces. His account also demonstrates how modernization has fragmented communities from within.[49]

Significantly, Brugge also remarks on how popular stereotypes of Navajos and Hopis have formed the basis for court decisions detrimental to Navajos. The Hopi legal counsel employed images of Navajos as latecomers to the Southwest, "cultural-borrowers," naturally nomadic, warlike, and aggressive. The Hopis were depicted as a passive and peaceful people unfairly trodden upon by their neighbors. Brugge expresses incredulity at how the court was influenced by stereotypes: "I was aware of the bias against the Navajos that was, and still is, widespread in the Southwest, but again I had been so convinced of the basic fairness of our society that I could not conceive of such prejudice influencing official government decisions."[50] Another personalized narrative, by law professor Charles Wilkinson, delineates the consequences of development for Navajos, Hopis, and Utes. In *Fire on the Plateau: Conflict and Endurance in the American Southwest*, Wilkinson shows how these tribes have been exploited for their natural resources—water and coal—for the benefit of larger American society, without seeing very much benefit for their own communities and governments. Peter Iverson's *Diné: A History of the Navajo People*, demonstrates how historians can weave oral traditions and oral history into their narratives. In addition to using extensive Navajo sources, Iverson brings Navajo history into the twenty-first century.

David Brugge's realization about the power of representations is examined by anthropologist James Faris, who deconstructs conventional images of Navajos to elucidate the ways that texts themselves are yet another form of colonization. In *Navajo and Photography: A Critical History of the Representation of an American People*, Faris examines a substantial collection of photographs of Navajos to determine how they have been represented from the mid-nineteenth century to the present. Photographs, which outnumber all other portrayals of Navajos, have shaped the discourse on them and have been instrumental in perpetuating stereotypes. The earliest photographs of Navajos, taken at Fort Sumner in 1868, fixed them as hostiles and savages even though in reality the U.S. Army had just defeated them. The most prevalent depictions of Navajos coincided with the rise of tourism that began in the 1900s. Clearly, Navajos were subjected to the popular Western misconceptions of American Indians and cast as the "bad guys" in the dichotomies of civilized/savage, sedentary/ nomadic, anthropological knowledge/local ideology, and West/other. Faris notes photography's power to shape the discourse on Navajos: "Navajo space is denied them by the Western rewrite of their history, by the anthropological evidence of their late arrival, their adaptation, their alien and exotic character." He continues: "Photography becomes a perverse asset in denying Navajo history, and they become subjects only of the West's history."[51] The power of the prevailing discourse about Navajos and the inability of scholars to recognize the colonial nature of their research is demonstrated by journalist Margaret Regan, who has examined photographs of Navajos and Hopis from the 1930s and 1940s and reiterates familiar themes about the culturally sensitive relationships that white women have had with their Native subjects and the notion that Navajo subjects "chose" to pose for the portraits, thereby demonstrating agency.[52]

More recently, historian Erika Bsumek has revisited historical evidence to raise questions about Navajos as cultural borrowers.[53] As Bsumek argues, the idea of Navajos as primarily cultural borrowers gained validity during the early twentieth century as white researchers worked with collectors and museum officials who placed Navajos within an accepted paradigm in which they believed that indigenous cultures resided on the lower end of the scale of civility but that they could advance with guidance from whites. Bsumek's study complements those studies that challenge conventional views about the Navajos and their past.

Expressing surprise that little analysis exists on the mammoth volumes of Navajo studies, James Faris has recently offered an archaeology of Navajo anthropology with hopes of demonstrating how the field has been hegemonic and that it has mostly ignored and dismissed Navajo truths.[54] My own examination of Navajo studies, including history texts, aims to move toward the development of a critical perspective in Navajo Studies, something long overdue. As Faris notes in his essay, although there has been outright censorship of Navajo views, which can be seen in what gets published as well as sharp exchanges between Navajos and "experts on Navajos," Navajos are slowly taking over Navajo Studies: "Some might consider it censorship according to some politically correct agenda increasingly dominated by Navajos themselves. But increasing domination by Navajo scholars can only be a good thing, and should ultimately be celebrated."[55]

Oral Tradition and History

My own Diné history is shaped by the historiography analyzed above, the need to deconstruct prevailing images of Navajos that have shaped how we are understood, and my desire to propose a history that simultaneously engages existing studies and offers one Diné woman's understanding of how Diné perceive the past. Importantly, the dialogue between anthropology and history has stimulated new interest in rethinking the analytic distinction between myth and history and informs my own efforts to create a Navajo-centered history. Many scholars have articulated the differences between Western and indigenous views of the past by examining how oral traditions serve as frameworks for understanding and talking about it. Revisioning oral traditions and history demonstrates that histories are constructed around social, political, and economic norms, and shows them to be reflections of how we see ourselves as a people, as a culture, and as a nation. Furthermore, the production of history occurs within a political context in which power and knowledge are intrinsically connected.

Anthropologist Julie Cruikshank's studies of how oral traditions can serve as frameworks for Native history narratives are excellent examples of shifts in history studies in which textual analysis illuminates the ways histories are narratives about how cultures see themselves and their past. Cruikshank collected indigenous narratives from the Yukon about the Klondike gold rush of the late-nineteenth century, in which Native men and women played parts. Comparing stories told by Skookum Jim's descendants, Kitty Smith and Angela Sidney, Cruikshank argues that dominant American narratives about the Klondike gold rush concentrated on dreams of wealth and getting rich quickly, stories still told about the promise of wealth and prosperity in America for immigrants.[56] In these narratives, indigenous peoples who provided assistance in the form of labor and service—as guides, cooks, and sexual partners—play minor roles and are relegated to the shadows of the larger adventure story of how individual white men stumbled upon fabulous riches and proceeded to spend their fortunes lavishly. As Cruikshank notes, these narratives embody the meaning of the American experience for immigrants who dream of wealth, fame, and prosperity. These stories render invisible the consequences of European, and then American, imperial expansion into indigenous lands and the exploitation of indigenous labor and natural resources to benefit American dominant society.

Indigenous narratives about the Klondike gold rush reveal a different history, one in which indigenous men and women reacted within a colonial space in which traditional practices that sustained self-sufficiency were disrupted. The fur trade devastated the animal population, and men, whose primary role was hunting, were forced to seek other means of livelihood. Many found work as laborers and guides for whites flooding into the region. According to Skookum Jim's female descendants, Jim worked with whites because he needed to provide for his family and ensure the safety of his sister, who was married to one of the white men involved in the gold rush. In narratives told by Jim's descendants, his traditional responsibilities to his sister obligated him to look out for her, hence his partnership with the gold miners. The narratives also note how Jim was guided by traditional stories in which animals and humans communicated with each other and they note how these stories could be used to foretell the future. In these narratives, the focus is on community stability and the importance of following the dictates set down in traditional stories. The gold rush that benefited a few whites and brought even more of them into indigenous land became part of the stories about how indigenous peoples strove to reclaim their communities and their lives. These stories reaffirm indigenous beliefs and values in the face of colonialism. As Cruikshank notes of the stories told by whites and Natives, "Both have to be understood as windows on the way the past is constructed and discussed in different contexts, from the perspectives of actors enmeshed in culturally distinct networks of social relationships."[57] Narratives about the Klondike gold rush told from white perspectives center on individualism and the American success story of fame and prosperity. Stories about the same events told by indigenous storytellers focus on the welfare of the community and cultural survival.

Julie Cruikshank's finding that history, like other narratives, is constructed around cultural, economic, and political values of a society is part of a growing literature at the intersection of oral tradition and history. Conventional scholarship held that indigenous societies that presented their pasts in orally conveyed origin and creation stories resisted historical change and existed in an atemporal order, whereas modern societies embraced irreversible, cumulative changes. It was assumed that societies with history had "progressed" beyond myth. However, reevaluation of oral traditions has led to recognition that both history and myth are representations of the past. Critical scrutiny has exposed imposed distinctions between myth and history, named both categories as narratives about a people's view of themselves, challenged history's claims to objectivity, and questioned the "accuracy" of history based on written accounts as opposed to oral traditions passed down for generations. Indeed, exploration of the ways in which different cultures have understood and talked about the past has led to realization that Native societies formulate the past according to their traditions and that different cultures use a variety of narrative genres in their historical processes.

Ways of seeing the past for the Western world and for Native peoples are not dichotomous polar opposites; rather, it would be more accurate to say that Native people's perspectives of the past must be understood within a history of conquest, in which Europeans and then Americans attempted to strip Native peoples of their land, resources, culture, and knowledge. Historically, Native peoples have experienced attempted extermination, termination, relocation, and then assimilation. As a result, Native peoples' recovery of their own knowledge, cultures, and traditions occurs within a colonial setting in which they strive to reclaim their sovereignty. For example, when I began to collect stories and learning about creative narratives, I assumed that oral traditions were largely fragmented and that much had been lost.[58] As David Cohen observes, we must revise our notions of oral traditions as unchanging and static:

> [W]hen one seeks the rich, formal narrative, there is bound to be a sense of disappointment concerning the articulation of the knowledge of the past. If one listens with a more open definition of the meaning of historical knowledge, however, one finds that it is not located most formidably in poetic verse or extended narratives of a formulaic kind; it is constantly voiced, addressed, and invoked all through every day life. . . . [T]his voiced knowledge constitutes a remarkable reservoir of evidence on the past.[59]

Certainly the fact that oral traditions have survived more than five hundred years of colonization is a testimony to their resilience and points to the value that indigenous people still place upon them. Recently, I was fortunate to attend a lecture by Cree historian Winona (Stevenson) Wheeler, who, in sharing Cree oral histories, reaffirmed that oral traditions are part of our lived experiences as Native people, and that they do not exist simply as bodies of ceremonial knowledge. It was inspiring to hear her reaffirm how they remain a conduit for revitalizing our indigenous traditional values within our own communities.[60]

Understanding how Native peoples talk about and understand our own past requires us to change how we write history, for differences include conceptions of time and space, and uses of the past. Furthermore, historians who work with oral history and traditions must use methodologies that are ethical and responsible to the Native communities about which they write. Stevenson (Wheeler) notes that Western, or conventional, historiography is firmly grounded in a number of tenets, which upon perusal explains why indigenous oral histories are still considered suspect as vehicles to write about the past. The writing of history requires attention to precision in form, in which we expect narratives to have a beginning, middle, and end, and to be documented through written reports. Time is important and historians must pay attention to how events are measured in a linear fashion that allows readers to visualize cause and effect. Plotting events on a timeline means that we assess the past and make determinations about how society has improved; thus, the meaning of the past is wrapped up in notions of progress. Historians continue to prefer sources that can be checked for accuracy, meaning that written documents are still considered veritable sources that can be checked for validity. Stevenson (Wheeler) notes that New Indian history, for all of its good intentions, has reinforced "the colonialist notion that Western historical canons and conventions are superior—that their methods and sources support 'true history' and that Native people have no historical traditions worthy of note."[61]

Indigenous scholars like Greg Cajete, Vine Deloria Jr., Winona Stevenson Wheeler, and Waziyatawin Angela Wilson have contributed significantly to the valuation of oral traditions across disciplines as an approach that facilitates stability and continuity with the past in Native communities.[62] In placing at the center of their inquiries oral traditions as vehicles for understanding the past, Native scholars and their allies are revising the definition of oral tradition and history, demonstrating how they remain integral to how tribal peoples see themselves, their past, and their future.

The attempt to define oral tradition has preoccupied many scholars, but there is no clear consensus. Conventional approaches to oral forms of conveying the past are classified in a number of ways, including characterizations of them as myths, legends, and folklore. Oral history, another category, is defined as the lived experiences of interviewees. Of "myths," Ruth Finnegan observes that they are "obviously fictional" because they feature deities, imaginary beings, or animals, and thus yield little historical evidence. According to her, they should instead be considered reflections of present realities and preoccupations.[63] Finnegan lists three main classes of oral tradition: "recognized literary forms, generalized historical knowledge, and personal recollections."[64] Historian Jan Vansina notes that throughout the world people who lack writing still rely on oral traditions to reconstruct the past. He defines oral tradition as the conveyance of knowledge handed down for at least a few generations and oral history as the study of the recent past by means of life histories and personal recollections that informants share when relating personal experiences.[65]

Angela Wilson also provides valuable insights into the nature of oral traditions and their uses for understanding the past from Native perspectives. In her article, "Power of the Spoken Word: Native Oral Traditions in American Indian History," Wilson suggests that oral tradition is contained within oral history:

> From a native perspective, I would suggest instead that the definition of oral history is contained within that of the oral tradition. For the Dakota, "oral tradition" refers to the way in which information is passed on rather than the length of time something has been told. Hence, personal experience, pieces of information, events, incidents, and other phenomena can become a part of the oral tradition at the moment they happen or at the moment they are told, as long as the person adopting the memory is part of an oral tradition. This definition also implies that while those belonging to an oral tradition would be able to relate aspects of oral history, not everyone relating oral history necessarily belongs to an oral tradition.[66]

Wilson's definition acknowledges a number of features that are important characteristics of Native oral traditions. The fact that oral traditions, of which the creation narratives are crucial components, have survived more than five hundred years of conquest attests to their tenacity and indicates that Native societies never severed their link with the sacred, with the cosmos, nature, community, and kin.[67] As Stevenson (Wheeler) notes, "Within the historical context of colonialism, it is a testament to People's spiritual strength and tenacity that so much oral history still exists in our communities."[68] Furthermore, these links are articulated through the creation narratives and include the following characteristics: they often reflect interactions between humans and nonhumans, as well as the memories passed down from the ancestors; and the retelling of creation narratives often incorporates new materials, thereby denying earlier anthropological assertions that oral traditions are static and bound by customs. Significantly, many Native people still consider their realities to include the power to speak to the deities and animals. Moveover, oral tradition "refers to the way in which information is passed on rather than the length of time something has been told."[69] For Native peoples, oral tradition encompasses personal experiences, pieces of information, events, incidents, and other phenomenon. As a person listens to the stories being relayed, she or he adopts the memories of the person who tells the narratives. Mexican scholar Enrique Florescano, in his examination of how the indigenous people of Mexico have incorporated into their histories those narratives often referred to as "myths," offers the valuable insight that myth is a form of narrating outstanding events that happen to a community and that it refers back to primordial times when all creation occurred, the perfect moment. Narrating history, then, for many Native peoples, means to refer to the past when perfection was achieved. In calling up the "mythic" past, Native peoples are reminded of beliefs and values that have stabilized their communities. As Florescano notes, recalling the past through the vehicle of creation narratives is a "rejection of the oppressive conditions of the present" that aspires to restore the lost past or to create a perfect community inspired by the idealized memory of the past.[70] Certainly for the Diné, invoking the creation narratives, the events and the beings who act in them, provides lessons for life, allowing listeners to reflect on how hózhó can be regained. Events that took place during the creation and the journey to the present world still take place. We also learn from the stories what can happen when we do not follow directives set down during primordial times.

My brief survey of the treatment of Navajo oral narratives indicates movement toward understanding how traditional narratives influence and shape Navajo societies, including understanding of the past. Studies have yet to formulate fully how Navajos have experienced history and to outline the ongoing means and processes of ethnogenesis by which they have struggled to make sense out of complex historical processes.

Recovering the Diné in Diné Studies

In the 1950s, the Navajo Tribe hired anthropologist Richard Van Valkenburgh to gather data for the Land Claims Commission. With colleagues J. Lee Correll and David Brugge, he brought together a variety of sources on Navajos that spanned the disciplines of archaeology, anthropology, history, and oral history. The accumulated knowledge, which ironically allowed for a reduction in lands that Navajos claimed because it formulated conventional wisdom about Navajos, found its way into Navajo communities via the tribal newspaper through publication of primary documents such as military reports and photographs. The researchers also published their own articles in journals and magazines meant for a popular audience. Dissemination of this knowledge about Navajos was their first exposure to Western concepts of Navajo history and has been instrumental in shaping a Navajo sense of the past. Today, the assembled information makes up the bulk of the archives housed at the Navajo Nation Library in Window Rock, Arizona, and is a valuable resource for engaging with the past.

The land claims research papers were followed by a number of Navajo-controlled publications like oral histories and the creation narratives that the Rough Rock Demonstration School and Navajo Community College Presses published.[71] From the 1960s to the 1980s, Diné educators like Ruth Roessel collaborated with white authors and collected interviews with Navajo community members who shared stories about Navajo life. Central to their narratives are the Long Walk, the Bosque Redondo experience, and the livestock reductions of the 1930s and 1940s, all of which are historical watersheds. Interviewees shared stories that make stark the brutality of federal Indian policies on Navajo life, and at the same time show resilience and determination in the face of colonialism. By understanding the relationship between oral tradition and history and how the creation narratives inform Diné historical processes, it becomes possible to ascertain how the Diné have responded to colonial domination and, importantly, understand the centrality of traditional narratives as a strategy of accommodation and resistance to ongoing cultural changes. Studies that center Diné philosophy challenge and counter the legitimacy of Western discourses that purport to represent the Navajo past, exposing many of them as the continuation of colonialism. These early efforts, which include the articulation of a Navajo-based history, are the foundations for the movement toward indigenizing Navajo education. Navajos' own stories about their identity and their past challenge established constructions of Navajos. Most importantly, deconstructions of the images clear the space for more accurate representations, including ones that Navajos themselves articulate.

As more indigenous scholars emerge from university programs with professional degrees, efforts to create academic programs relevant to our students is taking on an insistence also reflected in ongoing efforts to reclaim Diné studies. For example, Diné scholar Tiffany Lee argues that critical pedagogy should be linked to transforming social movements with the intention of realizing real Diné sovereignty. As Lee notes, Paulo Freire's articulation of education speaks to Native scholars and educators, who see in it a means to create critical consciousness that empowers individuals, who can then use education to better their communities and thereby transform oppressive conditions in the world.[72] Similarly, at a recent Navajo Studies conference, Diné scholar Larry Emerson articulated a decolonization methodology that exposes the ways in which the Diné have experienced colonialism, including their continued colonization through publications. Emerson emphasized the central place of our philosophy of hózhó in all of our studies as a major movement toward decolonization. The next section discusses what it means to place Diné philosophy and concepts at the center of our studies. For my purposes, I consider how the Navajo past looks when Diné philosophy becomes the point of reference.

Historian Kenneth Pratt offers his understanding of Diné perceptions of the past with his exploration of *Ałk'idáá*, our word for the past, which means "a long time ago." Translated literally, *Ałk'idáá* means "on top of each other in the past," or "experiences or events stacked up through time."[73] *Ałk'idáá* references events that occurred during primordial times, beginning with occurrences in the first world and the subsequent journey into the next worlds until the ancestors of the Diné emerged in the present world. The past is centered in the heartland of Navajo Country, in the present-day San Juan region in northwestern New Mexico. It is here that many of the events related in the creation narratives took place, beginning with the emergence from the lower worlds into the present world, the Glittering World.

In the unfolding events, Diné values were established. These included lessons learned as a result of transgressions. Ałk'idáá emphasizes place, direction, and the relationship between deities and humans/Diné and nature. In multiple ways, the belief system established during primordial times manifests itself in Navajo society. For example, the Blessingway (Hózhóji) was first performed by the Holy People to insure a state of harmony and balance. Today, Hózhóji remains at the core of Navajo life and is performed for prosperity. In particular, the ceremony is the focus of the Kinaaldá, which is performed for young women who have come into womanhood.

Ałk'idáá' is also a reference point for storytellers. In stories about the past, the primordial time comes alive as storytellers reiterate accounts of events that led to the establishment of the world, how the boundaries of Navajo Land were set and how the People learned the rules for proper living. Our ancestors play important roles in these stories. When my father shared one of his narratives with me about how Naayéé Neezghání (Monster Slayer) slew the giant at Blue Water and its significance, he began, "It is said," and noted that he had not seen the events himself but had been told about them. This way of beginning a story gives an indication of how old the story is, for it has passed through many generations since time immemorial. The phrase reflects an important measure of responsibility that the listener takes on to see that the story continues to be relayed.

Diné writer Rex Lee Jim provides an excellent example of how Diné philosophy, *Sa'ah naaghái bik'eh hózhóón nisłóo naasháa doo*, plays a central role in his life. He translates this phrase as "May I be Everlasting and Beautiful Living."[74] It also means to walk on the path of Beauty and Harmony to Old Age, which is the purpose of life. Beginning his narrative about his childhood, Jim describes the impact of boarding school on his life and how he was able to return to traditional teachings in spite of Western education. He references the nightmare of Hwéeldi, the Diné word for the Bosque Redondo reservation, how the People suffered and endured, and how the concept of hózhó was a path to healing and recovery for our grandparents. Jim considers Diné traditional teaching effective: "Today's teachers reach back into the past, beyond the present and this world, to bring into this world and present methods that work in creating a life that vibrates with happiness. Effective teachings defy death. They become traditions and are the foundation of effective living."[75]

Other Diné writers, like Luci Tapahonso, Ruth Roessel, Nia Francisco, Laura Tohe, Esther Belin, Irvin Morris, and Marilyn Help Hood, among many others, also convey the vitality of the oral tradition in their artistic expressions.[76] For example, in her poems, Luci Tapahonso reminds us of our relationships to the natural world and to each other. In "This Is How They Were Placed for Us," she invokes the four sacred mountains, Blanca Peak, Mount Taylor, the San Francisco Peaks, and Hesperus Peak, in the prescribed fashion, going from the east and moving in a circle westward. Each of the mountains imparts lessons about the stages of life, which are also reflected in the language of changing seasons. Values conveyed include ones about mothers' love for their children and the reasons why Navajos wear turquoise.[77]

In other poems, like "Shisóí" and "'Ahidzískéii," Tapahonso treats us to a sense of Navajo relationships.[78] "Shisóí" or "maternal grand-child" is about the delight that a grandmother feels at the birth of a grandchild. The grandmother simply cannot find words to express her love, and she says repeatedly, "All you can do is kiss her warm forehead and say, 'She's so sweet, I don't know what do.'" In particular, the love and nurture shown to a child is reminiscent of the care provided to the infant who became Changing Woman. "Ahidzískéii," translated as "two who sit together," is a poem about the meaning of marriage. This phrase describes the ideal marriage and it reflects a complementary relationship of mutual respect. Significantly, Tapahonso's poems indicate that the most enduring relationship among Navajos is the mother-child one, which anthropologist Garry Witherspoon describes as "Mother and child are bound together by the most intense, the most diffuse, and the most enduring solidarity to be found in Navajo culture."[79] Like other Diné writers, Tapahonso's prose and poetry transcends cultural boundaries, appealing to Navajos and non-Navajos alike, and it reaffirms the beliefs and values that sustained our grandmothers and grandfathers.

Although most writings by Diné are autobiographical and creative nonfiction, there are collaborations on life stories, such as that of anthropologist Charlotte Frisbie, who worked with Frank Mitchell and Rose Mitchell; and historian Robert McPherson, who published Navajo Oshley's story with afterwords by whites who knew Oshley.[80] McPherson also published John Holiday's life story.[81] All of these narratives focus on Navajo men and women at least one generation removed from the Bosque Redondo experience. Their stories depict the introduction of a wage economy among Navajos after the livestock reductions of the 1930s and 1940s, and show how individuals struggled to sustain themselves and their families. In Frank Mitchell's story, knowledge of tradition and ceremonies serves as the basis for centering his life and provides the foundation for him to become a prominent community leader. In her autobiography, Rose Mitchell states that she worked with Charlotte Frisbie because she felt that Navajos should have access to her story and learn about Navajo life and the importance of knowing about the past. The past remains a vital source for conveying knowledge about proper social relations that extend from the natural world to human society. Unfortunately, McPherson's supplement to Navajo Oshley's narrative, which was intended to provide a context to the end of Oshley's life, mostly perpetuates white stereotypes about Navajos.

My own research on the stories of my great-great-great-grandmother, in chapter 5, offers evidence of the ways in which oral tradition still informs Diné perspectives on the past and how the Diné looked to the past to meet the challenges of the present.

Personalizing the Methodology

Conducting research in our respective tribal communities entails facing a different set of issues, ones associated with "insider" and "outsider" issues. Decolonizing research is about centering indigenous worldviews and articulating theory and research from our own perspectives and for our own purposes.[82] Writing indigenous-centered histories has included interdisciplinary approaches such as poststructuralism, feminist theories, and postcolonial studies. My ongoing research projects acknowledge the nature of colonialism and its consequences for our society, and at the same time reaffirm the value of our own traditions and practices. By critiquing works that refuse to acknowledge the colonial nature in which we continue to live and then advancing studies that privilege a Diné worldview I hope to contribute to the betterment of our communities, for the Diné believe in the power of stories to transform, to move mountains. In particular, highlights of my own work have been a broadened understanding of my community, enhancement of my intellectual development, affirmation of my research from community members, and renewal of kin relationships.

Utilizing oral traditions to write Diné history requires changes in our approaches so that we become cognizant of community involvement and sensitive to Navajo needs. As Salish scholar Luana Ross notes, conducting research in our own communities leads to a personalized methodology that differs across tribal cultures. "As researchers, we must be compassionate and sensitive to decently interpreted experiences; we cannot pretend to remain objective," she writes. "When I interview people, I communicate in a meaningful, sincere manner. Moreover, the people I interview are not objects—I see them as real people. The goal of my research," she points out, "is to implement social change by taking their voices, their experiences, back to Native communities and policy-making officials."[83] During the course of my work in Navajo communities, I discovered that many Diné are willing to talk with Diné researchers. I hear community members and elders express concern and disappointment that the young people are forgetting cultural values. They welcome chances to share their knowledge and expertise in a number of subjects. Furthermore, cognizant of the effects of colonialism, community members support research that acknowledges our current state of dependency as well as research that revitalizes and contributes to our society.

For my own research, which was initiated as a dissertation project, I followed research guidelines set down by the Navajo Nation Historic Preservation Department and received an endorsement from my own chapter (Tohatchi) to conduct interviews with Navajos. I also received permission from the Navajo Nation's attorney general to examine the substantial collection of land claims papers, which are housed at the Navajo Nation Library. A novice researcher, I imagine that my experiences are similar to many Navajos of my generation. That is, my knowledge of Navajo and Native history was limited because the education system on the Navajo nation did not—and still does not—require that these subjects be a part of the curricula. I understand the Diné language like a fluent speaker and can speak it at a conversational level. As a child growing up in Ganado, Arizona, and then Tohatchi, New Mexico, I listened to my parents, who speak predominately Navajo. Although they spoke to my siblings and me in Navajo, we almost always answered them in English. The ban on speaking Native languages set down as federal Indian policy in the nineteenth century reverberates in our communities today.

Ethical research requires that the researcher become involved with the community she is studying. Unfortunately, researchers still think they can learn about a Native group's history simply by referring to archival documents and secondary history sources, which are still largely written by non-Indians. As Winona Stevenson (Wheeler) noted at a Western History Association conference, some scholars have refused to engage with Native peoples because they consider it onerous and time-consuming to be "traipsing around Indian country."[84] It is also relevant for becoming involved in the community to question whether or not a researcher has taken the time to learn the language or even become slightly familiar with it. Each language carries within it a culture's worldview. It is still the case today that Native peoples perceive the world in a vastly different way from Western worldviews.

For my study, which may also be the experience of other Native researchers, I gained the trust of elders with whom I worked because they are clan relatives, several of whom are my maternal grandparents. I prepared interview questions that my mother and I tested and worded in Navajo until I felt that the translations represented my intentions. As any researcher who works within the Navajo community knows, it is a feat to make an appointment and then actually find an interviewee home. There were countless times when we arrived at a grandparent's home, only to discover that he or she had accompanied a son or daughter into Gallup. It was also rarely possible to conduct a one-on-one interview since homes were often filled with two or three generations of family members. Almost always, interviews became storytelling sessions, and between questions and answers there were a number of stories shared with my mother and me about daily events and upcoming ceremonies. Community members were also intensely interested in what written documents say about Navajos. Their comments added significant details about beliefs, attitudes, and practices, some of which have changed. As Miwok-Pomo literary critic Greg Sarris notes, oral traditions are embedded in cultural contexts that are understood, and the histories of the speakers may or may not be evoked during exchanges: "One party may write a story, but one party's story is no more the whole story than a cup of water is the river."[85]

Initially, like many other researchers, I was hesitant to approach people—in my case, my relatives—for interviews. I was very relieved when most were receptive to my questions. Perhaps my elders agreed to share their stories with me because they respect my mother as their maternal niece, or "daughter," as they refer to her. One incident made it clear to me that how one's ancestors are regarded is also how one will be regarded. Early in my quest to find clan members able to tell me about Manuelito, Juanita, and their family members, my mother and I went to the home of one of her uncles. In the early 1990s, he was quite elderly and becoming forgetful. Although his daughter allowed us to speak with him, it was clear that we would not get much information from him. When we first introduced ourselves, my mother began by telling him that she was the granddaughter of Dághá Chíí. The elder responded with kind words, saying, "Yes, yes, Dághá Chíí. He was a good man." My mother was pleased to hear good words about her great-grandfather. One lesson I learned from this brief encounter, which was confirmed during other visits of ours to elders, is that we are responsible to our ancestors so we must always behave in correct fashion, especially since our children and great-grandchildren will be known by our behavior.

Interviews also facilitated my acquaintance with my grandparents, and, through their stories, with their immediate families. I grew to appreciate how they had lived their lives and endeavored to provide for their families. I remain deeply appreciative to have known them and their family. I remember the stories they shared with my mother and me. Mike Allison Sr.'s stories, especially, made me think of how Diné men fared during the early twentieth century when adjusting to new roles in the early reservation period. Although many Navajo men were forced to seek employment beyond Navajo Land's borders because there were few wage jobs available and the livestock industry had been decimated, Mike was fortunate to find employment at the Tohatchi Boarding School, where he worked for many years in facilities management. He worked close to home and was able to return each evening to be with his wife and growing family of nine sons and one daughter. Because he was able to work near home, he also managed his livestock—sheep, goats, cattle, and horses—which became the foundation for life lessons passed on to his children and grandchildren.

For Native researchers, many of whom prefer to work in their own communities, research can present opportunities to relearn cultural values and even the language. Another result of conducting these interviews, in addition to getting to know my grandparents, was that my fluency in Navajo improved considerably, as did my knowledge of local history and the continuing importance of ceremonies and other Navajo ways. Research became a method for strengthening kin ties, and with visits (called fieldwork) our relationships became stronger. In December 1999, I completed my dissertation and filed my graduation papers. I had finally arrived at the end of one stage in my life, ready to begin another. My grandmother, Joan Kinsel, presented me with a Pendleton shawl. I have a Pendleton shawl for every important passage in my life. I have one that my parents gave to me when I turned sixteen. I have one given to me as a wedding gift, and a couple from ceremonies. The fact that my grandmother gave me a Pendleton was very special. Over the years, my mother and I were invited to occasions held in honor of my grandparents, Mike Allison Sr. and Anna Allison. We attended their wedding anniversaries and grandpa Mike's birthday parties. In May 2005, Mike passed away at one hundred and four years of age. His wife Anna had died two years earlier.

Another benefit that comes with working in one's own community is that, in talking to clan relatives and community members, I discovered which issues were deemed important. Some of these have become the basis for new research projects. For example, being fully aware of the devastation that conquest has wreaked on the Diné, a factor that no doubt contributes significantly to the state of oral traditions today, we often discussed controversial issues, including ones that the Navajo Nation council was addressing. Rather than accept unquestioningly the stance that tradition as referenced in our stories is unchanging, we must acknowledge that five hundred years of countering colonialism has led to internalizations of Western beliefs, values, and practices that work to fragment our communities.[86] My research on the Navajo Nation government and gender came about as a result of my observations and conversations with other Navajo women and community members. Because of contemporary interpretations of tradition, Navajo women have been discouraged from full political participation in the Navajo government even as they are recognized as leaders at the community level and heads of household. Because of American assimilation policies, there are few, if any, Diné who have not been affected. Thus, when we consider the meaning and significance of oral traditions, we must also realize that, although they have the power to speak to the issues and problems we face today as Native peoples, oral traditions are also subject to interpretation within modern frameworks. Furthermore, engagement with community members as equals occurred as a series of dialogues in which I sometimes changed or was affirmed in what I had previously thought. For example, although narratives may often appear fragmented and incomplete on the surface, increasing familiarity with clan kin networks reveals a context that has foundations in the creation narratives.

Conclusion

Maori scholar Linda Tuhiwai Smith articulates very well the story of how non-Indians dismissed indigenous systems of order as they carved up our world to fit Western categories. The history of research and its practices is linked to imperialism and Western systems of knowledge that historically have exploited and destroyed indigenous communities. On multiple levels, from within communities to the academy, indigenous peoples are reclaiming their intellectual traditions. Important critiques of existing scholarship have revealed Western scholarship to be simply another kind of imperialism that reinscribes existing structures of power. Responding to larger calls that our research be transformative, Diné scholars are reclaiming the right to raise questions about the ways in which our people have been represented, and in the process they are theorizing and researching in ways that revalue Diné philosophy. Significantly, they also assert that our intellectual work should uphold Diné sovereignty, as leaders like Manuelito had envisioned. As Linda Smith declares of the transformative power of writing and theorizing, "It is not simply about giving an oral account or a genealogical naming of the land and the events which raged over it, but a very powerful need to give testimony to and restore a spirit, to bring back into existence a world fragmented and dying."[87]

In contrast to our presentation by non-Indians, Navajos have very specific things to say about how we see our past and ourselves. It is still the case that we privilege a worldview founded on the values and traditions embedded in our oral traditions. By first examining a body of Navajo Studies and then considering how a Navajo perspective might be advanced through the framework of oral traditions, I offer a perspective on Navajo history based on methodologies that use both written documents and oral history.

3/A Biographical Account of Manuelito

Noble Savage, Patriotic Warrior, and American Citizen

In 1990, Diné grandmother Tiana Bighorse published the stories that her father Gus had passed on to her about the traumas that her Diné people had endured during the American government's war on them. In 1863, the forces of the American military, New Mexicans, and Pueblo auxiliaries gathered against the Navajo people, burned their hogans and cornfields, slashed their fruit trees, and captured women and children for the slave market to force their surrender. Subjugated by such brutal tactics, more than eleven thousand Navajos were forced to march—their Trail of Tears—to the Bosque Redondo prison camp, where they endured harsh winters, forced labor, starvation, disease, sexual violence, and capture by slave raiders. Between 1863 and 1868, about twenty-five hundred Navajos died, many at the prison camp.

Gus Bighorse's life (1846–1939) spanned the nineteenth and twentieth centuries. Witnessing the war on his people and their subsequent imprisonment at Bosque Redondo for four years, and then adjusting to reservation life after 1868, Bighorse tells stories that make vivid the violence and brutality the Navajo people endured. His narratives impressed upon a young Tiana the meaning of warrior. To be a warrior means to be compassionate and loving and to defend Dinétah. Grandmother Tiana's goal, to remind present and future Diné generations of their ancestors' courage, is a lesson that many of my Diné students have taken to heart.

During this period of great trauma for the People, Gus Bighorse was only one of many warriors to whom the Diné looked for guidance and protection. One of the best known of the Diné warriors, Hastiin Ch'il Hajin (Man of Black Weeds), or Manuelito, fought against Mexican domination in the 1820s and then emerged as one of the most resistant warriors to oppose American expansion in 1846 and the invasion of Navajo Land from 1850 to 1868. With the Navajos' return to their homeland in 1868, Manuelito remained an influential leader, which Indian agents recognized. The early reservation period, from the 1870s into the late 1890s, was a time when the People strove to rebuild their society. It was a period characterized by conflicts between Navajo herdsmen and New Mexican ranchers who claimed the same grazing pastures. Manuelito attended to these conflicts, many of which seemed unsolvable and were often resolved in favor of white and New Mexican ranchers. By the 1880s, Indian agents reported that Manuelito was an alcoholic; his death in 1894 was related to his alcoholism, complicated by diseases such as pneumonia and chicken pox. American officials named Chee Dodge as Manuelito's successor, the next leader of the Navajos.[1]

Today, for both whites and Navajos, albeit in different ways, Manuelito remains a symbol—the spirit of Navajo resistance. The corpus of Western and Navajo histories to be analyzed include those published between 1960 and 2004. Currently, there are four short biographies of Manuelito, which span the twentieth century, published in 1908, 1965, 1970, and 1993. In 1965, J. Lee Correll published the first account of Manuelito in the *Navajo Times*. It was one of the first extensive treatments of Manuelito that Navajos themselves had read.[2] A draft of a longer biography of Manuelito that J. Lee Correll never published is part of the Navajo land claims papers in the Navajo Nation Library. Manuelito is also sketched in several encyclopedia entries.[3] Frank McNitt's *Navajo Wars: Military Campaigns, Slave Raids, and Reprisals* devotes significant attention to Manuelito's role in the war between Navajos and the Americans.[4] The biographical sketches by Maj.-Gen. O. O. Howard, Virginia Hoffman and Broderick Johnson, and Frank Waters were published several decades apart, but do not deviate from portrayals of Manuelito that place him within American frameworks for understanding indigenous leaders.[5]

This chapter recounts Manuelito's life and is based on published article-length biographies, secondary sources, and the few stories from Navajos that I have been able to recover. Influenced by New Indian history methodology that purports to offer a more balanced history by centering Native American experiences and presenting sympathetic portrayals, narratives produced by non-Indians portray the Diné leader as such a force of resistance that historian Clifford Trafzer named him "the defiant spirit of the Navajo."[6] At the same time, these narratives merely supplement the established narrative of Euro-American history by inserting Manuelito's story. The Diné leader's defiance, subjugation, and seeming capitulation are part of America's story of itself as a nation that embraces cultural diversity. In America's interpretation of itself, Indian men become part of the narrative in their portrayals as noble and ignoble savages who are defeated and relocated to reservations, where they become advocates of federal Indian assimilation policies. The depictions continue: if they fail to assimilate, they are cast as ignoble savages who must fall before the inevitable onslaught of American civilization.[7] Although historians are now more likely to be attuned to Navajo views on their past, presentations of Diné history still neutralize the meaning of the war on Navajos, deny the horrors that they endured, and ignore the inequalities and injustices that Navajos still face.

Manuelito plays a significant role in the narrative of Manifest Destiny and in New Indian histories, and his own people have memorialized him through stories, songs, and images as a patriot who would have willingly given his life for his people and his land. Remembering their leader in ways that highlight his dedication, the Diné depict Manuelito as a warrior who resisted foreign domination, voiced convictions about resistance as an appropriate response, and always fought for Diné sovereignty. After resettlement in Navajo Country, Manuelito advocated American education for our children, not because he believed we should resemble white Americans, but to ensure the survival of the People. I found a few stories of Manuelito among the Navajo and discovered two interviews recorded in 1966 with his son, Bob Manuelito, or Manuelito Number Two, known to Navajos as Naaltsoos Neiyéhí (Mail Carrier) (fig. 15). In one of the interviews, white researchers asked Naaltsoos Neiyéhí whether he had any stories of his father. He assured them that, indeed, he did, and that Manuelito had dedicated his life to his people, believing that the Diné must think always about 'Iiná—Life, the path to the future.[8]

Interestingly, one of the most popular portraits of Manuelito in Navajo Land is a reproduction of a photograph taken by frontier photographer Ben Wittick in 1882. Paintings, murals, Navajo Nation newsletters, and billboards (fig. 16) display this popular image of the Diné leader. In this portrait, a bare-chested Manuelito sits with a Navajo-woven textile draped across his lap. His eyes are downcast, his left arm cradles a quiver casing adorned with an eagle feather. A necklace with several strands of beads encircles his neck. The Navajos' embrace of this portrait of their beloved leader gives an indication of how reports and photographs of the Diné have become sources for reclaiming the Diné past, on the terms of our ancestors as well as our own.

Spaniards and Mexicans

The Diné have long been known for the ways in which cycles of con-quest have transformed their cultural, political, and social systems, beginning with the Spaniards in the late 1500s and continuing through American rule that began in 1846. A brief overview of Navajo history provides a context for Manuelito's life and indicates causes for his life-long resistance to colonial forces in which the Diné saw few, if any, differences among those who sought to claim indigenous labor, land, and natural resources for their own enrichment.

During Manuelito's lifetime, the indigenous people of the South-west had already witnessed at least two hundred years under the Spaniards, who ruthlessly exploited Pueblo lands, resources, labor, and women. Spanish treatment of indigenous peoples was initiated by Christopher Columbus, whom historian Jack Forbes declares "sin-gular in that he was, from the first, a dedicated slaver and exploiter with an extremely callous and indifferent attitude towards culturally different human beings."[9] The Spaniards also introduced domesti-cated animals like horses, cows, and sheep that revolutionized Diné society, transforming their lifeways from dependence on hunting and gathering for subsistence to pastoralism. Ironically, the adoption of the horse turned them into warriors who ably resisted conquest until 1864.[10]

The Spanish conquerors rarely saw the ancestors of the contempo-rary Diné. In 1626, Fray Gerónimo de Zarate Salmerón recorded the first known European reference to Navajos when he asked the Jemez people about Ute locations and was told that the "Apache de Nabajú" lived north of the Jemez, along the Chama River. The name *Nabajú* comes from a Tewa word that means "large arroyo with cultivated fields."[11] Three years later, in 1630, Fray Alonso de Benavides wrote a lengthy account of the Navajos. Describing them as a "vigorous and warlike people and very brave in war; even in the manner of speaking they stand apart from the other nations," Benavides reported on their religion and manner of dress and on the possibility of converting them to Catholicism.[12] The Spaniards' unabashed brutality toward the Pueblo peoples eventually led to a full-scale rebellion in 1680.

After the Spanish reconquest in 1693, the Diné were in constant conflict with them, especially when the Spanish governors organized slaving expeditions against the Diné. There are currently questions about the amount of influence that Pueblo refugees might have had on Navajos during this early period; however, archaeologists take the Pueblo-like fortresses that the Diné used for protection as proof that Pueblo peoples came to live with them.[13] In any case, Spanish rule transformed Diné relationships with Pueblo people. Traditionally, the Diné had traded with their Pueblo neighbors and established political and military alliances with them. In addition, their clan system indicates a history of kinship ties through marriage. At the same time, Navajo attacks on Pueblo and New Mexican villages, either for the purpose of adding to their growing flocks or for reprisals because their women and children were targets for the slave raiders, strained relations with the Pueblo peoples. This tension lingers in Pueblo memory and is reflected in Jemez historian Joe Sando's remarks that at Jemez traditional dances non-Indians are still viewed with suspicion, whereas former enemies like the Navajos are allowed and even welcomed.[14]

Historian Frank McNitt made note of the reprisals that Navajo suffered under the Spaniards. In 1675 and 1678, Juan Domínguez de Mendoza led three raids into Navajo Land. His men stole Navajo women and children, seized horses, and burned cornfields. Roque Madrid undertook another set of reprisal against the Navajos. Most likely, Madrid's first campaign, in 1705, was a response to two large parties of Diné warriors that had attacked San Juan, Santa Clara, and San Ildelfonso Pueblos and driven off their herds.[15]

Madrid's second foray into Navajo country is recorded in his journal, which was published in 1996 by Rick Hendricks and John P. Wilson.[16] Along with Madrid's descriptions of the countryside, which allowed Hendricks and Wilson to map the Spaniards' route through Navajo country, is his report on encountering two Native women. Madrid reported, "One was a Christian from the Jemez nation and

the other an Apache. I immediately separated them, putting them to
torture so that they would tell me where they were from, what they
were doing there, or where their camps were."[17] According to Hendricks and Wilson, the Jemez woman was married to a Diné man.[18]
No doubt, in addition to their own observations, the Navajos also
learned of Spanish cruelty and treachery through the Pueblo peoples
who came to live with them. It is no surprise that the Diné preferred
to live in mountainous regions that protected them from the Spanish
invaders.

A half-century of peace started in 1709, after Madrid led another
campaign into Navajo Country, causing untold suffering that led the
Navajo to sue for peace.[19] Frank McNitt suggests that the People's
desire for peace with the Spaniards was most likely shaped by pressure
they felt from the combined forces of the Comanches and Utes, who
were armed by other imperial forces such as the French. Consequently,
the Diné moved out of the San Juan region, dispersing north and west
toward present-day Mount Taylor and the Chuska Mountains. Spanish settlers began to infiltrate Navajo lands at Encino and Cebolleta,
places where Franciscan missionaries unsuccessfully attempted to con-
vert the Diné to Catholicism. When Spanish authorities issued land
grants between 1753 and 1772, the Navajos manifested their objections
in an alliance with Apaches that commenced 1772. Attacks on Pueblo
and Hispanic villages forced the Hispanic settlers to withdraw.[20] By the
1750s, the Diné grazed their growing flocks as far west as Wide Ruins
and Ganado. Their presence was noted from Chaco Canyon along the
entire Chuska Mountain chain, past Canyon de Chelly.[21]

Unwilling to submit to Spanish domination, live in villages, and
become Christianized, Navajos felt Spanish wrath. One incident that
remains in Navajo memory is the massacre of their people at Canyon del Muerto in 1805. In January 1805, Lieut. Antonio de Narbona
descended into the canyon to avenge an attack on Cebolleta the previous summer. Dispatching columns to Chaco Canyon and Canyons
de Chelly and del Muerto, Lieutant Narbona searched for his Navajo
victims. Above his head, Diné hidden in a cave were revealed when
an elderly woman, possibly a former slave of the Spaniards, shouted
expletives at the soldiers. The soldiers fired into the cave; bullets rico-
cheted and killed Navajos. When the firing stopped, more than 100 of
the People lay dead and more than 30 were taken captive. The Spaniards also took about 350 sheep and goats.[22] The Navajo experience

under Spanish rule did not change substantially under Mexican rule, from 1820 to 1846.

Manuelito was born into the Bit'ahnii clan near Bear Ears, Utah, around 1818. An interview by anthropologists J. Lee Correll and David Brugge with Naaltsoos Neiyéhí sheds some light on Manuelito's early life. The interviewers were particularly interested in Naaltsoos Nei-yéhí's father, and he shared several stories. Of his father's birth, he related the following:

> Manuelito was born after his mother endured three days of hard labor. When his father learned of his son's birth, he took the new-born outside and presented him to the east, to the Holy People, and prophesied that his son would be a great leader. He blessed his son, saying, "My baby will touch the earth with his feet. He will hold his head toward the sky, hold his right hand to the east and his left hand to the west. He will know everything on this earth. His thinking will be valuable and the People will listen to his words." Manuelito's father then placed in his infant son's mouth, *naat'ah*, medicine made by placing an object in an animal's mouth and then in the infant's mouth.[23]

The act of moving an object from an animal's mouth to that of an infant transferred powers to the child. Manuelito was accustomed to being around leaders in his early life. His father, Cayetano, was known as a resistor against the foreigners. His brother, Cayetanito, one of the leaders who went to Washington, D.C., in 1874, was prominent in the Mount Taylor area. Two of his other brothers, K'ayelli (One with Quiver) and El Ciego (the Blind One), followed Manuelito's lead.[24]

Known to the Diné by several names, including 'Askii Diyinii (Holy Boy), Naabaahi Jóta' (Warrior Grabbed Enemy), Naabááná badaaní (son-in-law of Late Texan), and Hastiin Ch'il Hajin (Man of Black Weeds), he is best known to non-Navajos and younger Navajos as Manuelito, a name given to him by the Mexicans and adopted by the Americans. Manuelito's names mark events and places in his life. Holy Boy indicates that he was blessed and recognized as a warrior by the Holy People. Naabááná badaaní means that he was the son-in-law of Narbona, a revered leader known for his avocation of peace. It is possible that Narbona's daughter was his first wife and that he married her when he was a young man, although not much is known about this marriage. With his marriage to Narbona's daughter, he moved closer to the Chuska Mountains, the residence of his father-in-law. His marriage no doubt provided him with the wise leader's insights and teachings. Hastiin Ch'il Hajin refers to his place of residence near Standing Rock, New Mexico. Ironically, the name most used to identify this great leader, Manuelito, is a Spanish name that indicates a diminutive, as the "ito" in Manuel means "little one." Based on interviews with Navajos, Richard Van Valkenburg created a genealogy chart that shows Manuelito had four wives. In his narrative about his wanderings among the Apaches, John Cremony reported that Manuelito had married the daughter of Mangas Coloradas.[25] In addition to the daughters of Narbona and Mangas Coloradas, Manuelito also married two other women: Asdzáá Tł'ógi and Asdzáá Tsin sikaadnii (Woman of the Clamped Tree People). Asdzáá Tsin sikaadnii was the mother of Naaltsoos Neiyéhí. My mother, who is descended from Asdzáá Tł'ogi and Manuelito, tells me that the children and grandchildren of Asdzáá Tł'ógi and Asdzáá Tsin sikaadnii maintained close kin relationships since both of these wives lived near Tohatchi.

Following the teachings passed down by his ancestors, Manuelito was trained as a medicine man and as a leader he knew about the warrior's ways. The way of the warrior was certainly needed during the period the People witnessed vast transformations in the Southwest. The way of the warrior is exemplified in the stories of Naayéé Neezghání (Monster Slayer) and Tó Bájish Chíní (Born for Water) and guide traditional Navajo men today.

In February 1874, William Truax was hired at Fort Defiance as a farmer.[26] Manuelito was often present there to conduct tribal business with the Indian agent, and Truax arranged an interview with the Navajo leader. Nothing more is known about the context of the interview. Traux began by asking the Navajo leader about his beliefs concerning the creation of the world: "Will you now give me your belief?"

Manuelito answered, "I know where they came from but it would take too long to tell. It would take four days and four nights."[27]

Manuelito then related the history of the Diné, our creation, and our journey into the present world, the Glittering World. Naming Changing Woman as the mother of all Diné, Manuelito explained how her birth, her rite of passage to womanhood, and then her pregnancy brought about harmony in the world. At the time Changing Woman lived, there was much chaos, particularly because giants roamed the earth. During one of her trips to the water, she was impregnated by Jóhonaa'éí, the Sun. Birth of the twins, Monster Slayer and Born for Water, reordered the world, bringing the return of harmony, of hózhó. During the time of Monster Slayer and Born for Water, their mother feared for their safety because giants were always around, looking for beings to eat. One day, because the boys noticed that other beings had fathers, they wondered where their father was. Changing Woman was reluctant to tell them because the Sun already had a wife. Finally, because of her sons' persistent questioning, she told them who their father was. The twins then decided that they wanted to meet him. After a series of adventures, during which they were assisted by a number of beings such as Spider Grandmother, the young men found him. Jóhonaa'éí initially refused to acknowledge them as his sons, and he sent them off on a number of harrowing journeys in which they could have been destroyed. Again, aided by beings with supernatural powers and natural elements such as the wind, the young men overcame all of the obstacles placed before them. Finally, and perhaps grudgingly, the Sun acknowledged them and gave them gifts with which they could protect themselves. Upon their return to their mother, the twins set about ridding the world of the monsters. After finishing, they underwent a healing ceremony, which is known today as the Nidáá or Enemy Way.[28] Monster Slayer and Born for Water were the first Diné warriors. Their birth, the journey to find their father, and their gifts from him gave them the power to save the world. Their powers also included the ability to call upon the natural elements for assistance and protection.

Manuelito's retelling of the stories of Changing Woman and the Hero Twins, narratives that model the warrior's role, are still stories that some young Navajo men hear as part of their journey to manhood. As Manuelito's narrative reflects, warriors have extensive knowledge of Navajo history and their stories have spiritual and practical applications. A warrior calls upon the Holy People for protection and guidance during times of strife. When there was prosperity, knowledge about proper prayers and rituals insured this order. Bighorse, a warrior who rode with Manuelito, told his daughter, Tiana, stories about what it meant to be a warrior:

> In Navajo, a warrior means someone who can get through the snowstorm when no one else can.

In Navajo, a warrior is the one that doesn't get the flu when everyone else does—the only one walking around, making a fire for the sick, giving them medicine, feeding them food, making them strong to fight the flu.

In Navajo, a warrior is the one who can use words so everyone knows they are part of the same family.

In Navajo, a warrior says what is in the people's hearts. Talks about what the land means to them. Brings them together to fight for it.[29]

For the Diné, the warriors were the protectors of the people. They fought to keep their land and community safe. As Bighorse declared about the resistance, "A man should be right to stand up straight for what he believes."[30]

Manuelito was involved in battles against the Mexicans. Although few stories of those battles exist, David Brugge unearthed one full account that involved a Mexican slaving expedition in Navajo country. Manuelito's son, Naaltsoos Neiyéhí, told of his father's role in battle against those Mexican slavers. In June 1823, Jose Antonio Vizcarra, the governor of New Mexico from 1822 to 1825, set out with about fifteen hundred men into Navajo country. Declaring that his brutal tactics would prevent Navajo attacks on New Mexican settlements, which they did from about June 18 to August 31, Vizcarra had his men scour Navajo Land for Navajos. Their course took them from Santa Fe to Hopi country, and to the region of present-day southern Utah.[31] By the end of the expedition, Vizcarra had engaged Navajo warriors at several points. On August 31, after his return to Santa Fe, he reported killing thirty-three Navajos, eight of whom were women, and capturing thirty. Five Paiutes mistaken for Navajos were also killed. Navajo livestock losses amounted to about eight hundred sheep, eighty-seven cattle, and twenty-three horses and mules. Vizcarra lost nine men, five of whom were killed and four of whom died from sickness. Thirteen were wounded, and twelve were taken as captives by the Diné.[32] Vizcarra's determination to force Navajo subjugation was not accomplished; rather, the alternative, continual war with the Diné, carried the day.[33]

From about 1690 into the mid-1860s, more than sixteen hundred Diné women and children were baptized in New Mexican Catholic churches and then taken into New Mexican households as servants.

As historian Lynn R. Bailey has observed of Navajo reactions to Mexicans, "Navajo hatred was well-founded. As the treaty of 1823, as well as subsequent ones hint at, this was a time when the tribe became a major source of captives for the slave trade."[34]

There is a record of at least one other battle with Mexicans in which Manuelito participated. In 1835, Mexican troops went into Navajo country, hoping to demonstrate their might by defeating the Diné and, more importantly, to capture women and children for the slave trade. At Red Copper Pass, currently known as Narbona Pass in honor of the Diné leader, Navajo warriors met Mexican soldiers who had among them their Pueblo allies. In 1943, Richard Van Valkenburgh published a Navajo account of this battle. In "Massacre in the Mountains," published in *Desert Magazine*, Van Valkenburgh related the story of that battle as Manuelito's son Naaltsoos Neiyéhí shared it with him.[35] Van Valkenburgh hints at the difficulty of getting Navajo elders to share their stories. He writes, "For a long time I had been hearing hazy tales of this epic massacre. But I could never pin a Navajo down to specific details."[36] Van Valkenburgh, standing on the site of the massacre, noted the number of skeletons, horses as well as human. He ended his narrative explaining how he verified the accuracy of the Navajo account by looking in archives. He observes, "Again Navajo unwritten history proved remarkably accurate."[37] During this period, New Mexican and Pueblo settlements suffered from Navajo and Apache attacks; however, Navajos and Apaches also endured a great deal of conflict and stress because their family members were targeted for the slave trade. Moreover, the people known collectively as Navajos experienced schisms because some leaders, like Antonio Sandoval, aligned themselves with the Mexicans to reap benefits that the conquerors offered.[38]

For the next sixty years, from 1800 to 1860, a pattern of violence, occasional formal campaigns, and short-lived peace treaties could be found in the borderlands.[39] In 1858, Kirby Benedict, chief justice of the Territorial Supreme Court, estimated that Navajos held in captivity in New Mexico numbered between fifteen hundred and three thousand. Out of an aggregate population of 61,525 (excluding Pueblo peoples), Navajo slaves made up roughly 3.2 percent.[40]

American Expansion

The Navajo story from 1846 to 1863 is one of resistance to American expansion. In this narrative, Manuelito plays a crucial role, for it was his voice and actions against those who sought to oppress Navajos and claim their lands and resources that shaped the balance of power in the Southwest in the mid-nineteenth century. On the one hand, Manuelito symbolizes the "defiant spirit of the Navajo." On the other hand, with his surrender he is depicted as a tool of assimilation into American culture and then as an indigenous man who, upon defeated, was unable to live successfully in a changing Navajo society. In contrast to these shifting images, which are present in American narratives, the Navajo sources on Manuelito remember him as a patriot who was intensely committed to the future of the Diné. Some of the Navajo narratives intersect with non-Navajo-produced narratives because he believed it was possible to use American tools for Navajo survival and prosperity.

As early as the 1820s, a few incoming American observers made favorable reports of the Diné and expressed admiration and sympathy for their efforts to resist Mexican occupiers. Josiah Gregg, one of the earliest Americans in the Southwest, observed that the government of New Mexico had "greatly embittered the disposition of the neighboring savages, especially the Navajos, by repeated acts of cruelty and ill-faith well calculated to provoke hostilities."[41] It was easy for the Americans to champion the Navajo cause against the Mexicans when they stood on the sidelines, but once they assumed power, their favorable reports quickly turned negative. Historian Carol Sparks observes that early American settlers saw it as their duty to "save" the West: "the land and its people needed the intervention of the would-be colonizer," she writes.[42] Contradicting Americans' declarations that the Southwest needed their protection, Navajo warriors led by Manuelito did not see the Americans as their saviors. Americans faced with the task of subjugating Mexico's former enemy certainly then saw the Navajos and Apaches as their enemies, particularly because Navajos did not perceive any differences among the waves of conquerors determined to rein them in and bring them under state control.

Manuel Armijo, Mexico's governor on the nation's northern frontier, wrestled with Navajo power for twenty-five years before the Americans finally made their claims to Mexico's northern frontier.

According to Chee Dodge, Manuelito's successor, the Mexican governor declared Navajos the "worst Indians in the country" and said that they continually carried off sheep, horses, and cattle, and made frequent raids on Mexican settlements. However, as Dodge observed, the real reason behind the Navajo's continual attacks on New Mexican settlements came as a result of Mexican abuse of Navajos, including enslavement.[43]

Beleaguered by Navajo attacks and retaliations, Armijo could only look on as American forces marched toward Santa Fe. American takeover of Mexico's northern territories came in 1846 with the arrival of Col. Stephen Kearney's Army of the West, from Fort Leavenworth, Kansas. Historians like Frank McNitt have perpetuated the ideology of Manifest Destiny with descriptions of U.S. expansion. McNitt described the arrival of Kearny's army: "like thunderheads moving before curtains of rain, the sweeping shadow of these forces moved down the Mora Valley in the form of a marching army of fifteen hundred men."[44] Such imagery strongly suggests that the land, like the people, was sorely in need of relief from a drought. Just as thunder, with its life-giving water, can revive the earth and all living things, so, too, did the Americans bring new life force into the Southwest, reviving the land and the people.

American claims to the Southwest met with little physical resistance from the Mexicans. Col. Stephen Watts Kearney announced to the New Mexican populace that he had come as a protector, not as a conqueror, "to protect the persons and property of all quiet and peaceable inhabitants . . . against their enemies, the Eutaws, the Navajos, and others."[45] Almost immediately, American forces recognized that they needed to confront Navajo resistance. Navajo forces held the balance of power in the Southwest until 1863.[46] Although the Americans might have announced their claim to the Southwest, Navajo leaders did not immediately acknowledge them or visit Santa Fe to meet American officials. Rather, based on reports of continued clashes between New Mexicans and Navajos, in 1846 Kearny ordered Col. Alexander Doniphan into Navajo Country to ascertain the Natives' acquiescence to American rule. Doniphan's meeting with Navajo leaders, which led to the first treaty signed between Americans and Navajos, was only one of a series of councils that ended in treaty signing.

At Ojo del Oso, or Bear Spring as the Navajos knew the place, Doniphan asserted to the assembled Navajo leaders that the United

States claimed New Mexico by right of conquest and that it would protect all of its new citizens, including the Diné. He made note of the ongoing war between New Mexicans and Navajos, emphasizing that Navajo attacks on New Mexicans must cease or Navajos would face war with the United States. Navajo leader Zarcillas Largos answered the Americans:

> Americans! You have a strange cause of war against the Navajos. We have waged war against the New Mexicans for several years. We have plundered their villages and killed many of their people, and many prisoners. We had just cause for all this. You have lately commenced a war against the same people. You are powerful. You have great guns and many brave soldiers. You have therefore conquered them, the very thing we have been attempting to do for so many years.
>
> You now turn upon us for attempting to do what you done yourselves. We cannot see why you have cause of quarrel with us for fighting the New Mexicans on the west, while you do the same thing on the east.
>
> Look how matters stand. This is our war. We have more right to complain of you for interfering in our war, than you have to quarrel with us for continuing a war we had begun long before you got here. If you will act justly, you will allow us to settle our own differences.[47]

Largo's speech attests to the Navajo's perceptions of their own place in the Southwest. In the nineteenth century, Navajo leaders saw themselves as the Americans' equals, if not their superiors. Largo's speech acknowledged the superior firepower of the Americans and points out their hypocrisy, but Americans were determined to claim the Southwest, including Navajo country, at any cost to the Navajos. The Diné had seen the Americans crush Mexican dominance, something they had tried to accomplish for more than a decade. Nevertheless, on November 21, 1846, the first of nine treaties was signed between the Americans and Navajo leaders after Largos agreed to American demands. Manuelito was one of the signatories. At twenty-eight years of age, he was young for a *naat'áanii*, a leader, but he had acquired the skills and qualities that a warrior needed.[48]

The Treaty of Ojo del Oso did not stand long; conflict between Navajos and the New Mexicans was almost immediate. Between 1847 and 1849, warfare continued unabated and a proclamation from Kearney that civilians could continue their war upon the Navajos if their women, children, and livestock had been seized did much to heighten hostilities in the Southwest. Reports of Navajo depredations on New Mexican settlements poured into Santa Fe. After several excursions into Navajo Country failed to end hostilities, and as conflict started again eight months after American officials had signed a second treaty with Navajos, Col. John Macrae Washington proceeded with plans to force Navajo acquiescence.[49]

Taking 178 solders, 123 New Mexico volunteers (slave raiders), and 60 Pueblo scouts, Colonel Washington left Santa Fe for Navajo Country. On August 30, 1849, the military expedition camped near Tunicha Creek, north of present-day Naschitti, New Mexico, and near Red Copper Pass (currently known as Narbona Pass). Several Navajo leaders approached Washington's camp. Washington immediately accused them of stealing livestock and killing New Mexican citizens. The leaders responded in much the same manner as they had in earlier communication with the foreigners and as they would in the future. The headmen told Washington that they did not have control of all their people, and that, yes, there were lawless men among them, but that they wanted peace and were willing to make some restitution for the livestock. Washington requested that the two parties negotiate a treaty the following day and indicated that he would meet the Navajos at Canyon de Chelly to sign it formally.

The Navajo leaders returned the following day. Among them was the revered Narbona, who was widely known for his efforts to keep the peace. The Navajo congregation also turned over livestock as a sign of good faith. The treaty negotiations commenced with Narbona representing the Navajos. At the end of the meeting, Narbona explained that he would not be at the formal treaty signing but would send two other leaders, Armijo and Pedro José. Washington agreed. Then Navajo leader Antonio Sandoval began to speak. He had accompanied the Americans and was not trusted by his fellow Navajos. It is not clear what message he was conveying to the Navajos, but the stirrings indicated that he was scolding them. Certainly he was speaking harshly. During his speech, a New Mexican with the U.S. military claimed that his stolen horse was among the Navajos. Washington ordered its immediate return. Panic and disorder set in and Narbona and the other leaders attempted to calm their warriors. Washington insisted on the return of the horse and when the Navajos failed to comply immediately, he ordered his riflemen to fire on them. The soldiers proceeded, also using the cannon they had brought. Some Navajos fled, but others fought back.

When the chaos ended, Narbona lay dead from multiple wounds. Exhibiting the brutality for which Navajos named the white Americans, Biláagana, which means "those who love to fight" or "the aggressive ones," one of the New Mexico volunteers scalped Narbona. Six other Navajos also died, but the military expedition lost only a few horses. Of Narbona's murder, Colonel Washington reported to his superiors, "Narbona, the head chief of the nation . . . had been a scourge to the inhabitants on New Mexico for the last thirty years." As Frank McNitt has noted, this statement was simply untrue. As part of the Navajo delegation, Manuelito witnessed American brutality and it no doubt confirmed his conviction that the Americans could not be trusted.[50]

Navajo leaders signed a third treaty with Americans on September 9, 1849. Its provisions called for the Navajos to surrender livestock taken from the settlements, promised free passage across Navajo country, and permitted the U.S. government to establish military and trading posts in Navajo Land.[51] The agreement to allow establishment of forts led to unremitting warfare and unimaginable suffering after Col. Edwin Sumner established Fort Defiance in the heart of Diné territory. Over the span of several years, Navajo leaders objected to the fort and the American military's claims to prime grazing lands that surrounded it. Manuelito claimed the lands for his own use, and the resulting dispute with the U.S. army led to war in 1858. According to white historians, Manuelito's conflict with the Americans served as the "final and fateful turning point in [white] relations with the Navajo nation." The conflict was the "cause of eight years of warfare that ended only with the tribe's surrender and finally with Manuelito's bitter acceptance of captivity at Bosque Redondo."[52]

In 1857, Maj. William Thomas Harbaugh Brooks assumed command at Fort Defiance. Manuelito did not immediately come to the fort to visit the new commander, which made Brooks wonder about the state of U.S. relations with the Navajos.[53] In a report to superiors, the major told of a visit from Manuelito, saying that the headman had informed him that Navajos would allow the military to graze their livestock at Ewell's Camp. Upon visiting the site, Brooks discovered that Manuelito meant to keep at least half the lands for his own use, much to the displeasure of the major. McNitt notes that Brooks and Manuelito most likely had an angry exchange.[54] In his report, Brooks noted that Manuelito had given notice he was resigning as chief and had sent Brooks a messenger with the baton and medal, symbols of office. Brooks refused to accept them.[55] Several days later, at a time set aside to distribute farming implements to Navajos, three or four hundred Navajos appeared, including headmen Zarcillos Largos and Hijo de Juanico. Brooks, noting that Largos did not stop to talk with him, requested reinforcements, for it seemed to him that conflict with the Diné was inevitable.[56]

As the dispute over the grazing fields continued, Navajo leaders recovered livestock that New Mexicans reported stolen by Navajos. On April 5, 1858, Capt. John Hatch, looking for stolen sheep, met Manuelito and Zarcillos Largos with large forces. Manuelito delivered 117 sheep to the captain and said that the remainder had been killed, sold, or distributed among the Navajos. Reports from this period repeatedly note that the Navajos attempted to return sheep and other livestock that others in their tribe had taken, and that, although some Navajos were indeed raiding the New Mexican settlements, others had had no hand in the depredations. The captain turned back, fearing an attack by such a large contingent of warriors.[57] On May 29, Brooks's men attempted to drive the Navajo's flocks, many of which belonged to Manuelito, out of Ewell's Camp. Manuelito witnessed the soldiers' attempts to drive out the flocks, whereupon he approached the fort with his men. Addressing Major Brooks, Manuelito claimed the "water, grass, and grounds," explaining "that he was born and raised there, and that he would not give it up." Brooks replied that he would retain the military's use of the lands even if it meant using force. That night, soldiers went to the field and slaughtered Navajo livestock.[58]

In the days that followed the slaughter of Manuelito's livestock, the U.S. Army kept a wary eye on Manuelito and the other Diné leaders. In his report to his superior, Major Brooks noted that the day after his troops killed the livestock, Zarcillos Largos had gone to the fort and said that he favored peace and that Manuelito had shown foolishness for insisting on ownership of the pasture lands. Brooks had handed Manuelito's baton to Largos, reporting it had been found in the field where the cattle had been killed. Largos shared information with Brooks about Navajo leaders, and Brooks sent a request to Santa Fe for reimbursement for Manuelito's livestock.[59]

Events moved toward war. A Navajo man, reportedly from Cayen-
tano's band, came into the fort, where he attempted to sell a blanket,
but then shot Brooks's black slave. Major Brooks sent this report of
the incident to his superiors on July 12:

> On Monday (July 12) an Indian came into the garrison and hung
> around for 3 or 4 hours, trying to sell a couple of blankets or more
> likely waiting the opportunity that finally presented itself. Hav-
> ing sold a blanket to a camp woman, and within 30 yards of the
> door of my quarters, he saw my servant boy, Jim (a slave), coming
> towards him and pass in rear of the camp woman's quarters; as
> Jim was about to pass him the Indian jumped upon his horse, and
> as soon as Jim's back was turned he fired an arrow, which passed
> under the boy's shoulder blade into the lungs. The Indian imme-
> diately put whip to his horse and left over the hill. The boy, strange
> to say, never uttered a word or exclamation, but attempted to pull
> the arrow out, in doing which he broke it off near the head; the
> head of the arrow remained in the body, the doctor being unable
> to extract it; the boy is still alive, but there is no doubt he is mor-
> tally wounded.[60]

Brooks's slave died four days later.

The issue of the slave's death became a major pretext for reprisals
against the Navajos. An enraged Brooks insisted that the perpetrator
be brought in for American justice. A Southerner, Brooks believed
that Jim was his property and that it had been taken. He also believed
that other "colored" races were inferior and that the strong arm of the
white man would teach them their proper places.[61] Zarcillos Largos
visited the fort after the incident and told the major that he had no
control over men from other bands. Besides, he added, the major had
not been in a hurry to compensate Manuelito for the slaughter of
his livestock. Largos agreed to look into the matter after he returned
home from an errand.

The officer demanded that the Navajos bring in the culprit,
whereupon the Navajos responded by producing the body of a Mexican slave as proof that they had brought the guilty party to justice.
Observers had reported that the man who had killed the slave had
been about forty-five years old, not the age of this much younger
man. Brooks then began war against the Navajos: "Since the arrival
of the commanding officer at this post (2nd inst.) sufficient time has

been given to the Navajo tribe of Indians, to seek, secure, and deliver up. The murderer of Maj. Brooks's Negro: to atone for the insult to our flag, and the many outrages committed upon our citizens." Brooks continued: "They have failed to do so. Our duty remains to chastise them into obedience to our laws—After tomorrow morning war is proclaimed against them."[62] Declaring war on the entire Navajo nation as result of Manuelito's refusal to relinquish his land rights forms part of the pattern of American conquest, in which attention was diverted from the real issue of forcing indigenous acquiescence. Major Brooks's insistence that the man who had killed his slave be turned over for American justice, coupled with reports of Navajo raids on New Mexican communities, led to a series of battles over the course of the next four months. These were costly to the Diné; at least two hundred of their warriors were killed, whereas U.S. troops saw far fewer fatalities.[63]

Once again, perhaps as a means to halt conflicts with the Americans temporarily, the Navajo leaders signed yet another treaty at Fort Defiance. This one, negotiated and signed by Cols. B. L. E. Bonneville and James L. Collins for the United States and fifteen Diné leaders, including Manuelito, established an eastern boundary for Navajo Land, called for payment of indemnification by the tribe for depredations committed by Navajos, provided for the release of all captives by both parties involved, and waived the demand for surrender of the murderer who had touched off the war. The United States also demanded the right to send expeditions through Navajo Country and establish military posts there.[64] However, the U.S. Senate did not ratify this treaty.

On April 30, 1860, Manuelito and Barboncito led an attack on Fort Defiance. In the early morning, approximately one thousand warriors stormed the fort. They were unsuccessful, largely because the three companies inside the fort had superior firepower.[65] The attack led New Mexicans and the army to agree that it was necessary to make war on the Navajos. As one New Mexican citizen declared, it was not possible to change the Navajos, "You might as well make a hyena adopt the habits of a poodle dog."[66]

President Andrew Jackson's Indian Removal Act of 1830 set the stage for the removal of all indigenous peoples who stood in the way of white settlement. In the Southwest, Gen. Edward R. S. Canby advocated Navajo removal from their homeland. In 1862, James H.

Carleton, governor and commander of New Mexico Territory, took command after Canby went east to fight in the Civil War. Carleton was thus left to implement the plan to relocate Navajos and Mescalero Apaches to a reservation at Fort Sumner, New Mexico. There, Navajos and Mescaleros would be grouped into villages and learn the arts of civilization. They would become farmers, be instructed in Christian virtues, and send their children to American schools. Carleton's rationale for his war against the Navajos is summarized in a letter he sent to his superior, Lorenzo Thomas:

> They understand the direct application of force as a law. If its application be removed, that moment they become lawless. . . . The purpose now is never to relax the application of force with a people that can no more be trusted than you can trust the wolves that run through their mountains. [The aim is] To gather them together little by little onto a Reservation away from the haunts and hills and hiding places of their country, and there be kind to them. . . . [S]oon they will acquire new habits, new ideas, new modes of life: the old Indians will die off and carry with them all latent longings for murdering and robbing: the young ones will take their places without these longings: and thus, little by little, they will become a happy and contented people.[67]

To force the Navajos' surrender and remove them to the reservation, Carleton enlisted renowned Indian fighter Kit Carson to convey his message, "Go to the Bosque Redondo, or we will pursue and destroy you. We will not make peace with you on any other terms."[68]

In the summer of 1863, Carson began his campaign against the Navajos. Moving with 221 men from Los Lunas to Fort Wingate (known to Navajos as Bear Spring), Carson added 326 men to his command. Carson fed his soldiers and livestock on Navajo wheat and corn and destroyed the rest of their harvest. Such action was key to their defeat. In his first attempts to force Navajo surrender, however, Carson was unsuccessful. His war was indiscriminate—he targeted women and children and allowed volunteers to take captives as payment. Carson's men also humiliated and murdered Navajos who surrendered. By the fall, Carson had failed to engage Navajos in open battle; rather, the Diné warriors who followed the militia, taking livestock and attacking army herds, continually embarrassed Carson's men.[69] As a result of the abuse they suffered and because stories that circulated told of Navajos being murdered, many refused to surrender. As Clifford Trazfer has noted, Navajos were convinced that Carson's campaign was a war of extermination. "Thus the Indians felt that they had no choice but to remain fast in their mountains and to avoid the onslaught of the troops, who they feared would murder them if they surrendered."[70]

After months of failure, and with the winter approaching, Carleton ordered Carson to continue the war against the Navajos with an invasion of Canyon de Chelly, the tribe's stronghold. In the 1960s and 1970s, Navajo elders recalled stories of this invasion. According to Eli Gorman, Bi'éé Łichíí'í (Red Shirt, Navajos' name for Kit Carson) kept the Diné on the run. There was no discrimination between peaceful and hostile Diné: Peaceful Diné were picked up and many women killed. Men were slaughtered. Children were taken as captives and sold into slavery.[71] The series of forays into the Navajo stronghold proved overwhelming for the Diné, who had already been severely weakened by Carson's scorched-earth tactics.

By late 1863, thousands of desperate Navajos had turned themselves in at the American forts. One of the first headmen to surrender was Delgadito, who with 187 of his people arrived in late November and was removed with them to the Bosque Redondo. After a brief stay, Delgadito and three other Navajos took Carleton's message back to Diné Bikéyah: The People must surrender and move to the Bosque Redondo reservation, where they will be allowed to live in peace. Delgadito told everyone he found that he had spoken personally to the American general and that the Navajos would be shown no mercy if they continued to resist. Some of the leaders listened to Delgadito's message. At the end of January 1864, Delgadito arrived at Fort Wingate with 680 Navajos.[72]

In March 1864, General Carleton reported to his commander, Lorenzo Thomas, that more than three thousand Navajos had surrendered at Fort Defiance and that they would join the other prisoners at the Bosque Redondo, which brought the total number of Navajo captives to six thousand.[73] The campaign was winding down; however, the attacks against Navajos did not cease because slave raiders found it profitable to continue their work. Some of the most distinguished Navajo leaders, including Herrera Grande, surrendered at the forts. Throughout the spring of 1864, Navajos had much to fear from raiders who attacked the Diné in their homeland and stole their children along the route to the Bosque Redondo.[74] Carleton made a few attempts to return captives to their Navajo families but found it difficult because captors refused to relinquish their stolen property. Certainly, the fact that Carleton himself held Navajo slaves probably did not persuade others that they should relinquish theirs.[75]

Although the military was finding it impossible to care for its Diné prisoners, Carleton was still eager to get Manuelito and Barboncito to surrender. The *Santa Fe (N.M.) Gazette* published one officer's report about the need to capture or kill Manuelito: "With his [Manuelito's] capture the last vestige of Navajo power in the Navajo Country will be broken up. The number of his band is not great, and its strength is comparatively little," read the report, "but his knowledge of the country and the control he has over his followers may delay the day of its doom, but that day is sure to come, and it will come before the snows of the next winter fall."[76] In early August 1864, soldiers surprised Barboncito and his people, who were in Canyon de Chelly. The leader surrendered with the remainder of his kin, which numbered only five men, a woman, and a child. Although Barboncito made the journey to the prison camp, he left within the year with a group of his people and lived among Apache allies in their mountains. However, the Diné leader was forced to surrender once again and arrived at Fort Sumner in November 1866.[77]

In the spring of 1864, military officers received word that Manuelito would turn himself in. Manuelito appeared at Fort Defiance but refused to go to the Bosque Redondo. An officer informed the Diné leader that he had no choice but to go to Hwéeldi. Having heard many of the horror stories about living conditions at the prison, Manuelito requested a visit from Herrera, one of the chiefs at the internment camp.[78] In a report dated March 21, 1865, Carleton related the results of Herrera's meeting with Manuelito. Herrera explained that Manuelito was in poor condition, that he had about fifty people with him, that he had few horses and sheep. Manuelito said, "Here is all I have in the world. See what a trifling amount. You see how poor they are. My children are eating roots."[79] Herrera reported that, after some thought, Manuelito declined to turn himself in, saying:

That his God and his mother lived in the west and he would not leave them; that there was a tradition that his people should never cross the Rio Grande, the Rio San Juan, or the Rio Colorado; that he also could not pass three mountains, and particularly he could not leave the Chusca Mountain, his native hills; that his intention was to remain; that he was there to suffer all the consequences of war or famine; that now he had nothing to lose but his life, and that they could come and take whenever they pleased, but he would not move; that he had never done any wrong to the Americans or the Mexicans; that he had never robbed, but had lived upon his own resources; that if he were killed innocent blood would be shed.[80]

Hearing their kinsman's declarations, the women in the camp began to cry in distress. Throughout 1864 and into 1866, Manuelito and his band did their best to elude the Americans and New Mexican and Ute slave raiders.

Tiana Bighorse's stories from her father, Bighorse, give an idea of the conditions that Navajos faced and indicate how leaders like Manuelito inspired their people to keep their courage. His own mother and father were murdered, by whom is not known. But the anguish that Bighorse suffered as a result led him to determine that he would not surrender. In his account, he notes Manuelito's influence, saying that Manuelito told his warriors not to be afraid. "Just because they capture you and even take your life, it's just you and not all your people who will suffer," he remembers Manuelito advising. "When you get captured, you just tell them, 'Go ahead and kill me, and I will shed my blood on my own land, not some strange land. And my people will have the land even if I die.'"[81] Bighorse shared more of Manuelito's counsel, noting that the leader often said the warriors must love the people and the land. "But we still are on our land. There's four sacred mountains. We are supposed to be here. The Great Spirit gave the land to us."[82] Bighorse's narrative reveals the extent to which the Diné suffered under the Americans' brutal conquest and how the People fought back. He also noted that they relied on their prayers and rituals for courage and strength.

Diné storytellers, poets, and performance artists have addressed the impact of the Long Walk and the imprisonment at Hwéeldi on their people. Their stories are contextualized around the larger events of dispossession, injustice, and violence that the Diné have suffered under colonialism.[83] Their remembrances tell of how their ancestors, in the face of starvation, death, and brutality, were forced to abandon the elders and pregnant women who could no longer keep pace with the group. Mothers killed their newborn infants because they did not want to see them suffer or because the children had been products of rapes by the soldiers or New Mexican raiders. In the face of starvation, they attempted to eat the crow and coyote, only to find them inedible. The memories are filled with such anguish, pain, and humiliation that we cannot help but feel overwhelmed with sadness for our ancestors, who were forced to debase themselves in order to survive. As Cherokee scholar Andrea Smith notes, the history of white-Native relationships shows that the colonizers sought "not only to defeat Indian people but also to eradicate their very identity and humanity."[84]

Although their stories unsparingly depict the utter brutality of Navajo experiences under American conquest, the Diné are moving toward reconciliation and healing with expressions of awe and appreciation as they reflect upon their ancestors' perseverance, courage, and integrity in the face of atrocity. Their songs include ones dedicated to their leader, Manuelito, whom they regard with love and appreciation.[85] For example, in his collections of songs, folksinger Vincent Craig remembers Manuelito's trials during the Fearing Time, the incarceration at Bosque Redondo, and his struggle to ensure that his people would return to Diné Bikéyah, their beloved homeland. Manuelito was under continual attack by the U.S. Army and New Mexico raiders. He finally surrendered and took his kin to Bosque Redondo. Craig's ballad inspires and reminds us that our leader battled almost insurmountable odds so that we could return to our beloved homeland.

Military officers were eager to either capture or kill Manuelito because he was the most defiant of Navajo leaders. Finally, in 1866, a wounded and ill Manuelito surrendered to Americans and was interred at the Bosque Redondo prison. His son-in-law, Dághá Chíí Bik'is, related the following story, which he heard from Manuelito about conditions at Bosque Redondo, when he gave testimony for the Navajo land claims hearings in 1951. "Many of them [Navajos] died from starvation. The kind of food they had to eat, many died from that. Also I think a larger percent of deaths was caused from homesickness." He continued: "They wept from day-to-day, many of them. 'I wish I was on my own land back at Chinle or Kayenta.' Places like that. Many died from those causes...." According to Dághá Chíí Bik'is, "Manuelito says that some of the people had no shelter so they would dig out a hollow space or bank and the people lived there."[86] For four long years, the Diné at Hwéeldi had attempted to wrest a living off the land with little success. Photographs of the fort show that the soldiers had adequate shelter and firewood to warm themselves, whereas the prisoners were forced to walk miles to find firewood and were terrified that Comanche and New Mexican raiders might capture them. The Navajos lived in ditches covered with wood and brush. Rations were often rancid and unfit to eat. Clothing and blankets were inadequate for the harsh winters. Of the approximately eleven thousand Diné who made the trek to Hwéeldi, more than twenty-five hundred died.

The Bosque Redondo Reservation was a disaster. In 1868, after four years at the prison camp, the Navajos' situation had not improved. The reservation's formulator, General Carleton, faced criticism from several fronts and the U.S. government was unwilling to continue paying the cost of the Navajos' upkeep. The plan to turn Navajos into white men had cost U.S. citizens at least ten million dollars. A substantial amount of this money lined the pockets of contractors, who had escalated prices for beef that was poor in quality, as well as other items, such as clothing and blankets.[87] The Diné were losing heart and threatening to rebel. Finally, military officers met with Navajo leaders to discuss conditions and solutions. On May 28, 1868, Gen. William Sherman and Samuel Tappan met with Navajo leaders to discuss the condition of the Navajos. Navajos selected Barboncito to speak on their behalf because he was known for his eloquence and ability to persuade. Asked why Navajos had not been able to improve their lives, Barboncito pointed to the severe conditions under which his people lived. He noted that the land was not agreeable: "Our Grand-fathers had no idea of living in any other country except our own and I do not think it right for us to do so as we were never taught to. . . . It was told to us by our forefathers," he said, "that we were never to move east of the Rio Grande or west of the San Juan rivers and I think that our coming here has been the cause of so much death among us and our animals."[88] General Sherman suggested the possibility of removing Navajos to Indian territory. Barboncito's reply was firm: "I hope to God you will not ask me to go to any other country except my own."[89]

The Diné had long recognized Barboncito's abilities to speak eloquently and persuasively. They had been wise to select him to address the U.S. military rulers. On June 1, 1868, Manuelito and other Navajo leaders signed the last treaty between their tribe and the Americans. Among its provisions were stipulations about land base size, American education for children, instruction in Christianity, and annuities for ten years. Even though the Navajos would be allowed to claim only a portion of the land they had once inhabited, they were still joyful. Seventeen days later, more than eight thousand began the journey home. The caravan extended for at least ten miles.[90]

Non-Navajo writers have offered their observations of the meaning of Navajo defeat and subjugation. Filtered through the rhetoric of American nationalist discourse that explains the experiences of people of color as a process of integration into the American mainstream, they suggest that the Bosque Redondo experience transformed Navajos into model American citizens who came to realize the benefits of white civilization. In one 1980 publication, historian David Lavender offered this interpretation of what the years of war and internment meant for the Navajos:

> Escorted by troops and carrying their possessions and their sick in wagons, the Indians released in segments, began their [second] long walk in June 1868. They took with them an improved knowledge of agriculture and vocational trades, better methods of constructing the hogans in which they lived, and an appreciation of wagons. . . . The people as a whole had a fresh, strong sense of the tribal unity, and a determination somehow to make their way peacefully in the Anglo world while retaining their own values.[91]

In 1998, in an update of his study on Navajos and the Bosque Redondo experience, historian Lynn Bailey delivered a similar interpretation. According to Bailey, during the years they were warred upon, Navajos had a "choice" to either retreat further into the homeland or surrender and march to the Fort Sumner internment camp. The "choice" to endure the prison camp was "not entirely without benefit."[92] Navajos exhibited some art at farming and the "irrigation system they constructed was probably the most intricate and best engineered in all of New Mexico." They acquired new technologies, replacing the digging stick with hoes, shovels, rakes, and plows. They learned about metal work to make nails, horse and mule shoes, and, of course, jewelry. One Navajo man acquired headman status after he demonstrated skill at forging iron.[93]

Historians and other writers have been slow to change their interpretations of the Long Walk, even as Navajos challenge those perspectives, and some still suggest that the American colonizing experience has been somehow beneficial, even benign. For example, in 2003, anthropologist Martin Link published a pamphlet on the Long Walk and declared that knowledge about the Navajo experience has been mythologized. Basing his conclusions on military documents and photographs from the period, Link argues that the soldiers treated the Navajos as humanely as possible during the course of the forced march to Fort Summer, that Navajos were free to leave the prison camp whenever they wished, and that, in addition to having enough to eat, they could pursue industries such as weaving.[94]

American narratives, such as those by Lavender, Bailey, and Link, reproduce colonial categories that justify conquest and dispossession and deny the horror, violence, and inhumane treatment of the Diné. Rather than positioning narratives about the Navajo experience as part of an appreciation for multiculturalism in which all perspectives are presented in a balanced manner and further entrenching the idea that writing Native history simply requires simply inserting Natives into the existing American narrative, it is incumbent upon us as scholars, educators, and community members to insist upon an analysis of the power and conditions of conflict within which cultural "encounters" occur, and to link our analysis to projects of political and social transformation.

The People still remember those dark years with pain and bitterness, and many refused to speak of the nightmare for decades afterward. In November 2005, the National Park Service held a conference in Window Rock, Arizona, to invite Navajo responses to a proposal to establish a memorial dedicated to the Long Walk and the Bosque Redondo experience. One day of listening to testimony about the Long Walk and Hwéeldi made it clear that the years have not dimmed the impact on Navajo consciousness. Waiting patiently all day and listening to speakers who explained the importance of establishing the memorial, local community members finally got a chance to share their stories. Just as their grandparents had heard them and conveyed them to the next generation, participants shared those same stories, which were filled with brutal images of violence, hunger, sickness, and loneliness. At various times throughout, there were many moments in which emotions threatened to overcome presenters and the audience alike. At the same time that they mourned, the participants also celebrated the courage and resilience of their grandmothers and grandfathers. They acknowledged that their ancestors persevered by remembering the teachings of the Holy People. On June 4, 2005, the memorial at Fort Sumner, New Mexico, was officially opened. Hundreds of Navajos and their allies attended the day-long event.

Return to Diné Bikéyah

In the years that followed their return, Navajos sought to reestablish their lives based on teachings that their ancestors had practiced. These teachings, based on Diné philosophy, had seen the ancestors through many trials and served as the basis for reestablishing life in the homeland. With surviving family members, Manuelito made his way to his old home near Tohatchi, south of Sheep Springs. Upon his return, the warrior retained his former status and Indian agents and other government officials solicited his advice and assistance to address the issues that faced Navajos in the late-nineteenth century. Just as the agents attempted to use Manuelito's influence to promote their assimilation program, the Diné leader was equally determined to reclaim Navajo sovereignty.[95]

The early reservation period was also one of adjustment and turmoil. Navajo leaders attempted to define the borders of the reservation, quieted conflicts among Navajos, and arbitrated disputes between Navajos and New Mexicans who claimed the same pasturage. They negotiated and made compromises with Indian agents who forced Navajo compliance with Western practices regarding education, health, marriage, and sexuality. In his biographical account of Manuelito, Frank Waters extolls the Diné leader's ability to transform himself from a noble savage to an American man. According to Waters, under Manuelito's direction, Navajo men found satisfaction in their jobs as laborers contracted to construct the railroad that snaked across their former lands, which the Diné had relinquished in the treaty of 1868. However, when the men began to break up wooden boxes bound with iron straps to get iron for their knives and arrowheads, Manuelito saw this activity as counterproductive to American values and cautioned them: "This is not right! We learned many things in the old days from the Pueblos, from the Spanish, the Mexicans. Now we must learn new things from the Americans."[96] The image of Manuelito rejecting the symbols of Navajo manhood, the knives and arrowheads, in favor of American ideals of industry affirms dominant society's assumptions that Native men had been domesticated. Furthermore, Waters reads the oppression of the Navajos under American rule as just one more instance in which they ably adapted, adopted, and borrowed to fit into modern America. William Haas Moore echoes Waters's sentiment when he notes that in 1892 Manuelito ran a successful farm: "[S]uccess has taught Manuelito the value of some Anglo-American ways. Although he had not abandoned his traditional values, he had used them to assimilate other values."[97] Writings about the Pueblo peoples rendered them "'civilized,' domestic, and feminized" at the same moment that Apaches had yet to be subjugated and recently defeated Navajos still adjusting to reservation life.[98]

In the 1870s, Manuelito was appointed to head a band of Navajo police given responsibility to quell conflicts among Navajos and between Navajos and non-Indian ranchers who claimed the same pasturing lands in areas decreed public domain. Many incidents of conflict from that time show that Navajos did not give up land without shows of resistance, even to the point that newspapers like one in Farmington, New Mexico, reported fears of an Indian uprising and calls to bring in the U.S. Cavalry.

One of the enduring narratives about Manuelito, seen in other Navajo stories as well, revolves around Navajo claims to land and sovereignty. Manuelito understood well that they were a sovereign people who had rightful claims to their homeland. Always intensely concerned about those lands, Manuelito traveled several times to Washington, D.C., to meet U.S. presidents. Manuelito's earlier experiences traveling east had made him aware of the incredible number of whites that populated the land. He knew that someday the sheer number of foreigners, who always lusted for Navajo land, could overwhelm his people. As his son, Naaltsoos Neiyéhí, related, Manuelito often had a difficult time sleeping because he was always thinking about his people's welfare: "My father would be overcome with the weight of his people's future. He said, 'If I don't stop thinking, my head will burst.' We would build a fire at his request and he would sit with his burden. After awhile, he would become calm and eventually sleep."[99]

In 1882, Ben Wittick photographed Manuelito, one of several, when he met him at the Territorial Fair in Albuquerque. According to Wittick's biographer, Patricia Janis Broder, the frontier photographer persuaded the leader to pose for a portrait and purchased the bow, fur quiver, moccasins, and other personal attire he wore at the sitting.[100] The portrait of Manuelito, taken after Wittick agreed to pay the leader, depicts him bare-chested and eyes downcast, a Navajo-made textile draping his lap. According to Wittick's daughter, who retold the story of the incident in a letter to Richard Van Valkenburgh, Manuelito seemed agreeable to having his portrait taken. Wittick had insisted that the leader remove his shirt to show a scar from a bullet wound inflicted by Kit Carson.[101] Manuelito removed his shirt for eight dollars, which he insisted on taking in silver quarters, whereupon Wittick rushed out to make change. The photo opportunity marks a moment when Wittick, perhaps in a fit of imperialist nostalgia, wished to present the leader as a noble savage. As Broder asserts, many of Wittick's portraits of Native peoples depict them living in an age of transition. "The willingness of an Indian to wear a costume, utilize props, and pose in front of a painted backdrop is a clear indication of the degree of the subject's acculturation and development of a dual cultural identity."[102] Certainly, such a declaration is in keeping with white Americans' desires to believe that Native people, especially men, had indeed successfully been assimilated into American society. For Manuelito, it seems that the silver coins were desired for the decorations they could provide on clothing.[103] Perhaps he intended to give them to one of his wives or his daughters.

Navajos leaders and community members favor this Wittick image to convey messages about the meaning of education for Navajo children and to link it with Manuelito's speech about education. According to several accounts, Manuelito had called American education a "ladder," by which the People "would again rise to independence, and regain their pride."[104] Raymond Friday Locke takes note of Manuelito's message about education, which he says Chee Dodge repeated to the Navajo people: "My grandchild, the whites have many things which we Navajos need. But we cannot get them. It is as though the whites were in a grassy canyon and there they have wagons, plows, and plenty of food. We Navajos are up on the dry mesa," he continued. "We can hear them talking but we cannot get them. My grandchild, education is the ladder. Tell our people to take it."[105] Navajo Studies scholars like Steve Pavlik and William Haas Moore echo the story of Manuelito's advocation of education and note this speech, saying that Manuelito revealed his education philosophy to Chee Dodge in the early 1880s.[106] Estelle Fuchs and Robert J. Havighurst say that Chee Dodge heard the message from Manuelito a few days before the elderly leader's death.[107]

In the 1950s, the Navajo Education Committee developed long-range plans to improve educational opportunities for Navajo students.[108] Under Chairman Raymond Nakai's administration, a tribal scholarship program was established to provide Navajo students with access to higher education. In the 1980s, the committee created the Chief Manuelito Scholarship for high-achieving college students. In both cases, Manuelito's speech and image are evoked. Prior to the Chief Manuelito Scholarship, awards were based on financial need, with academic success a secondary concern. William Nakai, who worked for many years as a counselor with the Navajo Scholarship Office, was instrumental in establishing the scholarship that valorized the great Diné leader and recognized the academic achievements of Navajo students. According to Nakai, one major influence on his decision to name a scholarship after Manuelito was the still-popular song, "Go My Son," composed and performed by Arlene Nofchissey and Carnes Burson. The song was composed and performed by the Latter Day Saint's Lamanite Generation, a group of Native Mormons who have performed throughout the world.[109] Nakai also noted that he had created a portrait of a fully clothed Manuelito. Years later, the scholarship office adopted the Wittick image as a logo for their Chief Manuelito Scholarship.

Today, like many Navajo leaders, educators, and community leaders, Diné College president Ferlin Clark invokes Manuelito's message about the value of education for Navajos. During his keynote address at the 2004 Navajo Studies Conference, President Clark reminded the audience that Manuelito had given counsel that we never forget our responsibility to protect our resources, culture, land, and language. One way to ensure that we remember is to provide our children access to education at all levels. According to President Clark, "Education is the key! Education is a tool, a weapon, a shield, a guide, a path to become self-sufficient."[110]

Interestingly, although Navajos and their white allies have attributed this speech to Manuelito and say that he addressed his words to his people, a written report gives a different story. According to it, during an informal council session between Diné leaders and Indian agent Dennis Riordan, the Navajo men had addressed Riordan upon hearing of his resignation as Indian agent. An aging Manuelito had stood up and declared, "My lips are very sore, I have just heard some news that makes my mouth sore, and makes me feel very bad, and I do not think I can say much." Expressing concern at the news, the

Diné leaders recalled the impact Riordan had made during his brief tenure. When Riordan came, "they had been groping along at the bottom of a deep canon where the sun never shone and they could not see anything but the rocky walls. Mr. Riordan had taken the lead," they continued, "and shown them the trail out of the canon and led them out and to the top where they could see the beautiful valleys beyond, with plenty of water and grass. Now he was going to abandon them and who was to carry out the ideas that he had put into their heads?"[111] In an unpublished manuscript, Richard Van Valkenburgh records the council, attributes the speech to Manuelito, and notes that the Diné leader spoke them to Dennis Riordan, not the Navajo people.[112] Although there might be a question as to whether the great Diné leader actually spoke these words, and to whom he referred if he did (no written document testifies to its authenticity), it is important to note that the Navajo people do remember him as a visionary who saw the benefits of Western education for Navajo children.

During the 1880s, Indian agents reported Manuelito's abuse of alcohol and declared him no longer fit to be a chief.[113] Their reports indicate that Manuelito's alcoholism was related to the death of his two sons, who had been sent to Carlisle, Pennsylvania, and died from diseases contracted at the school. Although non-Indians center their narratives on Manuelito's bitterness over his sons' deaths and link it to his drinking problem, Navajos emphasize Manuelito's vision of a better society. William Haas Moore has commented on the contradictory images of Manuelito: "This statement [about the value of Western education] along with several of his other accomplishments, would deny the charges of agents who claimed that Manuelito was simply an alcoholic and a beggar; instead; the old chief had also become a man of vision."[114] Indeed, Moore's understanding of Manuelito as a man of vision is more in keeping with the remembrances of Naaltsoos Neiyéhí and the Navajo community.

In 1882, as an example to his fellow Navajos, Manuelito had sent his sons to Carlisle School. Within a year of arriving, the boys succumbed to diseases. One son died at the school, where he was buried, and the other returned home, only to die within a few weeks. According to Dennis Riordan's report, a sorrowful and angry Manuelito recanted his earlier testament about the value of an American education for Navajo youths and demanded that all Diné children return home from boarding schools.

In 1966, Manuelito's son told a different story. Manuelito had sent his sons to Carlisle to demonstrate to his people that an American education could be an avenue for retaining Navajo culture, tradition, land, and natural resources. The two sons who were sent to Carlisle School were Naat'ahsilá (Leader Who Stands Back) and Naat'ahyisteel (Stubborn Leader). Naat'ahsilá was the son of Azdáá Tsin sikaadnii, Manuelito's second wife. Naat'ahyisteel, who died at Carlisle, was the son of Asdzáá Tł'ógi. Upon hearing about Naat'ahyisteel's death, Manuelito demanded the return of Naat'ahsilá. When that son died soon after his return, Manuelito was mournful. Great numbers of his people attended the son's funeral service. Naltsoos Neiyéhí remembered this service and Manuelito's address to the people who had come:

> [Manuelito said,] "I want to talk to you after you eat." They killed and butchered seven horses to feed the people. The people had stew and coffee. The horses [that the people had ridden] had saddles and bridles on while they grazed. There was a lot of grass in those days.
>
> After the people ate and rested, my father stood on a little hill and said, "I want all of you to think this over, what I'm going to say to you. Most of you think that Naabáána badaaní does not have sense. He sent his children to hell and only the evils came back to him. That is how you look at me. Isn't that what you think?"[115]

After some denials and affirmations from the people, Manuelito continued to speak. It had not been his intention that his sons die. He had meant to show the benefits of an American education. "As you know," Manuelito offered, "I made a speech at Fort Sumner about 'Iiná [Life]. 'Iiná doonti'da [Life does not end, it goes on]. I wanted to teach my people to hold on to the future with all of our strength." Manuelito continued his talk to the People, saying, "It should have been that my sons would be examples to follow, but it did not happen that way."[116]

In 1894, Manuelito died from a combination of alcoholism and pneumonia. Non-Indians like Ruth Underhill, Virginia Hoffman, Broderick Johnson, Raymond Friday Locke, and Frank Waters agree that, at the end of his life, Manuelito was "a pathetic, dissolute old man."[117] Such a reading of the end of Manuelito's life fits in well with American assumptions about the noble savage who has been contaminated by white vices. Cherokee scholar Jimmy Durham notes that white America prefers myths of Native leaders reduced by the reservation experience and dying miserably, usually as alcoholics. These are myths that the United States continually rebuilds in order to deny its inhumanity toward indigenous peoples.[118] As sociologist Bonnie Duran observes, the association of Natives with alcohol becomes a signifier of "Indian," fitting in with assumptions about Native peoples, including notions of Indians being at a particular stage in a social evolutionary ladder or the embodiment of wholism or degeneracy.[119] However, rather than taking alcoholism as acceptable and inevitable, Native people have struggled to eradicate the use and effects of alcohol in their communities.

Similarly, the Diné stories of Manuelito's commitment to the betterment of his people, as remembered by his son and through the speech that he made about education, belie the narratives that position Manuelito as defeated and unable to adjust to reservation life. Peterson Zah, former chairman and president of the Navajo Nation and an esteemed leader in his own right, recently shared his understanding of Manuelito's significance with me after I asked him what he thought of the contradictory images of Manuelito and the question of whether the leader had actually said, "Education is the ladder. Tell our People to take it." Zah asserted that his knowledge about the Diné leader was part of the stories he had heard in his community of Low Mountain, Arizona, "not from books." As a child, Zah had been exposed to great leaders, starting with his father, 'Ólta' Yázhi (Little Schoolboy), who had gone to a Western school and learned to speak English. Many leaders of the day had visited 'Ólta' Yázhi and Peterson had listened to their stories of the Navajo past, including those of Hastiin Ch'il Hajin. As Zah explained, Manuelito was a man of great vision who knew the consequences of white society for Navajos and had foreseen the benefits of Western education, not for turning Navajos into whites, but to be used as a tool to better our society.[120]

Although non-Navajos continue to perpetuate stereotypical views of the meaning of Manuelito's life, particularly at the end of his life, his widow, Asdzáá Tł'ógi, his daughters, and his son carried on his messages about the urgency to think always about 'Iiná. His fervent hope was that his people remember his teachings. Certainly Manuelito's family members remembered. Manuelito's son, who was ninety years old in 1966 when he told his story, offered his perspectives on the condition under which Navajos lived. Noting that many no longer sustained themselves but relied on the trading post for even the basic necessities of life, Naltsoos Neiyéhí explained how men of his generation had struggled to provide for their families. They had worked in the cornfields many hours, hoeing, plowing, watering, and planting seeds. His reflections on the meaning of his life, of efforts to sustain his family, indicate that he had listened to his father's teachings about living a good life. Manuelito Number Two had taken his father's teachings to heart, remembering, "These will be the stories you can remember in the future."[121]

Conclusion

American accounts of the meaning of Manuelito's life contrast dramatically with the ways in which the Diné themselves remember their leader. American accounts of the Diné warrior are shaped by prevailing views about indigenous peoples that have roots in the earliest European, and then American, thought. These accounts reflect shifting assumptions of Native men that move along a continuum from savage to noble savage to defeated savage who cannot live in civilized society. After conquest, Natives are depicted as having accepted federal Indian policies and seemingly taken their place in multicultural America. Furthermore, these narratives demonstrate how America as a nation sees itself as primarily a place where democracy reigns as freedom, independence, industry, and cultural diversity. Although the existing biographical accounts were written during a period that spans the 1960s to 2000, the language used, its themes and images, remain remarkably consistent and work to perpetuate stereotypes of Navajos that have roots in the earliest Euro-American encounters. As literary critic Louis Owens has asserted, "America's desire to control knowledge, to exclude the heterogeneous, and to assure a particular kind of being-in-the-world depends upon a total appropriation and internalization of his colonized space, and to achieve that end, America must make the heterogeneous Native somehow assimilable and concomitantly erasable."[122] As such, American historical narratives deny the horror of the Long Walk and the Bosque Redondo imprisonment. The history of America is one of a nation born from the genocide of Native peoples and built on slave labor. It is a nation that repeatedly undermines the values of liberty and equality it claims to hold dear. And it ignores what might be called a psychology of conquest.

Over the years, I have noted myriad ways in which the Diné remember their esteemed leader. Navajo perspectives on the past were created within the space of colonial discourse, and, in this particular instance, with all of its literary conventions about history and culture. As such, Navajo perspectives on the past have also been shaped by exposure to colonialist ideology in which biographies purport to convey meaning about history through the life of one individual, usually that of a man. Nevertheless, the People do revere their leader, but in ways that contrast with American notions about the meaning of the Navajo past. Navajo remembrances link the narratives and images of Hastiin Ch'il Hajin to the political message of resistance, survival, and cultural continuity. Remembrances of this great leader inspire and remind us that our ancestors battled almost insurmountable odds so that, as a people, we could return to our beloved homeland. As we reflect upon our ancestors' sorrows, we are also reminded of their courage and will to live. As one of our most celebrated leaders, Manuelito's words urge us to value 'Iiná and to walk into the future with the stories as our foundation. Surely, the prophecy of 'Askii Diyinii's father came to pass, that the People would value his son's thinking.

4/The Imperial Gaze

Portraits of Juanita and Manuelito, 1868–1902

In the early twentieth century, George Wharton James, a popular writer and lecturer on Southwestern indigenous cultures, met Juanita, a Navajo woman best known in the historical record as the wife of Navajo leader and war chief Manuelito. The encounter resulted in a series of photographs of Juanita and her family that James subsequently used to illustrate a number of his books on the Southwest and Indian cultures. Reflecting upon Juanita's portrait to convey his thoughts on the ills of white civilization, James grandly proclaimed Juanita "one of the queenliest women in dignity, grace, and character I have ever met."[1] Like many other white Americans of his generation, James imposed his own meanings on Juanita's life and on Navajos in general. Thousands of photographs of Navajos, including those by George Wharton James, lie in archival repositories all over the United States. Many of the Navajo subjects in these photographs are unidentified; in fact, Juanita is only one of two Navajo women who are consistently named in photographs. The other woman, Elle of Ganado, was employed by the Fred Harvey Company in the early twentieth century and wove rugs slated for the tourist trade.[2]

Although photographs of Native peoples were taken at different times from the late-nineteenth century into the twentieth, little has changed in their portrayals. This is also true of the portrayals of Navajo women and men to this day. Navajos are typically depicted in a setting associated with the beginning of the reservation period. Navajo men wear cotton shirts and trousers with moccasins and are sometimes depicted holding bows and arrows. Navajo women wear either the *biil*, a woven dress of their own manufacture, or blouses and tiered skirts modeled after those of white or Hispanic women's fashions of the day. Typically, both men and women wear their hair in a bun tied with white yarn. What do these predictable portrayals signify about Navajos? What can they tell us, if anything, about Navajos' historical experiences or the reality of their culture? In particular, what do photographs communicate about Navajo women? Studies of Native Americans in photographs demonstrate that dominant American society responds to these photographs based on stereotypes. These images reinforce reductionist representations while masking the unimaginable historical traumas Navajos have survived.

As it examines questions about the photographic representation of Navajos, this chapter focuses on photographs of Juanita in order to understand how photographs have ingrained popular perceptions of Navajos, particularly Navajo women, into the American imagination. As relevant, I also make reference to photographs of Manuelito. Ripped from historical and cultural context, the images frozen in these photographs have been placed in American frameworks for understanding Native American and Navajo women. Navajo women like Juanita have been cast by cultural producers into the predictable roles reserved for indigenous women, roles that non-Indian observers have found difficult to apply to Navajo women.[3] Reflecting the ways in which Navajo women have been stereotyped by dominant American society, the photos do not tell Navajo women's stories. The limitations of these representations for comprehending Navajo women's lives are revealed further when scholars use gender as a category of analysis.

History makes few references to Juanita, who lived from approximately 1845 to 1910, a period of tumultuous change for Navajos. During the "Navajo wars" in the 1860s, Juanita remained alongside her husband, Manuelito. Bighorse, a warrior who rode with Chief Manuelito, remembered: "Manuelito takes some warriors to Fort Sumner. I don't know how many days they ride. They take extra horses. Manuelito takes his wife, Juanita. She is a very tough lady. She is brave and uses guns and bows and arrows. She is always by Manuelito, her husband."[4] In 1866, Manuelito, Juanita, and their family and clan members journeyed to the Bosque Redondo prison, where they were incarcerated with other Navajos. In 1868, Manuelito and Juanita returned to their original home outside present-day Tohatchi, New Mexico.[5]

Juanita has been referred to as a Mexican slave who married Manuelito and subsequently became his favorite wife. In 1880, Navajo agent John Bowman ordered Manuelito to release his slaves, whereupon the Navajo leader replied that he did not hold slaves as they were free to go wherever they wished. Although historians have referred to Bowman's report as an indication that Juanita had once been a slave, in fact, Bowman does not name her explicitly.[6]

In 1894, Juanita was widowed and moved with her daughters and their families closer to the present Tohatchi community. Juanita's great-grandchildren still tell the story of her death, which occurred around 1910.[7] She is remembered and honored as a grandmother and mother who left a land base for her descendants.

Very little can be learned about Navajos from photographs. What can be learned is how the West privileges photography, how Navajos appear to the West, and how limited these representations are.[8] These limitations are directly related to a system of power that authorizes only certain representations.[9] Likewise, photographs of Juanita, which depict her at different stages in life, have been interpreted to reinforce popular American beliefs about Native and Navajo women, conveying messages about proper gender roles, the effects of assimilation policies on Native people, and the status of Native women in their societies. Failure to interrogate existing documents on women like Juanita undermines attempts to understand the past and present of Navajo women's lives.

Photography and Navajos

Numerous studies have tracked how the medium of photography has created and shaped popular understanding of the American West and, in particular, how American Indians can be understood. Photographs inserted American Indians into an existing discourse with predetermined meanings. Some images identified individual American Indians as the official representatives of their "race" and as stewards of the land. Other portrayals confirmed the popular American belief that Indians would vanish because of their inability to adjust to modern society.[10] Perhaps the most familiar portrayal of American Indians is that of bonneted warriors astride their horses.[11] Other studies have observed that photographs have confirmed anthropologists' ethnographic studies, thereby serving the interests of imperial or commercial expansion, particularly the nineteenth-century concepts of Manifest Destiny and white man's burden.[12]

In the American Southwest, the Pueblo peoples found themselves the focus of photographers and many others who promoted the region as a place for Americans to visit. These images of Pueblos as primarily passive, peaceful, and family-oriented peoples have not changed substantially since the first descriptions by Spanish observers. Literary critic Barbara Babcock has commented on these images: "Perhaps the only thing more surprising than the consistency and the popularity of such images is their longevity. The landscapes and peoples and distinctive objects being portrayed in Castaneda's chronicles of the sixteenth century, Cushing's descriptions of the nineteenth century, and in contemporary times, sound and look remarkably the same."[13] Photographs of Pueblos were created and conveyed by a system of power that authorizes "certain Pueblo cultural representations while blocking, prohibiting, and validating others."[14] With the emergence of a national marketplace for Indian arts and crafts, indigenous peoples came to be seen within its context. Images of sedentary Pueblo peoples drew curious travelers, quieted their fears about the "Wild West," and reassured them that Native peoples had accepted American beliefs and values—that they were not too different from white Americans.[15] Literary critic Leah Dilworth has pointed out that Americans understand indigenous peoples within a context that reflects their own concerns and fears. In the late-nineteenth century, those anxieties included uneasiness about rapid industrialization, urbanization, and shifting gender roles.[16]

Studies of photographs and American Indians have concentrated on the portrayal of men. Now emerging in the literature, however, are gendered critiques that examine depictions of Native women in literature, history, and photographs. These expand upon Rayna Green's classic study of representations of American Indian women. Green's examination of non-Indian literary and artistic depictions of Native women revealed that princesses and squaw-drudge depictions, rooted in Western traditions and reflecting colonizers' perceptions, were and still are tied to practices of conquest.[17] Interestingly, while Native women have been cast in these two roles, non-Indians have found it difficult to categorize Navajo women as either "princesses" or "squaw-drudges."

Anthropologists Patricia Albers and William James have noted that photographic depictions of Indian women, mostly in the form of postcards, have exhibited great variation in content and theme, but that they are also best understood within the context of popular "princess" and "squaw-drudge" images.[18] Specifically, prior to 1915, the images were produced for a national audience and emphasized the exotic. After 1915, portrayals were aimed at the local tourist and art market and depicted Native women situated in domestic scenes and engaged in crafts. Depictions also placed women in traditional native settings. Albers and James, like Green, noted that these images failed to acknowledge Native women's historical realities.

Heart of the Circle: Photographs by Edward S. Curtis of Native American Women, edited by Sara Day, is one the first books exclusively devoted to images of Native women.[19] Reevaluating Edward Curtis's photographs, Pat Durkin has written in her introduction that Curtis managed to capture American Indian women's lives realistically. Hundreds of images of Native women in tasks such as food preparation and childcare reveal the crucial roles of Indian women in their societies. Although women's presence was not obvious in political and economic realms, their voices were heard behind the scenes as men conferred with them.

Barbara Babcock has examined the images of Pueblo women in the Southwest, where they have been portrayed mostly as olla maidens in a discourse that assumes non-Western women as an unproblematic category that remained static and outside of history.[20] The images of olla maidens is part of a long "story of the aestheticization of the Other," in which Native women and the things they make become both the symbol and source of cultural identity, survival, and social continuity.[21] Native women become the mediators between cultures as well as vehicles of both stability and change.

Fascination with photographs has continued with recent publications that include gender analysis. *Trading Gazes: Euro-American Women Photographers and Native North Americans, 1880–1940*, edited by Susan Bernardin, Melody Graulich, Lisa MacFarlane, and Nicole Tonkovich; *Framing the West: Race, Gender, and the Photographic Frontier in the Pacific Northwest*, by Carol J. Williams; and *Picturing Arizona: The Photographic Record of the 1930s*, edited by Katherine G. Morrissey and Kirsten M. Jensen, are collections that examine relationships between white women, many of whom took photographs, and Native people.[22] The authors offer a range of interpretations that includes the usual observations about white women being more sympathetic toward their Native wards and neighbors and developing close relationships with them. They note that in formulating their perspectives on Native peoples, westering white women articulated their own positions as women in American society. Although these collections begin to offer a more complicated depiction of the nature of relationships between white women and native people, there remains a failure to examine how white women contributed to the racialized and gendered perceptions of native peoples that have sustained relationships based on inequalities and injustices. As historian Margaret Jacobs has observed, "While many other western historians have grappled with 'the legacy of conquest,' white women have remained largely immune from such scrutiny, with a few notable exceptions."[23]

James Faris's critique of existing photographs of Navajos has demonstrated that representations of Navajos have remained unchanged over the course of several decades and that they are tied to colonial enterprises. However, photographs of Navajo women have yet to be scrutinized. The American public of an earlier era saw few photographs and other images of Navajos and Apaches because they were still seen as "savage" at the end of the nineteenth century.[24] Faris includes standard portrayals of Navajo women in familiar roles with which Americans could easily identify. Navajo women were presented in domestic activities such as cooking, weaving, caring for children, and tending sheep flocks. They were also posed in much the same way privileged white families sat for portraits. In such settings, they were dressed in either the biil or the nineteenth-century white or Hispanic women's attire, which has come to stand for the "traditional" dress of Navajo women. Consequently, they become yet another signifier of Navajos as people who are primarily cultural adapters in American eyes. Although scholars have challenged portrayals of women in which domestic roles were devalued, it is still important to understand the meaning of domestic roles in Navajo society, in particular the meaning for Navajo women.

The most common portrayal of Navajo women presents them as weavers. Navajo women's woven textiles were renowned throughout the colonial Southwest. Previously worn as clothing for personal use, they quickly became valuable trade items sought first by the Spaniards and then the Mexicans. Indeed, ownership of one of these textiles was a mark of stature. By the late-nineteenth century, these waterproof, finely woven Navajo-made textiles were prized commodities important in the emerging national arts and crafts market.

Today, most people still know Navajo women primarily as weavers of these fine blankets. These stereotypical images have veiled the meaning of the textiles themselves, and, importantly, of Navajo women's labor, as well. As Kathy M'Closkey has argued, feminist anthropologists categorized Navajo women's knowledge as secular and considered their economic contributions to their families as "pin money."[25] These notions have devalued women's knowledge and suggested that women have made few economic contributions to their families' prosperity. In reality, weavers' knowledge, rooted in cultural knowledge that has ceremonial and spiritual significance, has been crucial to Navajo cultural survival. Their labor often meant the difference between starving and having enough to eat.

Photographs of Juanita, as with others of Navajos, became available to the Navajo public in the 1960s. Non-Indian researchers employed by the Navajo Nation uncovered them while canvassing archives for Navajo land claims. They subsequently published some of their findings in the *Navajo Times*, a newspaper that began operation under the auspices of the Navajo Tribe. In 1980, Robert A. Roessel Jr., a non-Indian educator, published the first collection of photographs of Navajos, making it the first time that Navajos actually viewed these nineteenth- and early twentieth-century photographs.[26]

Photographs of Juanita were taken between 1868 and 1902. These include single portraits of Juanita, ones of her with her husband and a son and as a member of a delegation to Washington, D.C., and ones with her daughters and grandchildren. The photographers who portrayed Juanita worked within the same ethos as other photographers of their day. Her portrayals reflect standard themes associated with American Indians, including ideas about the eventual disappearance of Native peoples, loss of tradition, and assimilation into American culture. Her photographs were also used to illustrate messages about the benefits of "primitive" life as white Americans eased their own anxieties about the ills of modern industrial and urban civilization. Images of Juanita as weaver foreshadow the prominence of Navajo women as weavers in the American imagination. By the early twentieth century, Navajo women as weavers had become linked to the emerging national Indian arts and crafts market.

Photographs of Juanita

Several photographs from the Bosque Redondo era depict groups of Navajos standing in cornfields, gathering food rations, and building the fort that housed the American officers and soldiers.[27] Portraits from this period include one of a young Juanita by Valentin Wolfenstein (fig. 2). A family photograph of Manuelito, Juanita, and a son was also taken, mostly like at the same time as the single portrait, since the props are the same (fig. 3). A series of portraits of the Navajo delegation to Washington, D.C., in 1874, taken by Charles Bell, shows Juanita to have been the only woman to accompany the delegation of Navajo and white men (figs. 4–6). The delegation series includes one of Juanita with William Arny (fig. 5). In 1881, Manuelito and Juanita sat for a photographer at Fort Wingate (fig. 7). Photographers repeatedly captured the two posed as a couple. In 1902, George Wharton James spied Juanita with her daughters at the Tohatchi School, one of the first of such schools established on the reservation, and persuaded them to sit for a series of portraits (figs. 8–12). One photograph from this collection of Juanita and her two daughters (fig. 11) appears to have been taken without their consent, for they seem to be waiting, sitting against a wall. A dog rests at one of the women's feet. James also used Juanita's portrait to illustrate some of his books, including *Indian Blankets and Their Makers* (fig. 12).[28] As James Faris has observed, "Poor Juanita, the wife of Manuelito and the most photographed of all early Navajo women, had to endure James's camera through numerous poses."[29]

The single portrait of Juanita, taken soon after Navajos had signed a treaty with the U.S. government in 1868 (fig. 2), shows a young Juanita posing in a standard posture associated with wealthy families who commissioned self-portraits.[30] Because of their influential positions in both white and Navajo society, several leaders such as Manuelito and Barboncito were the subjects of such portraits. Although white persons of financial means often commissioned these photographs for their personal use, Native peoples most likely did not, nor did they come to own them. This particular portrait of Juanita uses the same backdrop as the only existing portrait of Barboncito.[31] Juanita's travels with her husband are documented through a number of photographs, such as this one, and could be read as evidence of a long and lasting relationship, which their descendants have characterized as one of mutual respect.[32] More recently, during a conversation with Peterson Zah, I learned that he had heard similar stories of Manuelito's respect for his wife.

Juanita's manner of dress, her biil, a bead necklace, and buckskin-wrapped moccasins reflect the way Navajo women are presently portrayed and signify the "traditional" Navajo woman. Because the portrayals present Navajo women in a blend of indigenous wear and styles adopted from Pueblos and non-Indian women, they confirm existing ideas about them as primarily people who have adapted and incorporated cultural items from elsewhere. These sorts of interpretation fail to acknowledge that Navajos are indigenous to North America, that Native people have always experienced change, and that the ability to adapt and incorporate new forms and thought into existing cultural beliefs and practices has meant survival and prosperity.

Efforts to assimilate Navajos into American society began with the "experiment" at Bosque Redondo and were renewed under President Ullysses S. Grant's 1874 Peace Policy. For Navajos, reestablishing their lives in their homeland meant confronting American assimilation, which included those policies advocated by Grant's program. The program's goals were to change conditions that government officials saw as lawless, unethical, and immoral. The reforms included replacing army officers who served as Indian agents with males from specific Christian denominations. Assigned the Navajo reservation as their domain, Presbyterian agents were instructed to model moral and civilized behavior, eradicate drunkenness and polygamy, and inculcate Christian values.

On September 1, 1873, Arny replaced William Hall as Indian agent at Fort Defiance. As a new Presbyterian agent, Arny subscribed to the program to "kill the Indian to save the man." He was described as "the worse agent the Navajos ever had to contend with." Opposed to any behavior that deviated from Christian beliefs and values, Arny immediately banished from the fort white men who lived with Navajo women. For Arny, the Diné could do only two things right: raise sheep and weave blankets.[33]

During the formation of Grant's peace policy, Maj. Gen. Oliver O. Howard visited indigenous people in the Southwest, ostensibly to ease tensions between Apaches and Navajos. Howard's recollections of meeting with Manuelito led him to declare, "As he [Manuelito] and his men rode away my eyes followed this splendid leader, and I rejoiced that so fine a man was using every energy to bring joy and happiness to all about him—a war chief no longer, but a man of peace."[34] Because Manuelito was one of a few remaining leaders who had experienced the wars, it was in the interest of Presbyterian Indian agents to use him as a role model. Historian Norman Bender stated of Manuelito's influence:

> Barboncito and Armijo, two of the old chiefs, died during the year. Ganado Mucho, another old chief, then assumed a position of authority in the tribe. . . . However, in further restructuring of the tribal hierarchy, Manuelito, a younger and more militant subchief, ascended to a prominent position. Only time would tell how his role in tribal affairs would be defined, but the white residents at the Navajo agency certainly hoped he would also understand and appreciate the peaceful intent of the Grant Peace Policy.[35]

Photographs of Manuelito and Juanita intended to capture the intent of Grant's policy by suggesting that they were not unlike any other American couple (figs. 1, 3, and 7). Embedded in the portraits are notions about proper social relationships, ideal relationships between men and women, marriage, and monogamy. Cultural scholars like Laura Wexler and Judith Williams have explained how photographs convey messages about the integration of people of color into the American national family. According to Williamson, "Photographs played not merely an incidental but a central role in the development of the contemporary ideology of the family, in providing a form of representation which cut across classes, disguised social differences, and produced a sympathy of the exploited with their exploiters." Concludes Williams, "It could make all families look more or less alike."[36] As Wexler also observes, the use of photographs to create the semblance of American families "laid down the future possibilities for historical distortion and violent denial that operated both forward and backward in time."[37]

These portraits of Manuelito and Juanita also intimate that Navajos had adopted Victorian attitudes about marriage and sexuality. As Wexler notes, photographs were a mode of domestic representation that inscribed a set of relationships and created a system of meaning between subjects. Family portraits, with their origins in nineteenth-century bourgeois domestic photography, "related images to one another and to other cultural practices through a hierarchizing narrative of social signs. Thus, photographic sentiment helped to create the hierarchies of domesticity that, ostensibly, it only recorded."[38]

In figures 1 and 7, Manuelito's large stature is obvious despite his seated position. Juanita sits appropriately—for an American audience—in a lower position next to her husband. In figure 7, Manuelito wears a hat that appears to be perched on top of the headband that Navajo men customarily wore. The photographer seems to have provided the hat as an afterthought. In figure 3, a young man, probably a son of Manuelito and Juanita, stands with his hands touching the shoulders of his parents, thus forming an intimate family circle. In contrast to what the photographs imply about power relationships between women and men in Navajo society, Navajo women today still do not consider themselves subordinate to their husbands.

White Americans' fears and ambivalence about the nature of Indian societies are also suggested in these photographs. They would have been horrified and alarmed to learn that Manuelito had fathered numerous children with other women. Throughout the early reservation period, white missionaries, federal officials, and teachers attempted to abolish Navajos' polygamous practices. Some white men at Fort Defiance, like trader Thomas Keams and government employee Anson Damon, followed Navajo practice and married multiple Navajo women. Anthropologist Ann Stoler has argued that colonial authorities attempted to maintain racial and class hierarchies that separated themselves from the colonized, and one primary way was to regulate sexual relations between colonizers and the colonized.[39] Whites feared that prolonged contact with Natives and their environment would lead to physical and moral degeneration, and those men who dared to cross ethnic boundaries openly were censured and exiled from the reservations.[40]

As the wife of a prominent chief, Juanita was a member of the Navajo delegation that traveled to Washington, D.C., in 1874 to meet with President Grant. The Navajo leaders' determination to meet with the president and journey to the capital followed a tradition rooted in the earliest official meetings between Native and American leaders (fig. 6). Over the course of several decades, white Americans had brought Native leaders to the nation's capital hoping to impress upon them the power and resources of the American government and the benefits of white civilization. Manuelito, who remained a leader among his people, was an important delegate for the trip to the East.

Although scholars have echoed non-Indian observers who deemed the trip frivolous and self-serving, Manuelito believed that his right was to speak personally to the U.S. president.[41] Always concerned about Navajo land claims, Manuelito hoped to persuade President Grant to return more territory to his people and to try to resolve ongoing conflicts between Navajo herders and New Mexican ranchers. Although Arny had submitted the names of other Navajo leaders' wives for the journey, Juanita was the only woman to accompany the delegation.[42]

The delegation began its journey on November 15, 1873, in Santa Fe, New Mexico, where it spent several days before moving on to Denver, Colorado. At its final destination, Washington, D.C., studio photographer Charles Bell produced a series of photographs of the delegation. These reflect American beliefs and values about Native peoples, including ones about assimilation policies and family and nation. They mark the shifting meanings of Navajo women's lives as a national market for Navajo textiles emerged and they became best understood in the role of weavers.

Charles Bell's photographs of the delegation also reflect Manuelito's status. Manuelito, clasping a fringed quiver and flanked by his wife and their son, Manuelito Segundo, sits in the center of the group, signifying his privileged position among his people. William Arny, standing directly behind Juanita, has a Navajo-made textile, the message "1776 USA" woven into it, slung over his shoulder. Three of the Navajo men carry bows, items that signify warriors. Possibly the photographer provided the bows. Ironically, only a few years earlier Navajos had been militarily defeated, but in 1874, the men were portrayed as fierce warriors, noble savages.

Although a number of existing photographs of Manuelito and Juanita indicate their familiarity with studios and picture taking and suggest a level of experience and contact with whites and their institutions that other Navajos lacked, thus indicating some degree of collaboration between the photographer and his subjects, we must remain cognizant of the unequal nature of the relationship between the parties.[43] As Faris noted, "This is not an appropriate mode for subjects who have succeeded; it implies control, supervision, command, rule, test, defeat, arrest."[44]

In addition to conveying messages of Navajos' successful assimilation, the photographs foreshadowed the popular image of Navajo women as weavers. In one picture, Juanita and Arny face each other, with Arny seated gazing down at her (fig. 5). Surrounded by Navajo-made textiles and a fake boulder, Juanita holds a weaving implement in one hand. When the *Navajo Times* published this photograph, the caption indicated that Juanita was the weaver of the textile on the loom.[45] The copy of the photograph in the Smithsonian Institution's collection has written on the back, "Juanita and Gov. Arny showing blankets, etc." Juanita, although never recognized for her abilities and skill as a weaver, is portrayed as a "living" exhibit, the weaver of fine woven textiles that were gaining national recognition by the late 1870s.

In the summer of 2003, I conducted additional research in the National Anthropological Archives at the Smithsonian Institution. There, a photo archivist informed me that the archives has in its collection the textile shown in the photograph of Juanita and Arny (fig. 5). I was surprised to learn this, especially since I had not known about it when I had made my first research trip there in 1997. Arny had offered the textile to the Smithsonian Institution in 1875.[46] How had he acquired it? Not long after the Navajo delegation returned to Navajo Land in 1875, Navajo leaders forced the Indian agent's hasty departure after accusing him of stealing annuities provided for them under the Treaty of 1868. Did Arny take the textile with him when he fled?

Textile scholar Kate Kent Peck names this textile as one of the first pictorials woven by a Navajo woman. Incomplete, half of the textile depicts the American flag; the other half is an "eye-dazzler," so named for its brilliant colors. Navajo women began weaving eye-dazzlers only after gaining access to brightly colored yarns manufactured after 1868. Initially, textile experts ignored these weavings because they did not fit into notions about "natural" and "authentic" textiles. No doubt a textile that depicted the American flag and had brilliant colors did not catch textile scholars' attention, so it languished in the Smithsonian's collection for decades. As museum specialist Felicia Pickering informed me, the museum staff had not associated the flag blanket with Juanita until 2000.[47]

Why would Juanita weave an image of the American flag? Navajo leaders were aware that they continually needed to engage American officials' interests in Navajo causes, namely sovereignty, to which Manuelito and Juanita were committed. Just as later pictorials of trains and other signs of American influence on Navajos are reflected in late-nineteenth- and early-twentieth-century weavings, so Juanita's weaving of an American flag demonstrates awareness of cultural changes

to which the People were subjected and indicate critical consciousness about the politics of attracting the attention of federal officials.
A woven depiction of the American flag was one way to capture their
attention, for these officials had some say about the Navajo future.[48]

Soon after his arrival in Navajo land, Arny saw the potential for a
national market in Navajo arts and crafts. He most likely took advantage of Juanita's presence to enhance art and craft exhibits he set up
in major cities where the delegation stopped; certainly, the photograph of Arny and Juanita implies his intentions. In each town the
delegation stopped, Arny promoted Navajo crafts. At the delegation's
first stop, hundreds of curious spectators turned out to marvel at the
"dusky sons of the forest" and view Navajo textiles and other crafts in
one of the Denver Hotel's bridal suites.[49] The fact that Navajos were
not inhabitants of forests but people of a terrain that encompassed
both arid and forested regions was lost on white Americans. The caption on the photograph of Juanita and Arny indicates that they were
"showing blankets," and, at the same time, that she was on exhibit.
Although many Navajo women had donned American/Hispanic-style
skirts and blouses after 1868, Juanita continued to wear a woven biil
and moccasins with buckskin leggings. For the white spectators, Juanita epitomized Navajo weavers. As the maker of woven textiles, she
must have conjured up visions of the primitive American past.

Photographs of Juanita as a member of the delegation to Washington, D.C., foreshadow the emergence of national interest in Indian
arts and crafts; however, it was the establishment of the Santa Fe Railway in the Southwest that allowed development of a market for them.
Railroad companies formed business links with entrepreneurs like
Fred Harvey, who worked with artists, writers, and photographers to
create interest in the Southwest. An explosion of information about
indigenous peoples there circulated in ethnographic reports, popular magazines, and tourist literature.[50] White Americans' interest in
indigenous life, in their arts and crafts, reflected their own concerns
and fears. Images of the Southwest stirred nostalgia for an idealized
American past, invoking a republican past in which the ideal society
was agrarian and artisan labor was valued. Images of Indian women
attending to their families and domestic tasks also spoke to America's
preoccupation with shifting gender roles.[51]

Among the influential popularizers was George Wharton James,
who traveled throughout the Southwest and collected indigenous

material culture. He published his observations and lectured to interested audiences. James's work established a set of standards for collectors and others to ascertain the quality of their purchases. These standards, including an insistence on the use of hand-spun wool yarn, natural dyes, and wool warps, influenced the Indian arts and crafts market for generations. During one of James's travels around 1902, he met Juanita and her family and took a series of portraits with which he illustrated a number of his books. His use of these photographs reflected white American beliefs about Native people and demonstrated a facet of the relationships between collectors, Navajo artisans, and the developing ethnic art market. Juanita, the wife of war chief Manuelito, became a symbol, a living relic, linking the traditional and primitive Diné past to the increasingly modern twentieth century. James also managed to collect one of Juanita's biil, one of her dresses. Although Juanita treasured it as a link to the past, for James, it symbolized authenticity.

Manuelito's death in 1894 marked the end of an era. Juanita moved with her two daughters and their husbands (who were brothers) closer to Tohatchi, onto lands that their husbands' clan had occupied prior to 1868. The Manuelito family members were familiar figures in the Tohatchi region, where Juanita was often seen herding sheep with her grandchildren. It was at the Tohatchi School that George Wharton James spied the elderly Juanita. Perhaps to encourage other Navajos to enroll their own children, the Manuelito grandchildren attended the Tohatchi School.[52]

Most likely taken at the Tohatchi School, James's photographs (figs. 8 and 12) are probably the last ones taken of Juanita. James published the family photo (fig. 8) in *The Indians of the Painted Desert Region: Hopis, Navahoes, Wallapais, Havasupais* and titled it "The Widow, Daughters, and Grandchildren of the Navaho chief, Manuelito."[53] In this image, Juanita wears her biil, in contrast to her daughters, who have donned cotton blouses and skirts of the post-Bosque Redondo period.[54] The older daughter, Red Mustache's wife, was known to the school officials as Shizie. The other daughter is Ałk'iníbaa. Standing in the back of the group is Juanita's grandson, believed to be George Manuelito, the son of Red Mustache's wife. George wears American-style school clothes and his hair is clipped short. His was perhaps the first generation of Navajo men forced to have their hair shorn. An inspection of the photo reveals typical themes already noted:

Juanita and her family present yet another opportunity to gauge the effect of assimilation and change in Navajo life. Juanita, the elderly grandmother, is dressed in the fashion of Navajo women pre-Bosque Redondo, whereas the daughters and their children show evidence of adaptation. Juanita becomes a marker of continuity with the past, for Native women have often been represented as symbols of cultural continuity, embodiments of tradition. As James remarked, it was not that Indians were in danger of disappearing, especially the Navajos, but that the way of life was rapidly disappearing with the necessity of change.[55]

In this portrait of Juanita and her family, none of the party gazes back at the camera. Her eldest daughter, Red Mustache's wife, never looks at it, as if to hide her blind eye. These sorts of poses have often been interpreted as demonstrations of either "shyness" or reluctance, rather than resistance. Thousands of photographs with such poses lie in archives, and for the most part those that depict resistance have not been published. Perhaps the reluctance to gaze back at the camera's eye points to inequitable social relations inevitably part of these photographic encounters.

James's remarks on the photographs of Juanita and her family described Navajo cultural beliefs and practices. His derisive comments belittled Navajo values, marked them as superstition, and asserted the superiority of white culture. Using the photograph as an example, James wrote:

> The taboo is in existence in all its force among the Navahoes. The most singular of these is that which forbids a man ever to look upon the face of his mother-in-law. Among civilized people it is a standard subject for rude jesting, this relationship of the mother-in-law, but with the Navahoes, the white man's jest is a subject of great earnestness. Each believes that serious consequences will follow if they see each other; hence, as it is the custom for a man to live with his wife's people, constant dodging is required, and the cries of warning, given by one or another of the family to son or mother-in-law, are often heard. I was once photographing the family of Manuelito, the last great war-chief of the Navahoes. The widow of the chief, her two daughters, their husbands and children, made up the group. But there was no getting of them together. I would photograph the mother with her daughters and

grandchildren, but as soon as I called for the daughters' husbands, the mother "slid" out of sight, and when I wished for her return, the men disappeared.[56]

James's description of his session with Juanita's family explains why only the women and the children were present. Navajo tradition required that mothers-in-law and sons-in-law not inhabit the same social space. However, James did manage to take portraits of the daughters with their respective husbands and children in family-style portrayals (figs. 9 and 10). Certainly, even by the early twentieth century the Navajo conceptualization of family was still vastly different from that of white Americans. James's descriptions of other "irrational" Navajo customs, such as their aversion to fish, portray Navajos in caricature. Patronizingly dismissing his own and other white's egregious behavior towards Navajos and calling it "fun," he gleefully recounted an incident in which he "had a great deal of fun by innocently offering candy in the form of fish to Navahoes."[57]

George Wharton James also used Juanita's photograph and a rug she had woven to illustrate his *Indian Blankets and Their Makers*, published in 1914 (fig. 12). This book offered advice for collectors of Indian-made textiles and provided a standard by which they could evaluate quality and authenticity. Accompanying a portrait of Juanita, under which is written, "Manuelito's Widow Wearing Squaw Dress in Old Navaho Fashion," James related the encounter with Juanita that led to his acquisition of her biil:

> Specimens of this earlier type of woman's dress are very scarce. Only a few are to be found in the museums. The only one I was ever able to secure from the Navahos was one that was made and worn for years by the wife of the great warrior chief Manuelito. . . . As it was the last of its kind, and was very worn and much repaired, she had carefully washed it and put it away amongst her treasures, from whence she drew it forth to show to me. When I expressed my desire to purchase it she refused to let me have it on account of its dilapidated condition. But as later we became good friends she finally insisted upon my taking it as a gift.[58]

After referring to Juanita's biil as a sample of weaving from the Bosque Redondo, James explained that he lost track of the dress after he had lent it to an exhibit in Los Angeles.

James's cavalier attitude about the loss of the dress suggests that it was only one of many "artifacts" he had collected throughout his career. Furthermore, James's practice of taking artifacts through deceit and trickery are documented and makes his claims of a friendship with Juanita questionable. Leah Dilworth notes that the literature of connoisseurship is filled with collectors' accounts of noticing Indian people's possessions and desiring them, and encountering reluctance of the owners to part with them.[59] The notion of authenticity was crucial to the collection of Indian artifacts; authenticity included ideas that artifacts had been made by Indians, that they had worn them, or that the items were rare. James's reference to Juanita, the value she placed in her dress, and his tale about how he came to possess it increased its value. For James's purpose, as the wife of war chief Manuelito, "the defiant spirit of the Navajo," Juanita, or rather the objects with which she was associated or once owned, signified authenticity.

During the period that James traveled throughout the Southwest, many Americans attributed the region with rejuvenating qualities that could reinvigorate the body and mind, for it seemed that civilization was too materialistic and lacked spirituality.[60] James also saw that Native people's culture and practices could address White Americans' fears, and in *What the White Race May Learn from the Indians* he advised readers that living as simply and naturally as the Indians would help create a meaningful life. In one chapter, "Indian and the Superfluities of Life," James illustrates his thesis with a portrait of Juanita. Titling it, "The Widow of Manuelito, the Last Great Chief of the Navahos. One of the Queenliest Women in Dignity, Grace, and Character I Have Ever Met," James held her up for white admiration. Her simplistic style of dress told white women that they fussed too much about appearances and deprived themselves of "time that could and should be more wisely and profitably spent."[61]

In 1902, the Fred Harvey Company began to promote Elle, a Navajo weaver from Ganado, Arizona, as an icon of Indian crafts. Elle was one of the few named Indian artists, an exception since most Indian artisans remained anonymous. The objects they created were deemed more significant than their makers.[62] It is perhaps more than a coincidence that the two most frequently mentioned Navajo women, Juanita and Elle, were weavers. Although she was not widely known as a weaver, James's images of Juanita symbolized to Americans their primitive past. Her image spoke to American anxieties about women's proper roles, and she and her family stood as a gauge by which Americans could measure Navajos' acceptance of American beliefs and values about family, marriage, religion, and education. Juanita may not have been promoted as an accomplished weaver because in the 1870s Navajos were still seen as "savages," in contrast to the Pueblo peoples, who were studied and photographed more often than Navajos and Apaches. In contrast, Elle of Ganado became known for her weaving because Navajo arts and crafts had emerged into the national vision and market by the early twentieth century.

Non-Indian representations of Juanita and her family negate Navajo women's lives and history. Juanita was a Navajo woman whose life spanned two centuries. She experienced the horrors of the Americans' war on her people and saw her children stolen by slave traders. She actively resisted American invasion of her homeland. After 1868, she experienced the effects of American civilization on herself, her family, and her Navajo people. Today she remains a grandmother still remembered by her descendants as one who was generous, beneficent, and wise. Yet Juanita as a representative of Navajo women could still have all of her experiences reduced to a trope—such as Navajo weaver. Such images of Navajo women continue to define them today.

Although non-Indian representations of Navajo women and Native peoples have negated indigenous peoples' own perceptions of their beliefs, values, and history and substituted their own meanings, it has become increasingly difficult to ignore Native people's criticisms of those depictions. Reevaluations of the meanings of photographs now include Native people's responses.[63]

For many Native peoples, photographs housed in archives and museums or owned by private collectors have become a rich source for remembering the past. Native people's reflections on these photographs have added another dimension to the dialogue about the meaning of their lives and realities. As historical documents, they have become catalysts for people who find them useful in ways that promote and create a sense of community. As indigenous people across generations share their responses to documents long removed from Indian society, stories are told and retold. The process of remembering the past through the photographs becomes yet another vehicle for resisting the ongoing insistence that Native people take their places as "normal" Americans.

During the process of searching for information on Juanita, after I had discovered these photographs of her, I began to take them back to her descendants, whom George Wharton James had captured on film. The great-grandchildren of Juanita and Manuelito are now elderly, great-grandparents and grandparents themselves. Their responses upon seeing their grandmother lose richness when written down. As my grandfather, Isaac Allison, grandson of Juanita's younger daughter, Ałk'iníbaa, said with emotion, "It is just like I'm seeing my grandmother again." The photographs call up memories of the past, memories in which Juanita and her daughters played important roles in the continuity of Navajo family and society.

Conclusion

Little has changed in the portrayal of Navajo women since the earliest photographs of them after the Civil War. Between Flagstaff, Arizona, and Albuquerque, New Mexico, Interstate 40 is a tourist's paradise. It is an interesting slice of highway because of its colorful billboards and tourist attractions. One billboard outside Winslow, Arizona, claims that a great-granddaughter of Manuelito owns a curio shop. The image of Manuelito, the one in which he sits shirtless and straight-backed, looms above passing motorists. Going into Gallup from the east or west, travelers are welcomed to the "Indian Capital of the World," with images of young attractive Navajo maidens dressed in the style worn after 1868. On a regular basis, the *Navajo Times* features images of young Navajo women in the "traditional" style of velveteen blouses and volumes of three-tiered skirts. At all of the annual parades that occur within and around Navajo Land, scores of Navajo princesses wave enthusiastically and beam winsome smiles at crowds that obligingly wave back. Pick up almost any magazine that focuses on the Southwest and a Navajo woman in the "traditional" dress will gaze back. The magazine could be aimed at the tourist trade or published for Navajo readers. Moreover, as historian Colleen O'Neill remarks about the display of traditional values when Navajo women don their beautiful velveteen and calico cotton ensembles, "tradition and modernity sit side by side on the same stage, not in conflict with the other, but in harmonious conversations."[64]

The standard portrayals of Navajo women have been primarily understood within Western frameworks rooted in nineteenth-century American concepts of American Indians. These perceptions shift slightly when applied to Navajo women and reflect American concerns and fears about the changing nature of their own society. Furthermore, beginning in the late-nineteenth century, these images became increasingly tied to the market, so that Navajos became a commodity to be consumed. As Leah Dilworth points out, efforts to represent Native peoples serve to textualize or objectify them, thereby creating relationships based on inequalities.[65] Navajo women, like other Native women, have persisted, and the project to understand their historical realities better is ongoing. Because much of what is known about Navajo women is directly related to photographs that validate Western representations of them, these discourses tell us very little about their historical realities or experiences. Navajos have not controlled the representations of who they are, past or present. Yet, although it is not the subject of this chapter, Navajos themselves have claimed the image of the "traditional" Navajo woman, thereby making statements about Navajo femininity.

Figure 1. A group that includes Manuelito (sitting) and wife, ca. 1868. This photograph was probably taken soon after the signing of the Treaty of 1868.

Figure 2. Juanita, or Asdzáá Tł'ógi, in 1868. She often traveled with her husband and, as this photograph suggests, she was frequently present at council meetings between Diné leaders and American officials.

Figure 3. Manuelito, Juanita, and their son in 1868. This image suggests that Navajo families fit within American ideals of family as primarily nuclear. Manuelito actually had several wives and many children, though Juanita was his constant companion and his favorite wife.

Figure 4. Juanita (Asdzáá Tł'ógi) in Washington, D.C., in 1874. One story that her descendants remember tells of her journey to the nation's capital.

Figure 5. Juanita with William F. Arny in 1874. Juanita wove the textile shown in the background. Arny later donated it to the Smithsonian.

Figure 6. The Navajo delegation in Washington, D.C., in 1874. Juanita was the only woman to travel with the delegation, although the Indian agent had submitted the names of other Navajo leaders' wives. In 1951, Dághá Ch'íí Bik'is identified Manuelito's son, sitting second from the right in the front row, next to his father, as Naat'ahsilá.

Manuelita__Navajo Chief and wife.
New Mexico, 1881.

Figure 7. Manuelito and Juanita in 1881. Their Navajo names include Hastiin Ch'il Hajin (Man from Black Weeds) and Asdzáá Tł'ógi (Lady Weaver). After 1868 they returned to their former residence near Standing Rock, New Mexico.

Figure 8. Asdzáá Tł'ógi with her family in 1902. Left to right, they are
Dłíhaazbaa', Dághá Chíí be Asdzáá, Asdzáá Tł'ógi (sitting), George
Manuelito, Ałk'iníbaa, and Ałk'iníbaa's daughter. This photograph was
probably taken at the Tohatchi School, where the Manuelito family was
a familiar sight.

Figure 9. Dághá Ch'íí Bik'is and his wife, Ałk'iníbaa, in 1902. Ałk'iníbaa's husband was one of the council delegates who signed oil leases on behalf of the Navajo tribe in the 1920s. Their daughter was enrolled in the Tohatchi School.

Figure 10. Dághá Ch'íí doo be Asdzáá, Dłíhaazbaa', and George Manuelito in 1902. The Manuelito family, especially Dághá Chíí be Asdzáá, assisted school officials in recruiting students.

Figure 11. The Manuelito family in 1902. Members of the family seemed either unaware of James's camera or were resisting capture one more time by the photographer.

Figure 12. "Manuelito's widow," Juanita, in 1902. George Wharton James used this photograph to illustrate his messages about the ideals that Native women's roles might hold for white women. Her descendants remember her as a generous grandmother who was often seen herding sheep with her great-grandchildren.

Figure 13. Dághá Chíí and his granddaughter, Marie Dennison (Benally), at the Tohatchi Trading Post, ca. 1938. In his old age, Dághá Chíí received a pension from the U.S. government for his service as a Navajo scout. He used his pension to care for his great-grandchildren, like Marie.

Figure 14. Juanita's granddaughter, Dłíhaazbaaʼ, ca. 1939. She is remembered by her descendants as a loving grandmother and mother.

Figure 15. Naaltsoos Neiyéhí with his daughter and grandson. His mother was Asdzáá Tsin sikaadnii. In 1966, Naaltsoos Neiyéhí (also known as Bob Manuelito and Manuelito Number Two) gave interviews to white researchers. He told stories about his father, Manuelito.

Figure 16. This billboard sponsored by Diné College in Tsaile, Arizona, hails motorists as they leave Gallup, New Mexico, 1996.

Figure 17. Arthur and Theresa Holyan in Flagstaff, Arizona, in 1997. Art is descended from Ałk'iníbaa, the younger daughter of Manuelito and Juanita. He shared stories of Ałk'iníbaa with me.

Figure 18. Charles and Esther Manuelito at home in Toadlena, New Mexico, in 1997. Charles encouraged me to do research on his great-grandparents Hastiin Ch'il Hajin and Asdzáá Tł'ógi.

Figure 19. Rose Nez, Joan Kinsel, and Jennifer Nez Denetdale in 1997. Joan is the last surviving great-granddaugher descended from Manuelito and Juanita's elder daughter, Dághá Chíí be Asdzáá.

Figure 20. Faye Yazzie in Tohatchi, New Mexico, in 1997. Faye remembered stories about her great-grandmother's trip to Washington, D.C., in 1874.

Figure 21. Juanita's dress in the Southwest Museum, in 1998, when I viewed my great-great-great-grandmother's dress for the first time. A textile that Juanita wove is also part of the museum's collection.

Figure 22. Mike Sr. and Anna Allison on their seventy-fifth wedding anniversary at their home in 2002. Mike Sr. had stories to share about his great-grandmother Asdzáá Tł'ógi.

Figure 23. Nelson and Helena Bitsilly in Tohatchi, New Mexico, in May 2006. Helena is descended from Ałk'iníbaa, the younger daughter of Manuelito and Juanita.

5/Stories of Asdzáá Tł'ógi

Diné Traditional Narratives as History

In 1992, Acoma poet Simon Ortiz composed "Juanita, Wife of Manuelito" after viewing a photograph of her published in a Navajo newspaper.[1] Offering a moment to reflect upon Native people's experience
under colonialism, the photograph also provided a moment for Ortiz
to pay tribute to Navajo women like Juanita, who showed courage
and resilience in the face of the American war on her people and land.
Ortiz's honoring of Native women's places in ensuring the cultural
survival of their people is also reflected in the narratives that descendents of Juanita, or Asdzáá Tł'ógi, still remember about their great-
grandmother.

Narratives that I gathered from the descendants of Asdzáá Tł'ógi
about their great-grandmother appear fragmented, existing as images,
genealogy, biography, autobiography, creation and traditional narratives, and history. These remaining narratives begin with the return
of Asdzáá Tł'ógi and her family from Bosque Redondo in 1868 and
offer insights into how Navajos talk about the past, especially how
the creation narratives shape an understanding of its meaning. Placing these narratives within Navajo historical and cultural contexts
demonstrates that Navajo perspectives on the past contrast and even
counter perspectives presented in conventional Navajo histories.

Significantly, the stories from Asdzáá Tł'ógi's maternal clan, the
Tł'ógi, illuminate women's roles in the reestablishment of Navajo
homes and communities after the devastations of the "Navajo wars."
As the stories remind us, women's roles, modeled on those of the

female deities who figure so prominently in the Navajo creation narratives, indicate that women are conveyors of Diné beliefs and values. Although Navajo women have experienced changes under colonialism, they look to the roles set down in the traditional stories as guidelines for life. As the stories from Asdzáá Tł'ógi's descendants illustrate, women continue to be held in high regard in their communities, where they exercise authority and enjoy a measure of autonomy through their roles as grandmothers, mothers, and daughters. In many ways, women also link the traditional status of womanhood to their roles outside of the home, in the workplace, in professional settings, and in other public arenas.

The Storytellers: The Great-grandchildren of Hastiin Ch'il Hajin and Asdzáá Tł'ógi

As a child, I had heard stories from my mother but did not realize she was talking about Manuelito's wife until I was much older. Years went by before I realized the need to recover these stories, especially because the great-grandchildren of Manuelito and Juanita were growing older. The impetus to record narratives of my ancestors is motivated by the same reasons as those expressed by other Native scholars, who note that the history of Indian education has meant a loss of traditional knowledge and Native languages and little if any access to our own histories. Furthermore, our research aims to rewrite our histories in ways that more accurately reflect our experiences, especially under colonialism. As a result of time spent in my own community, with my clanspeople and my own family, my consciousness changed. I came to appreciate more fully the importance of oral tradition and affirmed for myself the importance of our cultural values. My grandparents and other relatives were eager to participate in my research project for they are also worried about the future of our children and grandchildren. Writing down the remaining stories of our grandparents thus is a way to reaffirm clan ties and the value of Navajo cultural teachings.

Elders of the Tł'ógi clan from Tohatchi, New Mexico, and elsewhere, acknowledge their matrilineal kin ties to each other through their great-grandmother Juanita, or Asdzáá Tł'ógi, and her two daughters. A photograph of an elderly Asdzáá Tł'ógi with her two daughters and her grandchildren, taken by George Wharton James in 1902, depicts the family after the death of Manuelito in 1894 (see fig.

8). Grandmother Asdzáá Tł'ógi sits in the center of her family while her two daughters, Dághá Chíí be Asdzáá and Ałk'iníbaa, stand beside her. Dághá Chíí be Asdzáá's hand rests on her daughter's arm. Her son, whom descendants believe to be George Manuelito, stands on one side of his grandmother. George was most likely a student, as was the young girl also pictured, at the Tohatchi School when James took this photograph. Ałk'iníbaa was Asdzáá Tł'ógi's younger daughter, and she stands next to her own daughter, who is unidentified.

James also managed to get photographs of Asdzáá Tł'ógi's daughters and their families. In figures 9 and 10 the two daughters, of whom Dághá Chíí be Asdzáá is the oldest, pose with their husbands and children. Dághá Chíí be Asdzáá and Ałk'iníbaa married men who were brothers. Dághá Chíí be Asdzáá and her husband, Dághá Chíí, stand with their children, Dłíhaazbaa' and George Manuelito. In another James photo, Ałk'iníbaa poses with her husband, Dághá Chíí Bik'is, and their daughter.

To the Navajo elders I interviewed, Asdzáá Tł'ógi is *nihi'masain*, our maternal grandmother. Her two daughters, Dághá Chíí be Asdzáá and Ałk'iníbaa, are also our grandmothers. Anthropologist Gary Witherspoon in his study of Navajo kinship and marriage notes that the mother and child relationship determines all others among Navajos. This is the relationship upon which concepts of *K'e*, or kin relationships, are based.[2] This is true of Hastiin Ch'il Hajin and Asdzáá Tł'ógi's descendants, who acknowledge K'e based on Asdzáá Tł'ógi's maternal clan, the Tł'ógi. The elders regard each other as brothers and sisters, equivalent to biological siblings in American society. When they refer to their clan relationships with each other, they use the word *biłhajiijeehigii*, which indicates that they literally emerged from one mother's womb.[3] The phrase also acknowledges that several generations of one clan trace their genealogy to one mother, to one grandmother, which in this case is Juanita. Today, the elders are concerned about younger generations who do not know about these clan ties, which bind us as grandparents, mothers, aunts, uncles, brothers, sisters, and cousins. The stories the elders shared with me was one way of remembering the kinship ties begun with Hastiin Ch'il Hajin and Asdzáá Tł'ógi.

During my search for information about my great-great-great-grandparents, Hastiin Ch'il Hajin and Asdzáá Tł'ógi, I visited my maternal grandparents, who name either Dághá Chíí be Asdzáá or

Ałk'iníbaa as their maternal grandmothers. I didn't consult with all of the great-grandchildren, but focused on those who maintained communication with my mother in various ways, including expectations that she would attend traditional ceremonies and invitations to weddings, anniversaries, birthday and graduation parties, and other social events. First, Charles Manuelito (fig. 18) and Joan Kinsel (fig. 19) are descended from the eldest daughter, Dághá Chíí be Asdzáá, and her husband Dághá Chíí. Dághá Chíí, shown in figures 10 and 13, was a Navajo scout who served with the U.S. military in the 1880s. In the late 1930s, when he was elderly, he was awarded a pension for his services.[4] The little girl identified as Dłíhaazbaa' in one of James's photographs (fig. 8) is Charles and Joan's mother. With the passing of Charles in January 2002, Joan is the sole surviving granddaughter of Dághá Chíí be Asdzáá and Dághá Chíí.

Charles was the first of my maternal grandparents I approached with my research project. Charles was generous with his time and shared what he knew with me. From our visits and my mother's stories, I came to see that, as a maternal uncle to my mother, Charles had taken responsibility for my mother when she was a child. It was Charles who placed her in boarding school at Fort Wingate, New Mexico, and in Stewart Indian School, in Carson City, Nevada. Charles made sure that his niece had adequate clothing and filled other needs of hers at school. His concern for his sister's children was reflected in his own sons, whom he also sent to school. In doing so, he followed the dictates of his extended family's belief that an American education could be used to better Navajo conditions.

My interviews with Charles took place at his residence in Toadlena, New Mexico, where he lived with his wife, Esther (see fig. 18). Esther is my mother's paternal aunt, of the Kinłichíinii (Red House People), and my grandmother, as well. At one point, my grandfather shared a number of newspaper articles that he had pasted into a notebook. He also brought out a set of letters that had once belonged to his great-grandmother and grandmother. Indian agents and school officials had written them on behalf of the Manuelito family at the end of the nineteenth century and the beginning of twentieth. His retention of these documents impressed upon me how Navajos are concerned about the past and how they hope to learn more about their history, including family stories. In particular, my grandfather's concerns about the family stories were directly connected to the land

and concerns that we descendants continue to hold onto it as a legacy for coming generations of Tł'ógi clan members.

My maternal grandmother, Joan Kinsel, is Charles's older sister. Today she resides in Yah-Ta-Hey, New Mexico, with her daughter, Gloria. As my mother tells me, when my grandmother was a young woman, she was a skilled horsewoman, which was true of most Navajo women in her generation. Joan speaks English well, and when she was young her family relied on her to convey messages to white traders and government officials. Joan remembers well her grandmother Dághá Chíí be Asdzáá and grandfather Dághá Chíí. During one of our visits, she gave my mother her grandmother's necklace.

Mike Allison Sr., Arthur Holyan, Isaac Allison, Faye Yazzie, Helena Bitsilly (figs. 17, 20, 22, and 23), and the late Robert Manuelito are among the great-grandchildren descended from Hastiin Ch'il Hajin and Asdzáá Tł'ógi's younger daughter, Ałk'iníbaa. Ałk'iníbaa had at least three husbands, so some of the descendants do not claim Dághá Chíí Bik'is as their grandfather. Her older sister also had several husbands. This experience appears to have been common in this period and may reflect ruptures created when men left to seek wage labor or died from epidemic diseases. Dághá Chíí Bik'is was appointed to the first tribal council in the 1920s and signed oil lease agreements on behalf of the Navajo tribe. It is very possible that Dághá Chíí found employment as a scout and Dághá Chíí Bik'is as a tribal councilman because of their marriages to Manuelito's daughters.

Of all of my grandparents's stories, I found those of Mike Allison Sr. most informative. Mike, who turned 101 years old in 2003, remembered seeing his great-grandmother, Juanita, when he was a boy. I attended several of my Mike's birthday gatherings, which included recognition of his wedding anniversaries. His wife, Anna Allison, is my mother's paternal aunt. Married for seventy-five years, my grandparents successfully raised nine sons and one daughter, all of whom cared for their elderly parents. During our interviews with Mike Sr. and Anna, I came to appreciate the lessons they had learned about marriage and raising a family. The life stories that they shared on several warm summer afternoons exemplify the meaning of Navajo teachings embedded in *Sạ'ah naagháí bik'eh hózhóón*. Just as their ancestors had relied upon Navajo philosophy to ground their lives, so did they.[5]

My own research and the histories I heard from my grand-parents, has led to my understanding of and appreciation for K'e, which shapes Navajo relationships. Today, my grandmother Faye Yazzie never fails to bring up our talks and trips to T and R Market, where we bought lamb, bread, and drinks for lunch. I recently attended the seventy-fifth birthday of my grandfather Art Holyan, in Grants, New Mexico. Art has been very supportive of my research. My initial visits to my grandmother Helena Bitsilly were made with hopes of talking to her mother, who remembered Ałk'iníbaa well. Unfortunately, that conversation was impossible because she had become forgetful. My grandfather, the late Robert Manuelito, was very gracious, as was his wife, Caroline, and invited me into their home. Robert's mother had died when he was an infant, and then his grandmother, Ałk'iníbaa, had cared for him until her death. Because he had been so young when both his mother and grandmother died, he had no memory of either.

The first responses to my queries about our grandparents included a litany of answers like "I don't know," "We didn't ask questions," and "We should have listened when we were told stories of our grandmother." Manuelito and Juanita's children were young men and women when they returned with their parents from Bosque Redondo. The next generation, the great-grandchildren of Manuelito and Juanita, also experienced boarding schools and were sent away for long periods. In the 1930s, other ancestors saw the beginning of reliance on wage labor, when livestock could no longer provide independence. Because of such historical experiences under federal Indian policy, which sought to exterminate the Navajos culturally, the oral tradition was profoundly disrupted. As a result, most of the narratives about Juanita and her daughters exist as fragments of stories, images, and an extensive genealogy that dates back to the 1860s. However, those beliefs and values embedded in the remaining stories are part of a rich cultural context still being passed on to the next generation.

The forms in which the narratives of Juanita exist suggest that we must redefine and extend the definition of history and oral traditions. Traditional narratives cannot necessarily be treated only as information to verify "facts" for Western histories. Neither should they be discounted and/or ignored when they contradict history. Rather, perspectives on the past are constructions that transmit cultural beliefs and values that allow for the reevaluation and revaluation of indigenous peoples' oral traditions as valid and legitimate histories.

This chapter is the result of my efforts to capture on paper the sig-

nificance and richness of Navajo oral traditions, in particular, the role
of Navajo women as conveyors of stories. To understand and appreciate my elders' stories, I provide a context that includes an introduction to traditional creation narratives. I emphasize the place of female
deities in my retelling, for they are important to understand the narratives about my grandmothers. Significantly, the remaining stories
of them reflect the framework of the creation narratives, especially as
the purpose of life is to return to hózhó.

Diné Creation Narratives

The Diné creation narratives are a vital part of Navajo life and culture. In order to illuminate their continuing significance to Navajos, it is necessary to revisit them, examine their import, and isolate
their relevant meanings. Traditional narratives have stood the test
of time, demonstrating a vitality and resilience to speak to contemporary issues and problems. The narratives can be understood on
multiple levels. I pay close attention to female deities who are part
of the contingent of Holy People, for their roles remain the template
for how Navajo women see their own roles. An examination of my
elders' narratives reveals similarities between creation narratives and
stories of my great-great-great-grandmother. In particular, a closer
look at Juanita's role illuminates Navajo women's traditional status
and sheds light on how the stories of female deities like Changing
Woman are the template that shape Navajo perspectives on women's
roles in Navajo society.

Traditional narratives outline how the world came into existence,
how the Holy People created the present world, and how the Diné
came into being. The narratives informed our ancestors, who relied
on them to practice and convey their beliefs and values. In the face
of the hardships that life meted out, especially the trauma associated
with colonization, they relied on the traditional narratives for spiritual and physical renewal. The stories are also a vehicle for reaffirming
community and kin relationships.

The Creation Stories

We Diné point to a specific place in Dinétah, in present-day northeastern New Mexico, as the site of our emergence from the lower

worlds into this one. Our stories tell us how our forebears journeyed through a series of worlds to emerge into the present one.[6]

The first world, which was black, was small in size and appeared as a floating island in a sea of water mist. Here, only spirit people and Holy People lived. Here, First Man and First Woman were formed. Insect people also lived in this world. The various beings quarreled among themselves and they began their journey, which started in this place of darkness and chaos. The beings continually moved through the second world, precipitated by their own transgressions, and emerged into the third world, the Yellow world, with the Bluebird being the first to enter. After him came First Man, First Woman, Coyote, and one of the insects.

The beings continued their journey, again because of quarreling among themselves and with their hosts, and emerged into the third world. Here a great river, the Female River, crossed the land from north to south. The Male River flowed east to west. The place where the rivers crossed is known as Tó Ałnáozlí (Crossings of the Waters). The Bluebird emerged first, followed by First Man, First Woman, Coyote, and one of the insects. First Man gathered soil from the mountains in the third world and used it to form the four main sacred mountains. These mountains, which demarcated the boundaries of Navajo Land, were dressed, and various Holy People entered each of them. Each of these was fastened to the earth with elements as follows: Sisnaajiní (East), with a bolt of white lighting; Tsoodził (South), with a stone knife; Dook'o'osłííd (West), with a sunbeam; and Dibé nitsaa (North), with a rainbow. Two other sacred mountains were also formed: Dził ná'oodiłii (Center, Huerfano Mountain) and Ch'óol'í'í (East of Center, Gobernador Knob). Animals such as squirrels, chipmunks, foxes, turkeys, spiders, lizards, and snakes also lived in this world. From these previous worlds, our ancestors brought valuable things and knowledge that we continue to utilize. For example, after learning how to make a fire with flint brought from the third world, they learned how to calm the fire with a poker stick. To this day, then, the poker stick is source of protection and lessons about living well.[7] Many other lessons were learned in the days after the emergence, including how to make a proper hogan, medicines for specific illnesses, and so forth. All of the teachings and values embedded in the creation narratives are embodied in the concept of Hózhó, our philosophy of life.

Events and interactions that occur in the various worlds have
come to form many traditional Navajo thoughts and values. Several
of the narratives feature relationships between the sexes, which scholars have labeled "complementary," meaning that gender roles are different but equal and necessary.[8] The natural world reflects the duality
of male and female. We have female and male rains, for example. The
earth is mother and the sun is father. Both female and male are crucial to the creation of all life. The story of the separation of the men
and women details what happens if we do not work together.[9] Tasks
performed by males and females are equally crucial to the survival of
the clan and community.[10]

One of the Holy People is Asdzáá Nádleehé (Changing Woman),
who is also known as Yoołgai Asdzáán (White Shell Woman). Traditional scholar Ethelou Yazzie published this version of Changing
Woman's birth:

> One morning at dawn, First Man and First Woman saw a dark
> cloud over Ch'óol'í'í (Gobernador Knob). Later they heard a baby
> cry. When they looked to see where the crying was coming from,
> they realized that it came from within the cloud that covered the
> top of Ch'óol'í'í. First Man searched and found a baby girl. She
> was born of darkness and the dawn was her father. First Man and
> First Woman brought her up under the direction of the Holy
> People. They fed her on sun-ray pollen, pollen from the clouds,
> pollen from the plants and the dew of flowers. This baby became
> Asdzáá Nádleehé (Changing Woman), one of the most loved of
> the Navajo Holy People.[11]

First Man and First Woman were so pleased with their new baby
that they made arrangements for a Blessingway for their daughter,
which the Holy People performed. The new parents made her cra-
dle from elements like the rainbow. Today, babies are celebrated and
blessings bestowed upon them so that they will lead lives according
to Navajo philosophy. Recently, I had the opportunity to hear traditional educator Ernest Harry Begay share stories from the creation in
workshops designed to develop parenting skills. During one of the
sessions that I attended, Begay noted that Asdzáá Nádleehé had been
born during the month of February and that, as Navajos, we should
be celebrating her birth, for her birth brought about harmony and
balance in the world. Begay especially felt that our Navajo leaders

should declare a national Navajo holiday in honor of Asdzáá Nádlee-hé's birth.[12]

When Changing Woman reached womanhood with her first menses, the first Kinaaldá was performed for her. She was dressed ceremonially and thereafter known as Yoł gai Asdzáán. The Holy People came to the ceremony and blessed her with prayers and songs that today are part of the Blessingway Ceremony. Her birth, coming of age into womanhood, and the birth of her own sons, Naayéé Neezghání (Monster Slayer) and Tó Bájísh Chíní (Born for Water), furnish the template for women's roles in Navajo society.[13] As Gary Witherspoon recounts, the ceremony and the accompanying prayers and songs enabled Changing Woman to have the power to create a new people who would transmit this power to the next generations.[14] Today the Kinaaldá remains an important ceremony for many Diné girls who reach womanhood.

One day, Asdzáá Nádleehé was out gathering wood when a force held her down. She looked around and finally spied Sun, who was a handsome man. She began to visit Sun and often went down to a spring and allowed the water to drip into her, which she found pleasurable. From her relations with Sun, she gave birth to her two sons. In Navajo life, mothers create and sustain life. Just as Changing Woman sustained her children, so do Navajo women today. All things that sustain life, including the earth, agricultural fields, corn, sheep, and even men who are nurturing, are called mother.[15] Furthermore, motherhood is the role from which Navajo women speak with authority.[16]

Naayéé Neezghání and Tó Bájísh Chíní often played outside and Changing Woman was always fearful that the monsters who roamed the land would discover and devour them. One day, Changing Woman's sons questioned her, "Who is our father?" She was reluctant to tell them, for their father was a powerful force who could harm them. Finally, after her sons asked their mother for the fourth time, she answered. The twins were determined to search for Jóhonaa'éí, the sun and their father, even though their mother pleaded with them to stay home.

Naayéé Neezghání and Tó Bájísh Chíní began a journey to find their father. They went east. Along the way they met Grandmother Spider, who gave them protection for their trip. As they continued, they encountered obstacles, which they overcame with the help of the deities and elements like the wind. Finally, they reached the home of their father. When they introduced themselves to him, he did not believe that the two boys were his sons. His wife looked on with jealousy because he had told her that he was faithful when he made his daily journey across the sky. Jóhonaa'éí asked, "What do you want? What are you after? Where are you from?"[17] He refused to acknowledge them as his sons. Sun picked up the boys and threw them at sharp spikes that hung in the east. The two were unharmed. Sun threw them in the other three directions, and still the twins were unharmed. Sun continued to subject them to a series of ordeals, all of which they successfully overcame.

After numerous tests, Sun admitted that the boys were his children. He offered them gifts like fields of the finest corn and other plants and seeds, and jewels and wild animals that included horses, all of which the twins admired and said that they would need at a later time, but that they had come for weapons with which they could kill the monsters. Sun was reluctant because the monsters were also his offspring. Finally, although troubled, he gave them suits of flint armor and a shield and a bow and arrow made of thunder and lightning. At this time Sun named his sons Naayéé Neezghání and Tó Bájísh Chíní. The twins left their father early in the morning and journeyed across the sky. They returned to their mother, Asdzáá Nádleehé. They eventually rid the land of the monsters. After their deeds were completed, they underwent purification rituals, the Enemy Way, which warriors still undergo.

Another narrative, which is important for understanding the stories of Asdzáá Tł'ógi and her daughters, is that of how Asdzáá Nádleehé created the first Diné clans. Asdzáá Nádleehé was living with her two sons when Sun visited her in her home. Sun tried to persuade Changing Woman to move to a place in the sky where he could visit her each time he crossed it. When he became insistent, Changing Woman told him that she would consider his request, but that she must think about it; if it suited her, she would comply. Such narratives indicate Navajo women's sense of self and the autonomy that they enjoy in their society.

After a time, Sun and his sons convinced Asdzáá Nádleehé to live on the Western Ocean. Some of the People went with her, but then they became lonely and went home. According to Ethelou Yazzie:

Changing Woman thought that there should be more people, so she created more of them (humans) by rubbing the skin from her breast, for her back and from under both arms. In this way she created the first four clans. Changing Woman rubbed the skin from her breast and formed people who became the Kiiyaa'áanii clan. From the skin rubbed from her back the Honáháanii clan was formed. From the skin under her right arm the Tó'dích'íinii clan was created, and from the skin under her left arm the Hashtł'isgnii clan was made.[18]

When these people left to go east, Asdzáá Nádleehé gave pets for guardians. Today, many clans claim kin ties to these original clans. They trace their lineage matrilineally, a practice begun with Asdzáá Nádleehé during creation. These stories exemplify ideal relationships between humans and deities and humans and the earth, and teach us how we should treat each other. Animals and nature are also reflected in these stories.

Traditional stories are sources that remind us about what is important in our lives. Through them, we express appreciation for the power and sacredness of language. We also note that the goal of life is continually to seek a state of hózhó, harmony and balance. Seeking hózhó means that we wake up and face the dawn each morning to accept the Holy People's blessings as they pass and that we express thankfulness that each day is an opportunity to begin anew. Telling these stories also offers us an opportunity to remember that, in the face of incredible trauma, our ancestors responded with courage and integrity. The fact that we are still here to tell the stories attests to their resilience. The elders are especially thought to be wise and worthy of emulation because they have traveled the road of life and reached the goal of Old Age. As Rex Lee Jim declares, "Reaching Sá is a lifelong goal for the individual, and an everlasting goal for a people."[19]

In my search to learn more about my grandmothers, Juanita and her two daughters, I discovered that the elders' narratives mirror the creation stories in form and motifs. As the mythical beings traveled through the five worlds and entered the Glittering World—the present one—they set about establishing order. In much the same way, my grandparents' stories are accounts of leaving the Bosque Redondo reservation, moving across the land, and resettling at former residences to reestablish order and harmony. The elders' stories refocus

the meaning of the "Navajo wars," traumatic years of loss and imprisonment, to stories in which Navajos endeavored to recover their families and communities. In them, Asdzáá Tł'ógi and her two daughters
play a significant role in the survival and continuity of their families
and clan members. Rooted in creation stories, our grandparents' stories testify to the bravery, courage, and resilience of their ancestors.

Remembering Our Grandmothers

The elders begin their narratives with their ancestors' return from
Fort Sumner to Navajo Land in 1868. After 1868, the People came
under American rule and were assaulted with American values about
education, religion, family, health, and sexuality, many of which con-
tradicted Navajo values. In the face of ongoing colonialism, these stories about our grandmothers offer evidence about their efforts to create continuity between the past and the present, to name once again
the value of our own traditions. Finally, the characteristics of these
stories, the themes woven within them, the ways in which they are
told, and what is told and remembered mirror the shape and form of
the creation narratives.

In the early nineteenth century, Navajos experienced vast historical transformations, which shaped Juanita's life. Although there are
no written or oral accounts of her life prior to 1868, we can speculate
based on what is known about the colonial Southwest. For example,
although non-Indian accounts claim that Juanita was a Mexican slave
whom Manuelito married and favored among his wives, Navajo oral
accounts depict her as a Navajo woman. Mostly, her descendants say
they have not heard stories that she may have been a Mexican slave
adopted into a Navajo clan.[20] Indeed, sometimes when I return to
Tohatchi, I inevitably come across some relative who has heard of my
research project and asks, "So, was Juanita a Mexican?" It is interesting to note what pieces of information and knowledge linger, whereas
others receive little if any attention. No doubt, Navajos' knowledge
of Juanita is informed by non-Navajo accounts. Our grandmother's
identity is shrouded in the history of the slave trade, in which indigenous women and children were targeted. Taken as captives and forced
to become part of their host society, many crossed cultural boundaries. Being adopted into a host society in the Southwest during colonial

times meant that people's identities were constructed differently then than they are today.

Born around 1845, Asdzáá Tłʼógi witnessed, and may have been a victim of, the slave trade that characterized cross-cultural relationships in the Southwest. Although slave raiding had been known in the region prior to Euro-American invasions, the practice intensified under the colonizers. As James Brooks notes, Kit Carson's campaign on the Navajos followed an established practice of raiding for captives. Indeed, during the course of his campaign, Carson pleaded with his superior for "continued rewards in Navajo captives for local militias and Ute scouts."[21]

Navajo relationships with neighboring Pueblos fell along a continuum of acknowledged kinship through peaceful trading through hostility marked by Navajo raids and attacks on New Mexican communities and Pueblos, in many cases as reprisals for attacks on their own families and clans. Although the prevailing thought in American histories makes Navajos the instigators, in fact, they had both friendly and hostile relationships with their neighbors.[22]

It was under American rule that began in 1846 that war and conflict escalated. By the 1860s, slave raiding had reached an all-time high since the American military encouraged such enemies of the Navajos as the Utes, Comanches, and New Mexicans to attack Navajos, which they eagerly did because Navajo women and children were very valuable in the slave markets.[23] As late as the 1880s, well into the reservation period, Navajos were still looking for family members in New Mexican households and insisting that the Indian agents assist them in their search for captive women and children.[24]

Recent studies of slavery in the Southwest illuminate the complexity of cross-cultural relationships as slaves entered culturally different societies. Captive Navajo women and children were baptized as Catholic Christians and entered Hispanic communities as servants in a hierarchical society in which race and class were demarcated.[25] Generally, Navajos did not conduct slave raids, but usually bought captives from raiders or at the trade fairs, which were widespread. Although many women experienced violence and rape, others carved out spaces within their host society, within which they rebuilt their lives with some autonomy. It was possible for slaves to change their status to become full-fledged members, either by marriage, whereby their children were considered Navajos, or through their skills and intelligence. Navajo society was fluid, captive women's children taking on either the Navajo father's maternal clan, the master's maternal clan, or, if the mother was accepted, the identity of her master's maternal clan. For example, there are many stories of how Mexican women's children identified with the Mexican clan, which is still present in the Navajo clan system.[26] Furthermore, because Navajos rely on kin relationships for all manner of communication, it was necessary to create kinship. Thus, identity was not based solely on biology, but also on culture.

If Juanita had been a slave successfully adopted and incorporated into Navajo society, she must have been a child when taken from her natal society, for by the 1860s, when in her twenties, she was already acknowledged as a Navajo woman. The fact that Juanita's descendents know her as a Navajo woman demonstrates her full integration into her host society, even if she had been Mexican or came from elsewhere. As Navajos see matters, her identity as someone other than Navajo is simply not an issue. The fact that indigenous identity is presently a topic of discussion reflects contemporary preoccupations with biological identity and blood notions of authenticity. Studies that discuss these issues also demonstrate that identities are cultural constructions that differ across time, culture, and race.[27]

My great-great-great-grandmother's public name was Asdzáá Tł'ógi, and can be translated as "Lady Weaver." Tł'ógi also translates as "Zia" and refers to Zia Pueblo, approximately seventy-five miles northwest of Albuquerque, New Mexico. In Navajo, Zia also translates as "weaver." The Francisan fathers at St. Michael's Mission translated Tł'ógi as "fluffy, or grass-mat people, because they wove mats of grass and yucca."[28] The fact that my great-great-great-grandmother was named Lady Weaver indicates a number of things. She may have been Zia or had kin ties with Zia Pueblo. The name also indicates that she was a weaver herself. Mike Allison Sr., as others of the Tł'ógi clan, notes that at one time his great-grandmother's maternal clan had been Tódík'ozhí (Salt Water People). The Tódík'ozhí clan is related to the Tó'dích'íinii (Bitter Water People), one of the original clans that Changing Woman created. The Tódík'ozhí clan is also related to the Tł'ógi clan, as I will explain with a story from Mike Allison Sr. in the following section.

The great-grandchildren of Asdzáá Tł'ógi began their stories with her return—along with her family and kin—from Hwéeldi, the Bosque Redondo reservation. Juanita, her family, and kin relied on ancient teachings to guide them back to Navajo Land, where they reestablished their lives. Just as the People's ancestors journeyed through various worlds in search of hózhó, Asdzáá Tł'ógi, Manuelito, and their kin left years of chaos at the prison camp to reestablish their lives, to seek hózhó. The great-grandchildren's version of their ancestors' return to Navajo Land highlights their grandmother's role.

The following story from Mike Allison Sr. was his response to a question from me about our grandmother's origin and how she came to be Tł'ógi. As members of the Tódík'ozhí clan began their return from Hwéeldi, Asdzáá Tł'ógi and her family decided to stop at the home of their old friends, the Tł'ógi (Zia Pueblo). Although there is no evidence to determine Manuelito's position in his wife's clan group, this particular narrative provides an occasion to think about how men were integrated into their wife's clan and whether Manuelito traveled mostly with his wife's clan. One part of the clan opted to continue its travels and the other decided to stop. Allison then related the following story:

> I don't know the origins of the clan. . . . They just said the Tł'ógi came. They journeyed. They came from Tódík'ozhí [Salt Water]. I don't know where that place is, Tódík'ozhí. My grandmother, the one I told you about, she had a donkey. This was her story. [She said,] "We are Bitter Water." So we are Bitter Water. I don't know where they had traveled [return route from Fort Sumner]. They had run out of food. Part of the group stopped at the Kiis'áni [Pueblo people]. The group that was known as Tódík'ozhí split up and one part kept going. I don't know how many of them were hungry and they slowed down.
>
> They said, "Let's drink some coffee from the Kiis'áani. Let us eat there." And they went in that direction. The Kiis'áani fed them. The Kiis'áani shared their food with them. The Kiis'áani that the Tódík'ozhí had come to were the Tł'ógi. They ate from the Tł'ógi and were given bread to take.
>
> As they were leaving, they were told, "You will be Tł'ógi. You will be our relatives. Now you are Tł'ógi, not Tódík'ozhí. Not Tódík'ozhí. Now go."
>
> And the group journeyed on to meet their relatives. So when they

met, one group was called Tł'ógi and the others were Tódík'ozhí. That is how they came together. My grandmother said, "The Kiis'áani named us that, Tł'ógi." The real Tł'ógi are the Zia Pueblo.

They said, "We will be your relatives." So we have relatives at Tł'ógi.[29]

Grandfather Allison's story is remarkably similar in form and theme to the creation story that relates how the Diné came to live within the four sacred mountains. Both narratives begin with a journey. Allison's story strongly gives an indication of how clans are connected to specific places. Although he says he does not know specifically where Tódík'ozhí is, somewhere, someone knows where the Tódík'ozhí clan originated. Furthermore, as I have noted elsewhere, it is part of Navajo storytelling to begin with the phrase, *'Alk'idaa 'jini'* (A long time ago they said). Although those of us present, storyteller and listeners, did not witness the events or see the actors in the story, there is faith that the events occurred at some time and that the actors were living beings.[30]

Each journey entailed movement from a place of darkness and chaos, and ancestors endured much hardship as they searched for hózhó. In the creation narratives, they were forced to continue their journey because of transgressions by a few members in their group. As Navajos acknowledge, some of their people had committed transgressions against New Mexicans and neighboring Pueblos and there was certainly cause for retaliation. Yet Americans named all Navajos as criminals and punished the entire nation.[31]

At the beginning of the creation narrative as well as Allison's story, our ancestors are depicted as impoverished and hungry. In both of these stories, the Diné meet Pueblo peoples who come to their aid. Paul Zolbrod's translated account relates the encounter with Pueblo peoples in the fourth world after scouts looked for signs of life:

Finally, two scouts were sent to explore the land that lay to the north. And when they returned they had a different story to tell. For they reported that they had found a strange race unlike any other. These were people who cut their hair square in front. They were people who lived in houses in the ground. They were people who cultivated the soil so that things grew within. They were now harvesting what they had planted, and they gave the couriers food to eat. . . . On the very next day, two members of the newly found race came to the camp of the exiles. They were called *kiis'áanii*, they said, which in the language of the Bilagáana, the White Man, means People Who Live in Upright Houses. And they wished to invite the exiles to visit their village.[32]

The friendly Kiis'áanii shared their corn and pumpkins with the exiles and taught them how to irrigate the soil and plant corn. They became very close and called each other by family and kin names. The exiles resolved to stay and not make any trouble. However, as the story goes, one of members of the Diné made sexual overtures toward the Pueblo chief's wife. In anger and disgust, the Pueblo chief ordered the exiles to leave. And so from that day on, Navajos have lived apart from the Pueblo people.

Corn, which is offered to the Diné in friendship, remains a central food among them and has sacred symbolic meanings. Indeed, linguists suggest that the Diné word for corn translates as "enemy food." Asdzáá Tł'ógi and her kin, like their primordial kin, relied on old kinships with Pueblo peoples for a measure of security and replenishment. In the elders' narratives of their grandmothers, as in other stories, the Pueblo people extended friendship and kinship to their old friends, the Navajos. The kinship ties established in primordial times are remembered when Navajo travelers are invited to share coffee and bread with their hosts. The story of my grandmother is a reminder that, although some things may change—like the introduction of coffee and white flour—others, like kin relationships, have remained strong, even in spite of colonial invasions that created strife between former allies.

A closer look at Grandfather Allison's story illuminates the nature of Diné social organization, suggesting that women played central roles not only in the creation of identity but also in the establishment of kinship ties across tribal cultures. Traditionally, Navajos have established kin relationships before any communication could be initiated. Furthermore, as historian Theda Perdue notes, women have been central to establishing kin relationships between tribal groups.[33] Likewise, Navajo recognition of kinship with Pueblo people has been a prerequisite for communication. Allison's narrative indicates that Navajo women like Juanita often created and cemented kin relationships with other indigenous peoples. Most likely, traditions of matrilineality colored trade and other economic relations as well. For Navajos, then, clan identity determines the nature of relationships that extend beyond the nation to other indigenous peoples, and even to Euro-Americans. Even today, traditional Navajos must name a relationship to non-Navajos in order to communicate easily.

Allison's story also notes that Asdzáá Tł'ógi was associated with one of the original Diné clans, the Tó'dích'íinii, which is related to the Tódík'ozhí. Prior to becoming Tł'ógi, Juanita and her matrilineal kin identified themselves as Tódík'ozhí. Revisiting their Zia friends led them to cement a kinship in which Juanita and her kin agreed to acknowledge the relationship by identifying themselves as Tł'ógi. Today, the descendants of Juanita and Manuelito identify themselves as Tł'ógi, thereby continuing to acknowledge traditional kinship ties with Zia Pueblo. This story about Juanita's identity underscores the fluidity of identity and community building in the nineteenth century.

The visits to Mike and Anna Allison's home remain with me. During one of them, my grandfather announced that, as a boy, he had seen his grandmother Juanita. She often herded sheep with her grandchildren. That afternoon, Mike, Anna, my mother, and I sat silently as we imagined our grandmother walking across a familiar landscape, her figure outlined against the horizon. As we sat in the living room, my grandfather and mother exchanged news about other relatives. Pomo writer Greg Sarris has explained that it is impossible to capture the context of storytelling, that writing "fixes or makes permanent not only oral experience but what is actually an interpretation of that experience."[34] In similar fashion, the elders' narratives are embedded in a context that exposes the limited nature of our knowledge and the fact that it requires continual learning.

Return to Dinétah

Just like other families, Manuelito, Juanita, their children, and other family members returned home in 1868 to begin the process of reestablishing their lives. By the 1890s, the Navajo population had increased to twenty thousand. The Navajo's livestock had increased from fifteen thousand sheep, goats, and horses in 1868 to more than one million by the mid-1880s. Obviously, the original reservation of four million acres was inadequate, so from 1876 to 1901, federal executive orders added land to the original treaty reservation that tripled its original size.[35]

In 1874, Manuelito traveled with his wife, other Navajo leaders, and white officials to Washington, D.C., to meet the U.S. president. Asdzáá Tł'ógi's presence on this Washington, D.C., journey is evidenced in photographs (figs. 4–6); however, what she may have said or contributed to the delegation's objectives is not recorded in written documents. In contrast, Juanita's descendants remember her participation. Their memories illustrate the centrality of women's roles as wives and mothers, and, in particular, the reality that these roles extended beyond what is considered domestic space.

Traveling frequently with her husband, Juanita was privy to her husband's concerns about issues that faced the Diné. For Manuelito, land had foremost importance. Navajo leaders initiated the request to visit Washington, D.C., with a letter to the commissioner of Indian Affairs in 1873.[36] After a series of written exchanges between Arny and officials in Washington, D.C., the Navajos' request was reluctantly approved after it was agreed that the trip would be financed with their own funds.[37]

The Navajo delegation spent several months in the East, stopped briefly in New York City, and even traveled to Boston, where its members toured a textile mill and inspected the Corliss steam engine. The *Washington Evening Star* reported that the Navajos had been subdued with "great difficulty," but that they were "now all pastoral in their habits, and own about 130,000 sheep and 10,000 horses." "These Indians are of the pure aboriginal type," it reported. "Manuelito, the old war chief, is very sociable. They all have high cheek bones, straight black hair, and are of a deep copper color, . . ." the newspaper continued. "The chief wears black buckskin pants, with the sides of the legs ornamented with dashing silver buttons."[38] On December 10, the delegation met briefly with President Grant and explained its concerns about land, problems with trespassers on their lands, ongoing depredations by Mormons and miners, and the need to have Navajos still in captivity returned.[39]

The meeting between Navajo leaders and President Grant brought no results for the Diné, especially since the leaders met only briefly. In 1951, Dághá Ch'íí' Bik'is, Manuelito's son-in-law, testified before the U.S. Land Claims Commissions on behalf of the Navajo land claims. In his testimony, he retold a story he had heard from Manuelito about the 1874 journey. He reiterated:

Chief Manuelito and his wife and his son, Na-ta-dasilah [Naat'ahsilá], and Gas-donah, Manuelito's brother. Four of them

went. Chief Manuelito took a chief blanket to the president, and
when he embraced the president he gave him the chief blanket. The
president refused to accept this blanket as a token of friendship but
tossed it aside and said, "I cannot, as president of the United States,
accept anything like this." He offended Manuelito. The president of
the United States offended Manuelito, that he did not even speak to
the president again, and he stayed there two solid months until the
time he had a chance to speak to the president again.[40]

The story attests to the patronizing and racist attitude the U.S.
government held toward its Native wards. Indeed, indigenous leaders expected the U.S. president to honor treaty provisions, but once
the "Indian threat" had passed, indigenous matters reverted to lower
federal officials. Faye Yazzie's remembrances are filtered through her
matrilineal clan, thus emphasizing her great-grandmother's role. As
Faye Yazzie told my mother and me:

> Our grandmother took with her Navajo foods. When the men
> became homesick and hungry, she brought forth Navajo food:
> jerkied meat, parched corn, and a paste made from ground pinons
> mixed with parched corn. She took these foods in bags with her.
> Periodically, she doled the food out to the men who were grateful.
> Her husband Manuelito wanted his wife Juanita to go on the trip
> because she spoke well and maybe she could persuade the presi-
> dent to let the Navajos keep their lands. Manuelito said the pres-
> ident's back was "stiff" and perhaps Juanita's words could soften
> [persuade] him.[41]

The U.S. government sought to strip Navajos of their very identities; however, Navajo women were central in the struggle to retain
their cultural values and traditions. As the Navajo delegation traveled months in the East, they experienced loneliness, homesickness,
racism, and a distaste for strange foods. Once, in Washington, D.C.,
because they were Indians, they slept in a hotel basement, where mat-
tresses were thrown on the floor.[42]

Navajo women retained cultural values by imbuing traditional
foods with their former significance. One of the major reasons for
Navajo defeat in 1863 was the destruction of their food sources.
Faced with starvation, Navajos surrendered at the American forts.
The destruction of Navajo food sources and substitution of Ameri-

can foods was part of the assimilation process. As prisoners, Navajos received rations of white flour, beans, and coffee. Many Navajo stories relate ignorance about the preparation of these foods and the consequences, which included diarrhea, dysentery, and death.[43] Today, although many of these American foods have become staples for Navajos, many of the People plant cornfields and raise sheep as they have for generations. Replanting their cornfields and rebuilding livestock herds is a way to endow traditional foods with their former meanings. Food is connected to power.[44] Eating is more than a biological activity; it is a vibrant cultural activity.

As Faye Yazzie remembered, "Our grandmother used to say that they became homesick on that trip. They tired of the Bilagáana food." To ease the men's loneliness, Asdzáá Tł'ógi periodically doled out the foods she had brought along. In sharing familiar foods with the homesick and hungry men, Asdzáá Tł'ógi assumed a vital place in Navajo society, that of mother. According to traditional narratives, mothers provide the sustenance for life. For the Navajo men, Juanita must have reminded them of home. As feminist scholar bell hooks declares, homes are places where we could "strive to be subjects, not objects, where we could be affirmed in our minds and hearts despite poverty, hardship, and deprivation, where we could restore to ourselves the dignity denied us on the outside in the public world."[45] The act of remembering is a conscious gesture to honor the efforts of women like Juanita who endeavored to provide for their own.

Faye Yazzie's story about Juanita's role as a member of the delegation adds further evidence that Navajo women also played a role in the political arena. As the wife of a headman, Juanita had the privilege of speaking at political meetings between Navajo and non-Navajo leaders. A few historical documents refer to the authority attributed to Navajo women. For example, Capt. John W. Reid recorded a meeting between leaders of the U.S. military and the Diné in 1846. During the proceedings, in which the revered leader Narbona hoped to establish peace with the Americans, Reid described how Narbona's wife disrupted the meeting as she warned the Diné men of American treachery. Describing the Navajo woman as an accomplished orator, Reid noted that the warriors stirred at her speech and he grew alarmed that the warriors would reject a peace proposal. Fortunately for the Americans, Narbona motioned his men to remove his wife and the council continued.[46] A white man like Reid might read the event as an indication that, regardless of race and cultural differences, Navajo and white men both shared similar notions about women's proper places, which was that women were not politically astute. Certainly, another reading would attribute Navajo women with keen insight and political acumen, especially in regard to American motives for seeking a treaty with the Diné.

In much the same manner as Narbona's wife a generation previously, Asdzáá Tł'ógi exercised her privilege as a headman's wife to speak in public spaces. According to Grandmother Faye, Juanita accompanied her husband Manuelito to Washington, D.C., because he recognized her excellent oratory skills. Women's authority extended into the political realm of Navajo society. This glimpse of the relationship between Manuelito and Juanita reflects the ideal egalitarian nature of male-female relationships. Navajo marriages mean that husband and wife are in a partnership expecting that they will establish a home where children will benefit from both parents. Another value in Navajo society reflected in Grandmother Faye's story is the respect accorded to Asdzáá Tł'ógi. In Navajo society, to speak well and persuasively is a highly lauded skill and a sign of exceptional intelligence. Traditionally, male leaders were called *naat'áanii*, or ones who speak persuasively. In contemporary studies, only men have been associated with leadership roles in which the ability to speak persuasively and with eloquence is central.[47] In contrast, Juanita is associated with oratory skills, suggesting that some abilities in Navajo society are not limited to the male gender. Other family stories indicate that Asdzáá Tł'ógi's eldest daughter, Dághá Chíí be Asdzáá, carried on characteristics from her father and mother, since she was also known for her oratory skills and regarded highly as a community leader.

The Navajo delegation arrived back in the Southwest on February 1, 1875. Not long after, William Arny fled his Fort Defiance post after Manuelito and others accused him of stealing government rations meant for distribution to Navajos and selling them for his own profit. The Navajos were also angry because they had discovered Arny's scheme to exchange prime Navajo lands for less desirable ones.[48]

Navajo relationship with Pueblos is another recurring image in Juanita's biography. The establishment and recognition of kin ties with Pueblo people are central to Navajo identity, as exemplified in both the creation and Tł'ógi clan stories. After the delegation returned to Navajo Land, Juanita and Manuelito visited Zia Pueblo, where they engaged in trade, exchanging meat for jewelry and beaded bags. As Joan Kinsel recalled, "It was said that Juanita and Manuelito returned from Zia on horseback. Beaded buckskin bags, gifts from their friends, hung off of their saddles."[49] The relationship with the Zia was long lasting. According to Faye, "Dághá Chíí's wife, your grandmother [speaking to the author] was friends with the Zias. They used to travel and visit people. Dághá Chíí used to travel a lot, even to Ute. Back then," she continued, "they didn't have a lot of sheep. Just a few. Back then, they used to weave. They used to go to Zia and bring back bread. The horse would be packed with bread. And they used to bring back turquoise."[50] Today, some Navajos maintain kin relationships with their Pueblo neighbors, but probably not to the extent that previous generations did.

As a longtime leader, Manuelito had experience with Euro-American society. He knew personally Americans' willingness to use military power against his people and understood that American laws dictated Navajo life. On his travels, he had seen overwhelming numbers of whites who inhabited land of formerly indigenous peoples. In an effort to reclaim Navajo authority, Manuelito believed that Navajo children could benefit from American education and better defend their people and land. Tł'ógi clan stories also highlight Manuelito's convictions and indicate how women were instrumental in conveying his messages.

The high value that my grandfather, Charles Manuelito, placed on education stemmed from his great-grandparents' convictions. During one of our interviews, Charles reiterated one story about his great-grandfather that is part of historical accounts:

> I guess he [Manuelito] recognized the power of the Anglos. [The Anglos had] their weapons and the Navajos used bows and arrows. We knew that we can't overcome the U.S. Army. We start thinking, "How can we, at a future time, how can we increase our knowledge? Is there a time when our knowledge can be as high as the Anglos?" The best thing to do was to get an education. That's why he said use the stepladder. He used to think the Navajos were living at this level [indicates with hand gestures] and the Anglos were way up here [gesture indicates a level higher than Navajos]. So in order to reach the level of the Anglos, you have to get some knowledge, climb, climb and the time will come we'll be at the level of

the Anglos. And that's where education is the ladder, climb, step-by-step. That was his idea. So he introduced it. He sent his son to school.[51]

Two types of documents demonstrate the Manuelito family's long-standing commitment to education for Navajo children. In addition to George Wharton James's photographs of the Manuelito family, a set of letters preserved by Charles further confirms the family's commitment to conveying their grandfather's message about the importance of an American education.

In 1894, Indian agent Lieut. E. H. Plummer wrote the following letter on behalf of Shizie:

> The bearer of this is the daughter of Manuelito, the Old War Chief of the Navajos, and the friend of the white people. He was a strong friend of the school and assisted us very much in managing the Navajos when behaving badly. He sent two or three children to Carlisle and all died. His daughter has just put a boy in school at the Agency.
>
> I sincerely hope that they will always be kindly treated by all persons with whom they came in contact, as they are most worthy and deserving of such treatment, especially from the officials of the Government.[52]

In 1900 and 1909, Indian agent G. W. Hayzlett and Superintendent Peter Paquette endorsed the letter's contents.

In 1906, a school official named E. H. DeVorn commented on Shizie's stature among her people: "This certifies that Shizie, who is a daughter of the late chief Manuelito has much influence among the Navahos and has been very helpful in assisting me to fill the school."[53] George Wharton James mentions his acquaintance with DeVorn and his visit to the Tohatchi School in his publication, *The Indians of the Painted Desert Region.* Again, the Manuelito women demonstrated the influence and persuasive oratory skills of Navajo women. The fact that school officials relied on them to assist with enrollment also attests to the family's continuing influence and indicates that the women were respected in their community. As Faye remembered about Dághá Chíí be Asdzáá (my great-great-grandmother): "No one followed in her footsteps. They say that she was an orator. They would tell her to speak to people. She would get on her knees, rise on her knees, and her arms moved about as she talked. She would tell them about her father and what he envisioned." Fay continued: "She would tell people what was happening in Window Rock. She did not have difficulty with speaking. Now they make fun of us because we are not like her. They used to say, 'Your grandmother was formidable.'"[54] The stories remind us of qualities among our ancestors that should be emulated. On several occasions, my grandmother's oratorical skills have been pointed out to me, perhaps in hopes that I might cultivate them, for it is thought that our ancestors' qualities are transmitted to future generations. These stories are also reminders that our behavior must be exemplary, for we are models for later generations.

Manuelito and Juanita's great-grandchildren also emphasize efforts to maintain family closeness. As Faye related, "And so when Hastiin Ch'il Hajin died, it seemed that there was no place to go, and so the men, Dághá Chíí and Dághá Chíí Bik'is, brought them to Dibé bitó [Sheep Springs—not to be mistaken for Sheep Springs, New Mexico]. That's what she said."[55] Mike Sr. pointed out that the Manuelito daughters were originally Tódík'ozhí, related to the Tó'dich'íinii, and that Manuelito had objected to his daughters' marriages to the brothers.[56] With the Manuelito daughters' move to Dibé bitó, the land came under the control of their maternal clan, the Tł'ógi. Not long after their move to the base of the Chuska Mountains, the younger brother Dághá Chíí Bik'is took his wife and family and moved northeast.

Asdzáá Tł'ógi spent the remainder of her life with her extended family, caring for grandchildren and livestock. Mike Sr. mentioned that Asdzáá Tł'ógi preferred to stay with her younger daughter, Ałk'iníbaa. As she herded sheep with her grandchildren, she told them stories of her life, about the Long Walk and Hwéeldi, and about the journey to Washington, D.C. Mike Sr. recalled, "I often saw her in the distance. She would ride by on her donkey. She always wore a biil." Many years later, one of Juanita's granddaughters, Asdzáá Bigizhii, visited her clan relatives and retold her grandmother's stories. As my mother related with regret whenever we visited grandparents and begin to talk about our ancestors, "We never listened to our grandmother Adzáá Bigizhii. She would visit and sit on the floor, and, with her arms waving in the air, tell us the stories she had been told. We didn't listen."

Asdzáá Tł'ógi died around 1910. Several stories tell about her death and burial. This is Mike Sr.'s response after I asked him if he remembered her or had, in fact, seen her:

Yes. I saw her. I saw her death. I saw my grandmother. She was
among us. We lived mostly with her. Sometimes she stayed with
my mother. She stayed mostly with us. She didn't really want to
stay with Dághá Chíí. She liked coming to my mother's. She went
to Tohatchi. They were dipping the sheep. I was herding sheep by
Na'bigizhi. She was going by on a donkey, a fast donkey. The donkey was a little feisty. She was going to Dághá Chíí's place at Red
Willow, the planting field. And I was herding sheep. She went by
on her donkey and I watched them.

She had a stomachache. In the evening, she was lying down
because of her stomachache. The sheep were at Bisi's [a relative].
My mother was at Red Willow. During the night, some time,
maybe about three in the morning. I heard gunshots, those big
guns, coming from Red Willow. We woke up. I wondered, "What
was that they were shooting at?" What happened was my grandmother had lost consciousness. They were shooting outside to see
if it would wake her up. It was early morning. She didn't see the
next day. She had been riding her donkey home. She didn't wake
up. I remember that. She died in one night.

About Manuelito and how he went about, I don't know. We
don't know how he took care of his family before and after they
came back from Hwéeldi.[57]

From Faye, there is this story about Juanita's death:

Now Chief Manuelito one time went to Grants to buy some wine
and that's how he got sick. He died from chicken pox. They say. After
he died, his house was burned down because he died in it and today,
where he was buried, it's said that he was buried with so much turquoise that it came to the surface. Today if anyone goes near his grave,
a whirlwind appears above the grave. After he died, Juanita came
with her children to Dibé bitó. Juanita died from diarrhea. There was
a sheep dipping in Tohatchi and Juanita cooked a meal there, mutton stew. She got sick, got a stomachache, and didn't recover.

When I was younger, I was told that she was buried over in
the small canyon, way past my house. At one time there was horse
bones scattered over her grave. That's what they used to do, kill a
horse when someone died. Now those bones are gone. I looked for
them one time. . . .

[T]hey lived at Red Willow and they lived there for some time after [Juanita's death], maybe a year. Willie Nez was young then and when Juanita died, Willie Nez was sleeping in her arms. So they say. There was a sheep dip, where the Catholic church stands, in Tohatchi. I didn't see the sheep dip. They took the sheep there. My grandmother went there. They used to eat everything there. She made fresh corn stew. She got sick that same day. She did not see the next day. My uncle from Tséyi'bitó. He had a lot of horses. They used one of his horses to put on her grave. It used to be evident by the horse bones on top of her grave.

She is buried here [near Faye's home]. The grave is gone. Before, it was visible because of the horse bones on top of it. Now it's not visible. They say that a beautiful white horse was killed on top of Juanita's grave. They used to kill horses on top of graves.[58]

On various visits, Faye reiterated the story of our grandmother's death. To the end of her life, our grandmother Juanita played a vital role in her extended family. Although elderly, she herded sheep and cared for her grandchildren. Indeed, one final image shows her holding an infant grandchild in her arms, even as she is near death. As Kathleen Bahr has noted in her study of Apache families, grandmothers held the ultimate responsibility for the well-being of their grandchildren. As bearers of cultural heritage, they played a vital role in sustaining their families well into their old age.[59] In a similar manner, the stories of Asdzáá Tł'ógi indicate that she, too, held a place of importance in her family.

The place Asdzáá Tł'ógi is buried is on Tł'ógi lands, not far from where Faye Yazzie lives. It is a place east of Tohatchi, where the land folds into rugged slopes; in between, the slope's wild grasses grow. I didn't ask for the exact location, for I knew that I would meet reluctance, but the fact that our grandmother lies on Tł'ógi land is significant.

Land and Stories

Navajo creation narratives make central the emergence of pre-Diné beings into this world. These beings then became the Diné, as we know ourselves today. We name the specific place from which our ancestors emerged into the fifth world, which became the center of Dinétah. Like the creation narratives that anchor the People to Diné Bikéyah, family and clan stories are sources for laying claim to a place and act as vehicles to affirm tradition. Narratives about our grandmothers, of Asdzáá Tł'ógi and her daughters, evoke images that become the source for shared thoughts and feelings about our place, connecting our sense of it, identity to our ancestors, and their place on the land. As Klara Kelley and Harris Francis have noted about the meaning of land and stories to the Diné: "The story of the origin of the Navajo people, both as passed down among generations of Navajos and versions we have constructed, shows that the Navajo people and their culture came into being through the struggles of their forebears to keep control of the land," they assert, "and that the culture has survived because people have stayed on the land and adapted things that inevitably come from outside into an ongoing way of life to form a distinctive, integrated cultural whole."[60] The great-grandchildren's stories about their ancestors are about movement across the land, naming it and reclaiming it through stories, and about resettlement on that land.

Just as narratives are vehicles that connect us to the land, so also they are tools utilized for practical and political reasons. Remembering Juanita and her daughters and being able to name them as matrilineal grandmothers entitles her maternal descendants to land use privileges. The reservation, even with several increases, was always too small for Navajo use. By the early 1930s, federal officials began to report the need to reduce Navajo livestock, ostensibly because of environmental deterioration, among other reasons. By 1935, Indian Commissioner John Collier had ordered enforcement of livestock reduction regulations. In order to improve range, Collier imposed the livestock permit system, through which Navajo livestock was limited by the issuance of permits that stipulated the number of allowable horses, sheep, and goats. These were issued to heads of household, which the government considered to be men. In many cases, men turned livestock permits over to their wives, who then passed them to their daughters. These permits were also tied to specific grazing areas. As a result, families became tied to grazing land, although many continued to move seasonally with their herds.[61]

Today, the Navajo Reservation remains much too small for the burgeoning population, especially as the young Navajo population grows. As a result, there are competing claims for land use, and those who can name a succession of grandmothers who lived on the land are able to validate their own claims. Similarly, descendants of the daughters of Juanita and Manuelito who live on the lands of their grandmothers validate their land claims through livestock permits.

Those afternoons sitting in the living rooms and listening to my grandparents' stories will remain with me. The stories were punctuated with interruptions, sighs, laughter, and pauses, and we often reflected quietly while images of our grandmothers appeared in our mind's eye. Our grandmother Asdzáá Tł'ógi moves across the landscape with her sheep and goats. As she and her grandchildren herd the sheep, she tells them stories of her life and the Long Walk. She tells them of Washington, D.C. The stories give us cause to reflect upon our grandmothers' claims to the land, the struggles to survive against impossible odds, and the significance of staying on the land for future generations. As Keith Basso notes of Apache place-making, to tell stories is to "speak the past into being," to summon it and give it dramatic form so we can participate in our ancestors' quest for survival and the need to create a sense of community and kin.[62]

Conclusion

Navajo clan stories like those about Asdzáá Tł'ógi and her daughters demonstrate the continuing vitality of traditional narratives and the centrality of women in Navajo society. Importantly, creation narratives feature prominent female deities who provide the foundation from which Navajo women continue to define their traditional roles as grandmothers, mothers, and daughters. These maternal roles are positions of power for Navajo women. Also, the fact that Juanita and her daughters are remembered as grandmothers who were benevolent, generous, and loving is a testament to the centrality that Changing Woman holds for the Diné. Our stories of our grandmothers and grandfathers serve to renew our faith in the strength of the old ways. Just as clan stories may illuminate the Navajo past, they also indicate that clan kinship responsibilities are important to survival and the persistence of Navajo values. As Angela Wilson shares in regard to oral histories that are a part of her family, "The stories handed down from grandmother to granddaughter are rooted in a deep sense of kinship responsibility, a responsibility that relays a culture, an identity, and a sense of belonging essential to my life."[63]

Our history is similar to those of other indigenous peoples. Waves of conquerors wrested away significant portions of our lands. They sought to impose their political, cultural, religious, and economic institutions upon our way of life. As Navajos, we have retained many of our cultural traditions. One way to understand this process is to examine the ways in which oral traditions serve as windows into the past, the ways the past inform the present. Even as American institutions sought to undermine women's positions, Navajo women have struggled to retain positions of autonomy and authority in their society. The narratives of Asdzáá Tł'ógi and her daughters are not only testaments to the validity of the oral tradition, but also demonstrations of how oral traditions serve as vehicles to transmit the past, connecting it to the present.

6/Stories in the Land

Navajo Uses of the Past

In the previous chapter, I demonstrated how traditional creation narratives serve as the foundation for the ways in which the Diné talk about and experience the more recent past. Placed in a historical and cultural context, stories about Asdzáá Tł'ógi and her daughters indicate women's centrality to the reestablishment of life after the return from Hwéeldi in 1868. Just as our female deities act decisively and wield a significant amount of power and autonomy, Diné women are recognized as powerful beings who have influenced the shape of Diné culture and the course of the future.[1] Today, still, Navajo women who reflect Changing Woman's desirable characteristics are admired and looked to for leadership.

In this chapter, I extend my examination of how narratives about Adszáá Tł'ógi and her daughters serve as vehicles that link the land with stories that reflect distinct Navajo cultural values and identity. Conveyed within the matrilineal clan, these narratives demonstrate the continuing centrality of maternal clans in which women are at the center of daily life, wherein "daily" includes decisions that deal with the land, livestock, home, and children. I include in my examination the study of landscape, focusing on those stories relevant to Native and Navajo perspectives on the meaning of land, and then articulate the significance of land as refracted through the stories of my grandmothers, beginning with Adszáá Tł'ógi.

During the course of research conducted for this study, one of the most powerful messages brought home to me was how Navajos have been subjected to catastrophic transformations under colonialism. Studying about the consequences of conquest, the loss of self-sufficiency, and the struggle to reclaim autonomy is not an objective impersonal undertaking. Moreover, writing our own history means that as Native scholars we are obligated to expose the colonial structures that shape our lives as Native people and to become critically conscious of how we have taken American truths about Native people as our realities, thereby accepting our marginal positions in American society. For me, the consequences of colonialism are the realities of my life, as they are for my parents and grandparents. The stories from my grandparents make vivid the effects of colonialism, especially when they explained why they knew few, if any, stories about the Navajo past. The stories I heard of Manuelito and Juanita's daughters and their families were anecdotes and fragments of narratives. However, one thing that my mother and grandmothers could do readily was to piece together a genealogy that went back to Juanita and Manuelito. Prior to 1868, memory of lineage is hazy, although the fact that many families returned to traditional land use areas after 1868 is testimony to the resilience of tradition and memory.

When I interviewed relatives of my mother's generation, I encountered narratives that were similarly fragmented and sparse. Stories of my aunts and uncles, their experiences as children and young adults, were filled with accounts of struggles to maintain a sense of stability in the face of extreme loss and absence. They had lost grandparents and parents to diseases such as tuberculosis and diphtheria. Some had gone blind with trachoma. Some had stayed years in sanitariums far away from home. Others had spent childhood at boarding schools in Albuquerque, Wingate, and Tohatchi, New Mexico; Riverside, California; and Stewart, Nevada. Families had scattered and regrouped. In some cases, brothers and sisters did not see each other for years; neither did they see their parents. When they became adults, they had faced chronic unemployment on the reservation, and so again had to seek work away from home. One common theme in their personal histories was their return home as adults, to the place where the daughters of Manuelito and Juanita had settled with their husbands.

My own experiences echo those of my clan relatives, for I received a Western education that emphasized Western values even though the schools were on Navajo land. Like my clan relatives, I was also unacquainted with Navajo history and our own extended family history. Significantly, although there are periods of loss and absence in our respective lives, the places to which we eventually return—or to which we refer when we acknowledge maternal clan relationships—are shaped by the fact that our grandmothers and grandfathers lived on the land that we still claim. The fact that my grandparents' and my mother's generations retain connections to lands where their ancestors had once lived, in spite of all these dislocations, attests to the enduring relationships created and recreated through narratives, narratives that link us as Navajos to the land. As I searched for stories of my ancestors, I came away with only glimpses of their lives, yet from these fragments, new stories are woven. And one of the most important ingredients for effective storytelling, nonverbal and prosodic language—the laughter, sadness, love, and affection—effectively communicates the meaning of these narratives for the present.

Today, the places where the daughters and their mother Juanita established their claims remain within control of their descendants. Stories of my ancestors unfold whenever we go for walks with my mother, who over the years has become more insistent that we remember our grandmothers and grandfathers. The descendants of Asdzáá Tł'ógi readily point out both natural and human-made features of the land. There are places where the extended family established residences. Remains of hogan sites are still there. Ringed sandstones mark the place where sheep were penned. Ash dumps are still visible. There are places where medicine people once placed their offerings and a shrine where a medicine woman prayed the eagles down. The land boasts a variety of medicinal herbs. Still visible are the sheep trails that go up and down the mountains. It is said that sometimes, when one listens closely, one can hear sheep bleating in the distance. The place where my parents live is still known as Dibé bitó (Sheep Spring) because of a fresh water spring that used to supply the family and livestock. There is the skeleton of a car that clings precariously to the steep wall of wash that gets flooded during the summer monsoons. That car also has a story.

Land and Stories

Studies of landscape remain popular among scholars and writers. These range in topic from the exploration of English colonists' experiences and those who looked upon the New World with a mixture of trepidation, fear, and wonder to westering white Americans who strove to recreate the land to fit their fantasies, fantasies in which land served as the basis for establishing a uniquely American identity. Credited with perhaps one of the best-known formulations of what it means to be American, Frederick Jackson Turner argued that the experiences of transforming the formerly "wild and savage" land and subduing the Indians had molded distinctly American traits such as individualism, a love of freedom, and the creation of democracy.[2] Although New Western historians have challenged Turner's vision of the American West, its efficacy is manifested in American neocolonialism, wherein American leaders reference their history of "Cowboys and Indians" to describe American presence in the Middle East.[3]

Feminist scholars Carolyn Merchant and Annette Kolodny have argued that a Euro-American perspective on land resulted in severe consequences due to disastrous environmental destruction and degradation. One major point of their argument includes the assertion that the violent ways in which the land was—and still is—treated is mirrored in the ways in which women have been historically treated under a Western patriarchy.[4] In a similar study, Merchant argues that white American women's perspectives on the land contrasted sharply with those of white males. Rather than attempt to transform the land through violence and aggression, as did the men, white women attempted to recreate a familiar place of home, by planting gardens, for example.[5]

Native scholars have also articulated the significance of land for Native peoples. Pointing out the sacred dimensions of the relationships between people and land, many Native people see the land as a living entity that has provided sustenance for all living beings, and is therefore known as Mother.[6] Indeed, at the heart of the conflict and struggle between Indians and whites have been claims to land. Even today, as Native activist Winona LaDuke writes so passionately, our lands have been under attack with renewed colonialism as our lands are used for bombing ranges, uranium mining, and repositories for the American nation's nuclear waste.[7] Moreover, Andrea Smith has argued that in order to realize fully indigenous sovereignty, the links between the rape of the land and the rape and violation of Native women must be exposed and then countered, for the status of women reflects the values of a people and a nation.[8]

One of the most eloquent studies of the relationship between

Native peoples and land is anthropologist Keith Basso's *Wisdom Sits in Places*, a study of Apache stories and land, which adds to our understanding of how perceptions of the land are culturally constructed. Basso begins his narrative with a report about his longstanding relationship with the White River Apaches, who have come to trust him as a responsible and ethical researcher. Of his study about land and stories, Basso notes that, upon first glance or perhaps because of unfamiliarity, a landscape initially appears to be part of the ordinary until something happens to dislodge this sense and it gradually comes to take on new meaning:

> Many of these places are also encountered in the country of the present as material objects and areas, naturally formed or built, whose myriad local arrangements make up the landscapes of everyday life. But here, now, in the ongoing world of current concerns and projects, they are not apprehended as reminders of the past . . . unless something happens to dislodge these perceptions they are left, as it were, to their own enduring devices. But then something does happen . . . any disturbance, large or small, that inscribes the passage of time—and a place presents itself as bearing on prior events. And at that precise moment, when ordinary perceptions begin to loosen their hold, a border has been crossed and the country starts to change. Awareness has shifted its footing, and the character of the place, now transfigured by thoughts of earlier day, swiftly takes on a new and foreign look.[9]

In his unfolding examination of Apache stories about the land, Basso realizes a new consciousness of Apache perceptions of place that is about cultural spheres and can tell us about conceptions of wisdom, notions of morality, particular ways of speaking distinctly Apache, and ways of imagining and interpreting the Apache past. His collaboration with Eva Tulene Watt, an Apache woman, reinforces an understanding of how indigenous people claim the land.[10] Stories act as vehicles to claim places, and in the process convey Apache cultural values. As Basso declares, part of the process of remembering, of imbuing a place with meaning, involves a "way of constructing history itself, of inventing it, of fashioning novel versions of 'what happened here.'" As N. Scott Momaday proclaims, "We are what we imagine ourselves to be."[11]

Places have long served as durable symbols of distant events and as indispensable aids for remembering and imagining them. Studies of Navajos and their relationship to the land have been articulated by Klara Kelley and Harris Francis, who have conducted a number of studies that map Diné relationships to the land. It has long been recognized that, to Navajos, the land is sacred. Navajos easily point out places in the original Dinétah where the Diné interacted with the Holy People. They can tell you where our ancestors emerged from the previous worlds into this one; where Changing Woman was born; and where Monster Slayer and Born for Water slew a giant at Blue Water. Navajos can often tell about the places where many of our ceremonies originated. In the late 1990s, one Navajo grandmother reported sighting Monster Slayer near her home in northeastern Arizona. Some Navajos interpreted her announcement as a sign that we were inattentive to our cultural values. As Kelley and Francis point out, creation narratives form the basis of our history; they are stories about the past and have culturally meaningful associations with the land.[12]

In recent studies, Kelley and Francis continue their examination of sacred stories that are part of ceremonies and trace them on the land. Their findings indicate that Diné oral tradition offers information on trade routes from Meso-America into the Southwest. Just as significant, their studies provide proof for claims of Navajos that their ancestors had relationships with the ancient peoples and exchanged material culture and ceremonial knowledge with them.[13] When the Ancient Ones dispersed, for reasons still to be advanced, some came to live among the Diné. In a similar manner, Diné scholar Richard Begay discusses Navajo relations with the people of Chaco Canyon, relating the story of the Gambler who went to Chaco Canyon and through a series of events claimed people as prizes for winning bets. Navajo stories note that Chaco Canyon became a place of vice and excess, resulting in the disappearance of its people. Some of those ancient people are the progenitors of Navajo clans. Begay's study offers significant insight into the nature of Navajos' historical and cultural relationships to the early indigenous peoples of the Southwest.[14]

Many of these studies of Navajo relations with the land offer new insights into the nature of Navajo senses of place. From a different direction, stories from the descendants of Juanita and Manuelito also offer insight into how land remains integral to the persistence of Navajo life and culture on a daily basis. As Keith Basso points out, upon first glance, it appears that land is made up simply of geographical features formed by thousands of years of climate, but more recently, it has also been seen to indicate the efforts of men and women to carve out distinct places for themselves. During the course of this research project, I learned a new appreciation for the land upon which my grandmothers had lived for generations. By listening to stories from my mother and her relatives and by visiting the places where they had lived as children, I came to see a storied landscape.

The stories from my clan are situated in a place where one comes across sandstone slabs still arranged in a circle—signs of hogans from an earlier time. There are ringed blocks of sandstone once used to corral sheep and goats. Abandoned dishpans are half emerged in garbage or ash dumpsites. I share first stories of the journey to establish a household after the death of Manuelito and then proceed to give some depth as to how the eldest daughter of Manuelito and Juanita, with her husband, endeavored to provide for their family. Although these stories appear fragmented, with no set chronology that strings them together in a coherent narrative that moves from past to present, the themes present illustrate the workings of families centered around a matrilineal clan, providing further evidence of women's centrality in kin and clan networks.

Tohatchi Community

Tohatchi (the word translates as "water seeps up when one scratches the earth") is a small community twenty-eight miles north of Gallup, New Mexico. Originally, Hastiin N'daaz (Heavy Man) claimed the land for his family's use. Stories give evidence that the land where the community now stands has seen long tenure. A stream runs on the east side, near the base of the Chuska Mountain. Years ago, people used the area around the stream for cornfields. In 1890, George Sampson, whom Navajos called Hastiin łibai (Grey Man), established a trading post. Two other traders came before Albert Arnold settled in with his Navajo wife Alice to run the store for more than forty years. Hastiin N'daaz consented to have some of his land withdrawn for a school, and in 1895 Tohatchi School opened. The first Christian church, the Christian Reformed Church, was established in 1910. A Catholic church followed, and was built over the site of a sheep dip. Years earlier, Juanita and her family had herded their livestock to that dip. This is the place she ate corn stew and became deathly ill. A wooden clapboard hospital building where a doctor treated Navajo patients also opened. Several years ago, it burned down. It was in this hospital that my mother says her brother and sisters were born.

Today, a more modern Indian Health Service hospital has been built. One of the streets near it is named Manuelito. A public school and a community school serve the area's children. On one of the two streets that lead into Tohatchi sits the chapter house, a central meeting place where political decisions are made. The chapter house is also a place where the veterans meet, where the annual Christmas dinner is held, and where families hold various family and clan celebrations.

Although many Navajos live in suburban-style housing within the boundaries of the Tohatchi community, other families reside beyond its boundaries. They live on lands that their families and kin have occupied for generations. Northeast of Tohatchi, the descendants of Juanita and Manuelito live on lands that their grandmothers—the two daughters of Juanita and Manuelito (figs. 9 and 10)—lived on with their families. Originally Dághá Chíí and Dághá Chíí Bik'is lived near each other, but a strong disagreement between the two brothers led to Dághá Chíí Bik'is taking his family northeast. Today, Highway 491 going northeast toward Shiprock, New Mexico, bisects the land use of both daughters' descendants. Dághá Chíí be Asdzáá and her husband, Dághá Chíí, remained at the base of the Chuska Mountains. Today, their descendants utilize these lands.

On the south side of Highway 491, all the way past the El Paso Natural Gas plant and going east, the descendants of Ałk'iníbaa live and raise their families. In various ways, the descendants of both daughters remember their grandmothers by keeping in contact with each other. Whenever we meet as clan relatives, the elders always remark that they do not often know the younger generations and that we have not taken the time to ensure that our children and grandchildren know their kin ties.

The stories of my grandmothers and grandmothers are situated in the early reservation period and mark Navajo responses to changes that Navajo faced, including livestock reduction, education mandates, the wage economy, and disease epidemics. Some of the first stories my maternal grandparents told me were intended to situate me within the extended family. They begin with our genealogy and then go on to the journey to a new residence after the death of Manuelito in 1894. Although there is some uncertainty about exactly when the extended family moved, my grandparents and mother know where Juanita and her daughters set up new households after the death of Manuelito. A sense of who we are as Tł'ógi Diné begins with the land. As my grandfather Charles Manuelito related to me:

> Chief Manuelito [had] two daughters. Tł'ógi clan [and the daughters] moved to Dibé bitó. My grandmother . . . Here's the way it goes: two brothers married to Chief Manuelito's two daughters. One is my grandfather. The other is the brother of my grandfather. My grandfather, his name was Pete Dághá Chíí. His brother is Dághá Chíí Bik'is. The two brothers didn't get along very well. My grandmother went to the agency in Fort Defiance and contacted the official there and the official came out and took a look at the land, the location. So the official told Dághá Chíí Bik'is, that's his real name, Dághá Chíí Bik'is to move out of the Dibé bitó. Originally, the two sisters moved to Dibé bitó at the same time, but afterwards, the feud.[15]

From this place, the extended family followed the seasonal pattern of following the sheep. There are many stories that descendants tell of herding sheep and how sheep embody Diné values such as industry and self-sufficiency. Farming was part of the way Diné claimed land. Red Willow, where Asdzáá Tł'ógi died and her daughters and their family continued to plant their fields, serves as a reminder of how Navajo families used to move seasonally. Following the sheep, in the late spring or early summer, some of the members moved midway up the Chuska Mountains, which we call the "middle mountain" in the Navajo language, whereas others stayed to care for the cornfield. My family continues to utilize the cornfield there, although in the past few years the harvest has been sparse.

All that is left of my grandmothers' home are rings of sandstone. Not far away, against a hill slope and just barely visible, a row of rectangular sandstone slabs once served as the pen for sheep and goats. My mother tells me that, as a child, she heard stories of the annuities her grandmother received, which she placed for storage and safekeeping in openings in the hillsides. Perhaps remnants of the items are still tucked away somewhere.

Moving toward the highway and further from the mountainside—but still hidden from the highway—a one-room structure made in the Pueblito style still stands. My mother tells me that Dághá Chíí built this. On my walks, I often stopped there and inspected stone walls, which are still chinked with dried mud. In one corner of the tiny room, a fireplace fashioned out of sandstone still stands. For a long time, there was an axe head, neatly broken in half, that rested on the fireplace. At some point, it disappeared. I wasn't the only one captivated by the places our ancestors dwelled.

Anthropologist Karen Blu observes that taking notice of places provides openings to multiple interpretations and gives cause to imagine whatever occurred here, as well as the significance of those occurances.[16] For me, visiting places my grandmothers set up their households sets me thinking about a sisterly closeness that existed between my grandmothers and provides an occasion to think about what Navajo life must have been like back then. In narratives about these places, the central image is one of women moving about, setting up their households. Movement creates a sense of vitality and stability; movement suggests life and well-being. Certainly, the photographs taken by George Wharton James in 1902 (figs. 8 and 12) are of the two women traveling with their mother, Juanita. As Blu declares, movement is a metaphor for health, well-being, and connectedness.[17] Looking at the evidence of our grandmothers and grandfathers going about the daily business of living reminds me to be respectful of their foresight. They moved about with a vision of grandchildren and great-grandchildren.

After 1868, Navajos struggled to recover a measure of their former autonomy and self-sufficiency. By the end of the nineteenth century, Navajos had increased not only their own population, but also their livestock. Taking care of livestock required a constant search for pasturing lands. In many cases, Navajo herders were forced to graze their animals on public domain, lands formerly their own territory, which resulted in conflicts with non-Indian herders and cattlemen who refused to share the pastures with Indians. Indeed, among the letters my grandfather Charles had in his possession was a "good Indian pass." Written by an Indian agent for my great-great-grandfather, the note indicates that Dághá Chíí was passing through the area and that he was a respectable person. In the 1880s, Indian agent Dennis Riordan reported an increase in Navajo livestock and called for reduction by at least one-half to two-thirds. Federal officials reported that the Navajos owned more than one million head of livestock, the majority sheep and goats. Severe drought from 1898 through 1904, combined with growing numbers of livestock, took their toll on the land.

In 1933, Indian Commissioner John Collier ordered Navajos to reduce their herds 50 percent by 1950.[18] Livestock reduction was only one of several recommendations made by forest rangers. Navajos resisted and Collier turned to the newly created tribal council to enforce his draconian measure. Navajos' stories of their responses to forced livestock reduction mirror those of Hwéeldi, in which they expressed fear, shock, outrage, and trauma at the loss their animals, which were essential to their livelihood. Navajos had so thoroughly embedded sheep, goats, and horses into their value system that their creation stories explained how the Holy People had gifted them to the People.

Livestock reduction is only one thread of the story about efforts to recreate life during the early reservation period. As historians Robert Trennert and Wade Davies point out in their studies of Western medicine among the Navajos, after 1868, Navajos were exposed to a number of infectious diseases and ailments that decreased their population and created conditions from which they easily succumbed to illnesses.[19] In the early twentieth century, Navajo families experienced disorganization and chaos as a result of diseases such as diphtheria, whooping cough, measles, smallpox, syphilis, and trachoma. There was also tuberculosis in the early 1900s, which federal officials attempted to deal with after it began to spread from the schools into the isolated areas of the reservation. By 1912, tuberculosis was still a growing problem and remained a major focus of public health officials attempting to contain it.[20] Trachoma was just as catastrophic, though federal officials were unwilling to admit how widespread it actually was. Attempts to contain the disease were initially made at the Phoenix School, though trachoma remained out of control and conditions did not improve because physicians were not trained to deal with the disease.[21]

Attempting to discover more about my great-great-grandfather, I asked my grandfather, Charles, "What do you remember about Dághá Chíí?"

He replied, "Not too much. Of course, when I was young, I was away herding sheep forever. But I know he was a quiet man. He used to go out with the sheep, with a stick laid across the back of his shoulders. He walked in front of the sheep and the sheep followed. Now there are not sheepherders like him" (see figs. 10 and 13).[22]

When my mother talked about her great-grandfather, she said,

"When I was a child, I used to take care of my grandfather. He was blind and I used to lead him out of the hogan. He would sit in the shade. He used to sit us children on his lap and sing Blessingway songs to us. He knew the Blessingway songs."[23] My grandfather became blind after he went into a sweathouse and debris fell into his eyes.

As family stories go, discoveries are usually situated within the domestic realm. During my search through documents, I discovered that Dághá Chíí had served as a scout with the U.S. military. Although studies devoted to Apache scouts who served under Gen. George Crook exist, there are few references in historical sources to Navajo scouts. According to historian William Hagan, in 1872, after a number of recommendations from Gen. O. O. Howard and trader Thomas Keam, Navajo men were recruited and placed under the command of Manuelito to quiet the disputes between Navajos and non-Indians along the reservation's borders.[24] The scouts also resolved tensions between Navajos, for there was always fear that the People would be blamed for the conflicts and imprisoned again.[25] Navajos also enlisted in the campaign to force the surrender of Apache leaders. According to Robert Collman, who examined Navajo scout files at the National Archives, Navajo men served from 1873 to 1894, and they performed a number of duties similar to those of the first Native scouts to ally themselves with foreign expeditions.[26] In the late 1920s, under the direction of Superintendent Samuel Stacher, the federal government compensated former scouts with pensions. By the 1930s and 1940s, they were elderly; the few accounts they told of their experiences were relegated to a small number of reports in the *Navajo Times* during the early 1960s.

It was among pension claims that I found Dághá Chíí's applications. Known by several names, including Pete Dougal Chee and Pete Scott, my great-great-grandfather began to serve in 1889. According to these records, he was born in 1857 and was about thirty-two years old when he became a scout. He died in 1942, at the age of eighty-five.[27]

Why did Navajo men join a branch of the U.S. military, where they were required to address hostilities between Navajos and non-Indians and serve as auxiliaries with the army to track Geronimo and other Apache leaders? According to Manuelito's son-in-law, Dághá Chíí Bik'is, the men were enlisted specifically to fight against the Apaches.[28] Remembrances of my grandfather, Charles Manuelito, and my mother bring in another dimension that illuminates Navajo life in the early twentieth century. In my great-great-grandfather's scout file, copies of which are among the applications for pensions in land claims papers in Window Rock, Arizona, there are letters written by Charles Manuelito. Charles assisted his grandfather in getting approval for a pension for his service. After being deemed eligible, Dághá Chíí received a lump sum payment, with which, according to my mother, he immediately purchased two mules and a wagon. A child at the time, she remembers that each month thereafter trader Eddie Arnold would visit to affix Dághá Chíí's thumbprint to a pension check, which was then paid out in bills and coins. Upon receiving the money, Dághá Chíí entrusted his daughter, Louise, with it, saying, "Here, granddaughter, take care of this."

Dághá Chíí's income from the pension was vital for the family. When his grandfather died, Charles sent letters to the federal government inquiring about the pension and letting the officials know that Dághá Chíí had provided the main financial support for his great-grandchildren. Replies to Charles' inquiries stated that pensions were provided only for pensioners' widows and offspring. Thus, the Manuelito family lost an important source of income. Given the context of the times, it must have been a hardship indeed for the family to lose this income. A glimpse of Navajo life during this period indicates that, as with many other extended families, Dághá Chíí was responsible for several generations. No doubt when he was a young man, there had been few options for Navajo men to support their families. Serving as a scout brought in some income, even though scouts were either poorly paid for their services or often not paid at all until much later in their lives.

In contrast to stories about the scouts' feats in the military, then, these family stories have a different focus, and they indicate that Navajo men signed up for scout duty as a way to support their families. Charles's letters, some of which were written on behalf of his mother, Dłíhaazbaa', further indicate that Navajo men were enmeshed in matrilineal extended family concerns. Just as Dághá Chíí was responsible to his children, his grandchildren, and his great-grandchildren, so, too, did Charles recognize a responsibility to his maternal clans-people.

Stories of Juanita and Manuelito's granddaughter Dłíhaazbaa' (fig. 14) and her husband have the power to elicit storytellers' emotions. Whereas my great-great-grandfather Dághá Chíí was known as a kind, generous, and quiet man, his wife, Dágha Chíí be Asdzáá, is remembered as a strong woman who took care of her family. As Charles remembered his grandmother, his voice became tender: "I loved my grandmother very much, but don't remember clearly everything. Anyway, when I was in school, in Albuquerque, someone wrote me a letter that my grandmother passed away. At that time, all the graveyards were across from the Christian Reformed Church [in Tohatchi]. That's where she is buried."[29] What are remembered in stories about our ancestors are their traits. At the same time that Charles demonstrated his love and respect for his grandparents, he also asserted that the care of children must be done with love, not harsh words. The ways in which he linked the memories of his grandparents' care of him to present-day child rearing practices served as a moment to reflect on how one should raise children. Indeed, Charles was very much like his grandfather Dágha Chíí, for he, too, had been a kind and generous man who had spoken softly.

Just as Charles's stories provide a sense of our ancestors' attributes and their endeavors, my mother's stories about her grandmother, Dłíhaazbaa', the daughter of Dágha Chíí and Dágha Chíí be Asdzáá, add further evidence of ongoing efforts to keep family together. My mother tells stories of learning how to herd sheep when she was a child. After the death of her great-grandfather, her grandmother cared for her. Dłíhaazbaa' also took care of her, her brother, her sister, and her clan brother, Sherman. Recalling the annual trip in summer up to pasturing grounds in the mountains, my mother shared this story:

> In the spring, in the summer, we moved to the mountains with our grandmother. When we lived with her, she was sick but I didn't know that. She kept getting sick, it seemed. But there was not a word about a ceremony. I don't know. In the middle mountain, where the cornfield is, that's where we moved. That's the only place we moved. Every summer. Every summer. We never deviated from that. There was a hogan.
>
> I was very young. We moved in a wagon. The wagon was filled with our belongings. We didn't have many belongings. Just enough to fill the wagon. We children sat in the back. Up there, the sheep were herded. In the morning we left, slowly. Toward evening, late evening we arrived. The sheep would already be there when we arrived in the wagon. The hogan door would be covered. The

wagon stopped, and my grandmother would instruct us, "Stay in the wagon."

My grandmother went into the hogan to sweep the floor. Maybe she sprinkled water, I don't know. She swept the floor and started a fire on the ground. There was no stove. She lit a fire and blessed the hogan with corn pollen. Then we brought in our belongings.[30]

My mother notes that her grandmother was ill, something of which she unaware until much later. Dłíhaazbaa' died of tuberculosis. During one of the seasonal moves up to the mountain, after she had prepared the hogan for her grandchildren, she left and went back down. My mother reports that she never saw her grandmother again. About this part of her life, my mother remembers: "She [Dłíhaazbaa'] was very ill and taking care of us. We didn't know about it. We moved up to the mountains. I don't know how long we were up there and soon she was very ill and she left on the horse to the hospital." My mother continued: "She may have gone down the mountain with my brother [Wilbert Dennison], I don't remember. In the evening Wilbert returned alone. Our grandmother was admitted to the hospital in Tohatchi. From there, she was sent to Fort Defiance Hospital. She never came back."[31] According to remembrances of my mother, her grandmother might have been in a tuberculosis sanatorium up to two years. After she died, Rose's mother, Louise, whose Navajo name was Naałíí'baa', began to care for the family. When my mother was about twelve years old, she was taken off to a boarding school. Her maternal uncle, Charles, made the arrangements for her enrollment. When she tells me about this time in her life, she speaks with affection for her uncle. Her fondness reflects the traditional ordering of a Navajo household and the important roles that maternal uncles have played, in which kinship revolves around the matrilineal clan.

Recently, I had the opportunity to hear Winona (Stevenson) Wheeler speak about the value of oral tradition in the academy. Her presentation was heartening, for I was reminded about the significance of remembering stories that our community and family members tell us. She noted that many times the stories we relate may seem to lack specific teachings, but that such absences are acceptable because part of the nature of oral traditions is that we draw our own lessons from the stories and these offer moments upon which to reflect and find teachings for ourselves. Wheeler touched upon the meaning of memory and how it is a gift: "To remember those times spent listening to old people tell histories at the kitchen table, on a road trip, or in the warm glow of a campfire, is to relive them."[32]

These are only a few of the stories from my grandparents and mother that illuminate how families and clan persevered under the most trying conditions. Today, we still experience the consequences of the past, including livestock reduction and the introduction of a wage economy after the 1940s. As a result of livestock reduction, many Navajo families no longer know the land as their ancestors did. In some cases, following the sheep to pastures has almost disappeared. Nevertheless, those movements are recalled in stories such as ones to which I have referred in this chapter.

Another way that the livestock reduction is referenced and has great import is the use of livestock permits. These were issued to control livestock population, to ensure that Navajos did not overgraze the land to exhaustion. In many cases, although Navajo men as heads of household often received the permits, they immediately turned them over to their wives. The permits were then passed down through the wife's matrilineal clan. Today, it is extremely difficult to discuss these permits, particularly in relationship to the land. Each time they are passed to family members of the next generation, they allow fewer and fewer animals because each family member receives only a portion. This system has fostered serious tension and conflict within clans, with extended and immediate family members.

Prior to livestock reduction, Navajos gathered at multiple sites to participate in ceremonies, several of which were expensive. It is said that a person's herd could be decimated by the cost. Participation in the ceremonies required traveling great distances, so journeys were not undertaken lightly. Extended families often stayed at the ceremonial site for days, or even weeks. Thus, ceremonies served as vehicles to maintain clan ties. After the livestock reductions, people could no longer pay for the ceremonies, and under the permit system they were restricted to one or two locations. Moreover, with the introduction of wage work, there was no longer any reason to move to seasonal campsites. In many cases, only stories remain about the relationships shared across great distances, about the cornfields at Red Willow and how the Tohatchi Mountains were often filled with the sounds of bleating sheep, their bells clanging in the distance. One evening in

Robert Manuelito's home, my mother and he reminisced about how the Chuska Mountains had always been alive with human activity. One always knew a visitor was approaching because he or she sang riding songs while riding up to a relative's home. Remarking on the changes in Navajo life, Robert said to me, "Even the woodpeckers no longer send their clatter up to the skies."[33]

Whenever I go home, my relatives tell me that I am truly fortunate to have my mother and father, who live at Dibé bitó. Parents, grandparents, and great-parents, they are at the core of our family life. We look to them for guidance and teachings for our own lives. There are many days I go for walks and sometimes take the few of my mother's sheep to graze. As I revisit the places where my grandmothers and grandfathers walked, the land comes alive and I remember the stories of our ancestors as they moved about the daily business of making a living. I imagine them herding sheep, planting cornfields, cooking meals for children and grandchildren. I imagine them arranging healing and blessing ceremonies for their children and grandchildren. Surely, their determination to ensure the future of their people was not in vain. During one of our visits to Mike Allison Sr., as we were leaving, he told my mother, "Hold on to your land with sheep."

Conclusion

The historical picture often paints Navajos as thoroughly chastised by the U.S. military and then forced after 1868 to eke out a living on the reservation. In contrast, like other stories recorded by Navajos, those by Tł'ógi clan members shed light on how Navajo families strove to recreate family and community and maintain a grip on the land. Their stories are about survival and persistence. The process of recovering them has led me to affirm kin ties and reconnect with community and family members across generations. Old stories take on new forms as I become part of the process for reimagining and imbuing them with new meaning.

Today, the descendants of Adszáá Tł'ógi and Hastiin Ch'il Hajin make efforts to maintain Tł'ógi kin ties that began with Adszáá Tł'ógi and her daughters. In 1993, my aunt, Julia Burbank Thompson, a descendant of Adszáá Tł'ógi's younger daughter, organized the first Tł'ógi clan reunion. The descendants shared a day of stories under the shade of a tarpaulin stretched over poles. Over roasted mutton, mutton stew, tortillas, and Pepsi-Cola, several generations remembered our ancestors. Just as we always have, we endeavored to remember and value our ancestors' teachings. After all, these same teachings enabled our grandmothers and grandfathers to move beyond some of the worst times in our history. It becomes the responsibility of each generation of Navajos to recover the past and convey its meaning to future generations. We have not forgotten the teachings of the Holy People. As Diné poet Luci Tapahonso gently reminds us: "Before this world existed, the holy people made themselves visible by becoming the clouds, sun, moon, trees, bodies of water, thunder, ran, snow, and other aspects of this world we live in. That way, they said, we would never be alone. So it is possible to talk to them and pray, no matter where we are and how we feel. *Bíyázhi daniidlí*, we are their little ones.[34]

7/Conclusion

The Diné is one group of indigenous people that has maintained a distinct cultural cohesiveness to the present day in spite of the destructuring effects of American colonization. Until fairly recently, the Navajo past has been largely studied, classified, and written by non-Navajos with reliance on Western categories of historical production for meaning. These renditions of the Diné past have not adequately represented our own perspectives on the past. In my work, I have critiqued the existing body of knowledge on Navajos that dates back to the first known written accounts penned by the Spaniards. These have become the basis for stereotypes about Navajos. By the early twentieth century, as interest in the Southwest intensified, the notion of Navajos as late arrivals and cultural borrowers was firmly established. Although more recent studies, particularly collaborations with Navajo scholars and community members, are countering stereotypes, there is still much more work to be done.

In seeking to approach the Navajo past through oral traditions, which have served as authoritative explanations for the cultural and social transformations that have occurred in Navajo communities, I examine the interconnectedness of oral traditions and history, in which Western senses of past have been privileged and Native perspectives either dismissed or ignored. Scholars have begun to acknowledge that notions about the past are culturally constructed and that, by analyzing categories embedded in histories, we can better understand cultural beliefs and values that shape and inform history. I situate Navajo history within this evolving discussion of the relationship between oral tradition and history and argue that an approach that emphasizes traditional narratives is sorely needed for creating Navajo histories.

My examination of the Navajo past must necessarily engage with existing histories of it, thereby transforming the scholarship on Navajos and moving toward theoretical and methodological approaches aligned with Navajo objectives and goals. My chapter on Manuelito is a much-needed account that relies on both non-Navajo and Navajo sources. In my study, I discovered multiple layers of meaning about the past that go back and forth between history and oral tradition, for Navajo views on their esteemed leader are shaped by Western historical conventions as well as a Navajo nationalist project. Not surprisingly, Manuelito's portrayal in Navajo historiography follows a trajectory wherein indigenous men have been presented as noble savages who heroically defended their lands but are defeated and ultimately unable to live in Western civilization, thereby reaffirming Western beliefs about the vanishing American Indians. Western historiography thus justifies American invasion and the conquest of Navajos. My analysis clears the way for creating new biographies and histories of Manuelito that better reflect Navajo perspectives on their leader and their past.

Navajos have cast Manuelito as a cultural hero who exemplifies Navajo traditions and values; the deployment of narratives about him illustrates how Navajos empowered themselves as a group in relation to the dominant society. At the same time, the construct of Navajo nationhood, based on Western notions of nation and democracy, has taken on a patriarchical structure that has undermined Navajo women's traditional status, which has been one of autonomy and authority. Exploration of this important topic in detail awaits further research.

As with many other indigenous peoples, Navajos have been severed from their past because of American education imposed upon us beginning in the mid-nineteenth century. We were discouraged from retaining language and cultural traditions and forced to accept American gendered notions of family and nation. The introduction of a wage economy, chronic unemployment, and the prevalence of epidemic diseases, as well as the mandate for Western education, scattered extended families. Throughout the early twentieth century, many Navajos relocated to urban areas to support families and to take advantage of education opportunities. Yet Navajos remain rooted to the homeland and articulate their ties through a number of venues, including stories. My love of stories led me to examine more closely the existing narratives of Juanita and her daughters. We cannot understand or appreciate the significance of Navajo women like Juanita, who were and are the vanguards of Navajo society, if we rely on American historical and cultural context for interpreting Navajo history and Navajo women's roles in that history.

My fundamental argument is that clan narratives of Juanita, which are still part of her great-grandchildren's memories, shape Navajo perspectives on the past when placed within a historical and cultural framework that emphasizes the creation narratives as the foundation. These stories about Juanita are conveyed through the matrilineal clan members who claim Juanita and two of her daughters as their grandmothers. Navajos understand and talk about women's roles within a framework that values the characteristics of female deities such as Changing Woman. Navajo women who are honored and revered share Changing Woman's attributes. Oral traditions placed within a historical framework can offer rich insight into Navajo perspectives on the past, and especially the authoritative roles of women in Navajo society, past and present. In addition, photographs made by non-Indian photographers returned to Navajo communities have the potential to become sources for renewed storytelling.

Native scholars are presently engaging in a process of decolonization, which includes deconstructing the American master narrative and recovering and reclaiming traditions as part of our histories. As with many other Native scholars, my work has deeply personal meanings. In chapter 5, I offer stories from my clan relatives, mostly from those descended from the eldest daughter of Juanita, because those are the stories with which I am most familiar. Stories about Juanita and her two daughters also concern the land and have served as vehicles to convey understanding about its significance in Navajo beliefs, values, and identity.

Because I am the great-great-great-granddaughter of Manuelito and Juanita, chapter 6 is an illumination of one Navajo woman's search for her own sense of the past. Although I grew up in a Navajo community and am familiar with our own traditional practices and stories, only recently have I discovered that studying and critiquing Navajo history is part of an ongoing larger process, one in which many

Native scholars are presently engaged. This process encompasses the recovery and revitalization of our community, family, language, and traditions. It is my hope that this study will offer Navajos and other Native peoples an opportunity to share my journey of reclaiming the Navajo past on multiple levels that range from the personal to the national.

Appendix

Genealogical Charts

Understanding complex Diné kin relationships can be difficult even for the average Diné, like myself. In the hope of illuminating the complexities of matrilineal descent lineage, I include the following charts, which depict Manuelito's family from two of his wives, Asdzáá Tł'ógi and Asdzáá Tsin sikaadnii, both of whom resided in the Tohatchi region and were well acquainted with each other's families. The first chart includes these two wives and their children. The second and third charts trace the families of Manuelito and Asdzáá Tł'ógi's two daughters, with Dághá Chíí be Asdzáá's children on the second chart and Ałk'iníbaa's children on the third. The fourth and fifth charts indicate the lineage of the grandparents whom I interviewed. As noted in these charts, the grandparents are descended from one of Manuelito and Asdzáá Tł'ógi's two daughters.

An interesting aspect of creating the lineage charts was my work with genealogist Cheri Bytheway to modify genealogy chart designs that were intended to trace families through the paternal line. As I consulted with various grandparents, uncles, and aunts, I was sometimes given different information on the same person for such items as names, dates of birth and death, the order of siblings, and the names of husbands. It was interesting to listen to the conversation as relatives discussed their ancestors.

One of the reasons I include these charts is to remind us Tł'ógi of our kin relationships to each other. Also, to preserve privacy and confidentiality, I trace lineage only up to my grandparents' generation. I also include birth dates and dates of death if they are available to me. I want to provide the descendants with the charts so that they will understand the relationships of their grandparents, and I include my own lineage as well.

I appreciate the input and encouragement provided by Larson Manuelito, who is descended from Manuelito and Asdzáá Tsin sikaadnii and whose grandfather was Naaltsoos Neiyéhí. Of course, any mistakes are solely my own, and I provide these charts in the hope that my relatives will develop the lineage by adding their own family and relatives to them.

Descendants of Manuelito [Hastiin Ch'il Hajin] (---)

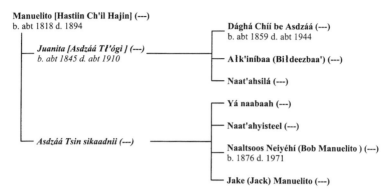

Manuelito [Hastiin Ch'il Hajin] (---)
b. abt 1818 d. 1894

Juanita [Asdzáá Tł'ógi] (---)
b. abt 1845 d. abt 1910

Dághá Chíí be Asdzáá (---)
b. abt 1859 d. abt 1944

Ałk'iníbaa (Biłdeezbaa') (---)

Naat'ahsilá (---)

Yá naabaah (---)

Naat'ahyisteel (---)

Asdzáá Tsin sikaadnii (---)

Naaltsoos Neiyéhí (Bob Manuelito) (---)
b. 1876 d. 1971

Jake (Jack) Manuelito (---)

Descendants of Dághá chíí be Asdzáá (---)

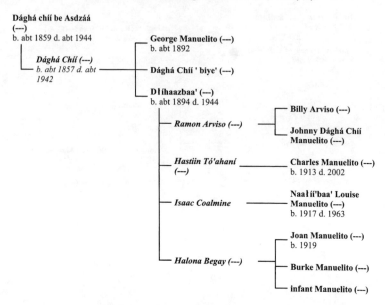

Dághá chíí be Asdzáá (---)
b. abt 1859 d. abt 1944

Dághá Chíí (---)
b. abt 1857 d. abt 1942

George Manuelito (---)
b. abt 1892

Dághá Chíí ' biye' (---)

Dłíhaazbaa' (---)
b. abt 1894 d. 1944

Ramon Arviso (---)

Billy Arviso (---)

Johnny Dághá Chíí Manuelito (---)

Hastiin Tó'ahaní (---)

Charles Manuelito (---)
b. 1913 d. 2002

Isaac Coalmine

Naałíí'baa' Louise Manuelito (---)
b. 1917 d. 1963

Halona Begay (---)

Joan Manuelito (---)
b. 1919

Burke Manuelito (---)

infant Manuelito (---)

Descendants of Naałíí'baa' Louise Manuelito (---)

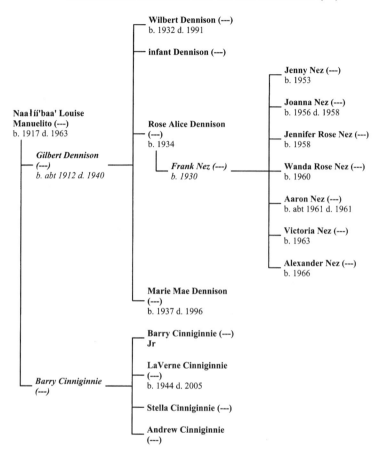

Naałíí'baa' Louise Manuelito (---)
b. 1917 d. 1963

Gilbert Dennison (---)
b. abt 1912 d. 1940

Wilbert Dennison (---)
b. 1932 d. 1991

infant Dennison (---)

Rose Alice Dennison (---)
b. 1934

Frank Nez (---)
b. 1930

Marie Mae Dennison (---)
b. 1937 d. 1996

Jenny Nez (---)
b. 1953

Joanna Nez (---)
b. 1956 d. 1958

Jennifer Rose Nez (---)
b. 1958

Wanda Rose Nez (---)
b. 1960

Aaron Nez (---)
b. abt 1961 d. 1961

Victoria Nez (---)
b. 1963

Alexander Nez (---)
b. 1966

Barry Cinniginnie (---)

Barry Cinniginnie (---) Jr

LaVerne Cinniginnie (---)
b. 1944 d. 2005

Stella Cinniginnie (---)

Andrew Cinniginnie (---)

Descendants of Ałk'iníbaa (Biłdeezbaa') (---)

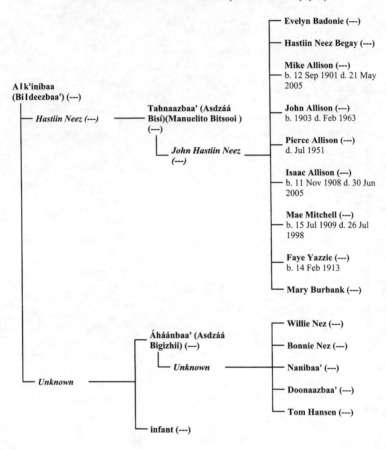

Ałk'iníbaa
(Biłdeezbaa') (---)

— *Hastiin Neez (---)* ——— Tahnaazbaa' (Asdzáá Bisí)(Manuelito Bitsooi) (---)

       John Hastiin Neez (---)

— Evelyn Badonie (---)

— Hastiin Neez Begay (---)

— Mike Allison (---)
b. 12 Sep 1901 d. 21 May 2005

— John Allison (---)
b. 1903 d. Feb 1963

— Pierce Allison (---)
d. Jul 1951

— Isaac Allison (---)
b. 11 Nov 1908 d. 30 Jun 2005

— Mae Mitchell (---)
b. 15 Jul 1909 d. 26 Jul 1998

— Faye Yazzie (---)
b. 14 Feb 1913

— Mary Burbank (---)

— *Unknown* ——— Áháánbaa' (Asdzáá Bigizhii) (---)

       Unknown

— Willie Nez (---)

— Bonnie Nez (---)

— Nanibaa' (---)

— Doonaazbaa' (---)

— Tom Hansen (---)

— infant (---)

Descendants of Ałk'iníbaa (Biłdeezbaa') (---)

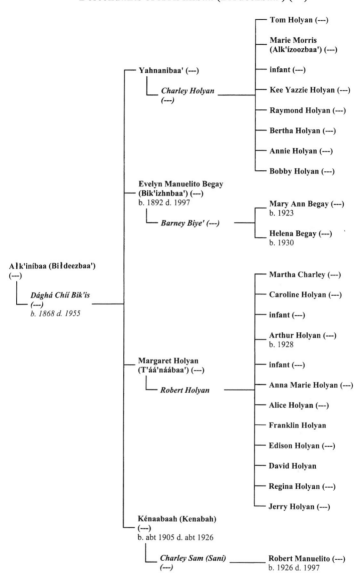

Tom Holyan (---)

Marie Morris
(Alk'ízoozbaa') (---)

infant (---)

Yahnanibaa' (---)

Kee Yazzie Holyan (---)

*Charley Holyan
(---)*

Raymond Holyan (---)

Bertha Holyan (---)

Annie Holyan (---)

Bobby Holyan (---)

**Evelyn Manuelito Begay
(Bik'izhnbaa')** (---)
b. 1892 d. 1997

Mary Ann Begay (---)
b. 1923

Barney Biye' (---)

Helena Begay (---)
b. 1930

Ałk'iníbaa (Biłdeezbaa')
(---)

*Dághá Chíí Bik'is
(---)*
b. 1868 d. 1955

Martha Charley (---)

Caroline Holyan (---)

infant (---)

Arthur Holyan (---)
b. 1928

**Margaret Holyan
(T'áá'náábaa')** (---)

infant (---)

Anna Marie Holyan (---)

Robert Holyan

Alice Holyan (---)

Franklin Holyan

Edison Holyan (---)

David Holyan

Regina Holyan (---)

Jerry Holyan (---)

Kénaabaah (Kenabah)
(---)
b. abt 1905 d. abt 1926

*Charley Sam (Sani)
(---)*

Robert Manuelito (---)
b. 1926 d. 1997

Notes

Chapter 1. Introduction

1. James, *Indian Blankets and Their Makers*, 112.

2. For spellings of Navajo words, I rely on Austin and Lynch, *Saad Ahaah Sinil*; and Wall and Morgan, *Navajo-English Dictionary*. Roseann Willink and Marilyn Help Hood were very generous in assisting me with Navajo spellings. Any errors I have made in translating or spelling Navajo words and phrases are my own. When referring to a specific work that utilizes Navajo words, I use the spelling preferred by the author. I find written Navajo and especially the dictionaries confusing and unfriendly to the average Navajo. Even though teachers of the Navajo language insist that there is a standard orthography, Navajo language teachers teach the written word differently. I look forward to the day when a Navajo language scholar or linguist creates a user-friendly orthography.

3. Juanita's dress is featured in Whitaker, *Common Threads*, 59. See also Whitaker, *Southwest Textiles*, 55–57, 206, 207.

4. Navajo textile studies provide histories, classifications, and descriptions of the various textiles that Navajo weavers have created. See, for example, Hedlund, "'More Survival than an Art.'"

5. James, *Indian Blankets and Their Makers*, 118.

6. See, for example, Lipps, *Little History of the Navajos*.

7. For example, at a Navajo Studies conference, anthropologist James Faris delivered a presentation in which he noted that Navajos and the specialists who study them often come to sharp disagreements over Navajo beliefs, values, and ways of being. Faris suggests that Navajo Studies scholars "scrutinize carefully non-Navajo explanations, and consider more carefully ways

of comprehending and understanding Navajo truths *on their own terms.*" See Faris, "Taking Navajo Truths Seriously," 182, 183.

8. Lyon, "Navajos in the Anglo-American Historical Imagination"; and "Navajos in the American Historical Imagination."

9. Trask, *From a Native Daughter*; Linda T. Smith, *Decolonizing Methodologies*; Stevenson, "Decolonizing Tribal Histories"; Cruikshank, "Images of Society," 20–41; and *Social Life of Stories*; Waziyatawin A. Wilson, *Remember This!*; Andrea Smith, *Conquest*; and Said, *Orientalism.*

10. Bsumek, "Navajos as Borrowers."

11. Rappaport, *Politics of Memory.*

12. I base this information on oral histories and Richard Van Valkenburgh's genealogy chart in the Navajo Land Claims Papers, Navajo Nation Library, Window Rock, Ariz.

13. Said, *Culture and Imperialism*, xii.

14. There are different meanings attached to Dinétah and Diné Bikéyah. Dinétah most often refers to the sacred ground that lies between the four sacred mountains as well as the region where the ancestors emerged from the lower worlds. Diné Bikéyah, which means Navajo Land, is also used to refer to our territory and usually refers to lands within the four sacred mountains and to the present Navajo Nation.

15. For English versions of Navajo creation narratives, see Zolbrod, *Diné Bahane'*; Yazzie, *Navajo History*; and Matthews, *Navaho Legends.*

16. Jim, "Moment in My Life," 232.

17. Brugge, "Navajo Prehistory and History," 489–501.

18. Spicer, *Cycles of Conquest.*

19. Forbes, *Apache, Navaho, and Spaniard.*

20. Young, *Role of the Navajo*, 19–23.

21. McNitt, *Navajo Wars*; Brugge, *Navajos in the Catholic Church Records*; Brooks, "'This Evil,'" 97–121; "Violence, Justice, and State Power," 23–60; and *Captives and Cousins.*

22. Locke, *Book of the Navajo*; Sundberg, *Dinétah*; Iverson, *Diné*; and Gerald Thompson, *Army and the Navajo.*

23. Gerald Thompson, *Army and the Navajo.*

24. See, for example, Broderick H. Johnson, *Navajo Stories of the Long Walk Period.*

25. Alexie, "Redeemers"; and "American Indian Filmmaker/Writer Talks."

26. American Indian and Alaska Native Population 2000

27. For studies of Navajo removal from Big Mountain, see Kammer, *Second Long Walk*; Brugge, *Navajo-Hopi Land Dispute*; and Benedek, *The Wind Won't Know Me.*

28. Tapahonso, *Sáanii Dahataał*, 3, 4.

29. Cruikshank, "Images of Society"; Cohen, "Undefining of Oral Tradi-

tion"; Faris and Walters, "Navajo History"; Pratt, "Some Navajo Relations"; Morrow and Schneider, *When Our Words Return*; Hill, *History, Power, and Identity*; Angela C. Wilson, "Grandmother to Granddaughter," 27–36; Waziyatawin A. Wilson, *Remember This!*; and Nabokov, "Native Views of History," 1–59.

30. Waziyatawin A. Wilson, *Remember This!*

31. See, for example, Hoffman and Johnson, *Navajo Biographies*; O. O. Howard, *Famous Indian Chiefs*; Waters, *Brave Are My People*; Kelly, *Navajo Roundup*; and McNitt, *Navajo Wars*.

32. In the last ten years, numerous studies of American Indians and photography have been published. See, for example, Lyman, *Vanishing Race*; Hales, *William Henry Jackson*; and Fleming and Luskey, *The North American Indians*. Faris's *Navajo and Photography* is one of the first studies that places photography and Navajos within a postcolonial framework. Other notable works that critically assess indigenous peoples and photography within postcolonial studies are Lippard, *Partial Recall*; Hartman, Silvester, and Hayes, *Colonising Camera*; Pinney and Peterson, *Photography's Other Histories*; and Ortiz, *Beyond the Reach*.

33. Angela C. Wilson, "Grandmother to Granddaughter," 29.

34. Juanita is listed in the 1880 census. Her name is faded and undecipherable. See Indian Census Rolls, 1885–1940, M595, #227 (with 1891 general schedule and letter, 1898). Listed with Manuelito and Juanita in 1885 are two daughters and four sons. Census data from 1910 at St. Michael's Mission, St. Michaels, Arizona, list Juanita with two daughters and two sons. The 1915 census lists Juanita and Manuelito's two daughters with their separate households. See Indian Census Rolls, 1885–1940, Navajo 1915 (with letters in 1919 and 1923) M595, #273, National Archives, Washington, D.C. Microfilm. Census data are confirmed by descendants of Juanita and Manuelito. Interviews are in the possession of the author.

Chapter 2. Recovering Diné Intellectual Traditions

1. Trouillot, *Silencing the Past*, 55, 56.

2. Native scholars have laid the groundwork for recovering our own intellectual traditions in a number of ways that span Western disciplines such as literature, history, and art. For example, Robert Warrior interprets the contributions of two Native intellectuals, Vine Deloria Jr. and John Joseph Matthews, and places their writings within a framework of reclaiming native sovereignty. Other scholars also look at how our intellectual traditions are grounded in traditional philosophies. See, for example, Warrior, *Tribal Secrets*; Womack, *Red on Red*; Cajete, *Look to the Mountain*; Vine Deloria, *God is Red*; and Cook-Lynn, *Why I Can't Read Wallace Stegner*.

3. Linda T. Smith in a pioneering study on how imperialism and colonialism have affected indigenous peoples provides an extended study of concepts of these terms and shows how they are used in relationship to describe the subjugation of indigenous peoples. See Smith, *Decolonizing Methodologies*, 19–35.

4. See Howard M. Bahr's *Diné Bibliography to the 1990s*.

5. Nasdijj, *Blood Runs Like a River; The Boy and Dog are Sleeping;* and *Geronimo's Bones*. Reporter Matthew Fleischer broke the story of Nasdijj's true identity in his story, "Navahoax."

6. Lyon, "Navajos in the Anglo-American Historical Imagination."

7. Sparks, "Land Incarnate."

8. Morgan, *Ancient Society*.

9. Halpern and McGreevy, *Washington Matthews*.

10. Faris, "Some Observations."

11. Ibid., 79.

12. See, for example, Matthews, "Cubature of the Skull," 171–72; and "On Measuring the Cubic Capacity of Skulls," 107–16.

13. Emerson, Afterword, 125–29.

14. Father Berard Haile's work spanned fifty years, and, although he published some of his studies, his death left others to complete and publish some of his projects. See, for example, Haile, *Origin Legend of the Navaho Enemyway*. See also, Bodo, *Tales of an Endishodi*.

15. Gladys Reichard's works include the following: *Spider Woman* (1934); *Navajo Shepherd and Weaver* (1936); *Social Life of the Navajo Indians* (1928); *Navaho Religion* (1963); and *Navaho Grammar* (1951). Her novel, based on her experiences and observations, is *Dezba: Woman of the Desert* (1939).

16. Reichard, *Navaho Religion;* and *Prayer: The Compulsive Word*.

17. Lamphere, "Gladys Reichard among the Navajo," 157–81.

18. A number of feminist scholars have critiqued the ways in which Western feminist approaches are inadequate in examining Native women's lives. For example, anthropologist Alice Kehoe observed, "The traditional picture of the Plains Indian woman is really that of an Irish housemaid of the late Victorian era clothed in a buckskin dress." See "Shackles of Tradition," 70.

19. For example, one textile expert once said to me that Willink and Zolbrod's assertion that bits of bird's feathers and pieces of buckskin embedded within some historical textiles are proof that the textiles had ceremonial use (and provide evidence that women possessed sacred knowledge) was unfounded. Rather, said the textile expert, what had probably happened was that a bird had flown over the textile and a bit of feather had become intertwined with the weaving. See Willink and Zolbrod, *Weaving a World*.

20. Frazier, "Genre, Methodology and Feminist Practice."

21. Oakes, *Where the Two Came to Their Father*.

22. O'Bryan, *Navaho Indian Myths*.

23. Zolbrod, *Diné Bahane'*.

24. Zolbrod, *Reading the Voice*; Swann, *Coming to Light*; *Native American Songs and Prose: An Anthology*; and Krupat, *New Voices in Native American Literary Criticism*.

25. Zolbrod, *Diné Bahane'*, 25.

26. Willink and Zolbrod, *Weaving a World*.

27. Ibid.

28. Zolbrod, "Squirrel Reddens his Cheeks."

29. Towner, *Defending the Dinétah*; Kelley and Francis, "Abalone Shell Buffalo People"; and Begay, "*Tsé Bíyah 'Anii'ahí*."

30. Faris, "Taking Navajo Truths Seriously."

31. Underhill, *The Navajos*, ix.

32. O'Neill, "Rethinking Modernity."

33. I find it very interesting to note how the Navajo newspaper, the *Navajo Times*, which began printing in 1958, was an important medium for conveying messages about the benefits of development, meaning transitions into modern American society. On a number of different levels, Navajos were bombarded with messages about the benefits of modernization. It would be interesting to examine how other scholars, like Clyde Kluckhohn and Leland Wyman, contemporaries of Underhill and Gladys Reichard, also disseminated beliefs about how development could benefit indigenous people like the Diné.

34. Fixico, *Rethinking American Indian History*. For New Western history, see Limerick, *Legacy of Conquest*; and Richard White, *It's Your Misfortune*.

35. Hagan, "New Indian History."

36. Vine Deloria, *Custer Died For Your Sins*.

37. Angela C. Wilson, "American Indian History?" 23.

38. Garrick Bailey and Roberta G. Bailey, *History of the Navajos*.

39. Klein, *Frontiers of Historical Imagination*, 10.

40. Brugge, *Navajos in the Catholic Church Records*.

41. Brooks, "This Evil"; and *Captives and Cousins*. New Mexico State historian Estévan Rael-Gálvez, in his dissertation, examined the presence and invisibility of Navajos taken as slaves into northern New Mexico households. See Rael-Gálvez, "Identifying Captivity and Capturing Identity."

42. Rael-Gálvez, "Testifying to the Present Tense."

43. Locke, *Book of the Navajo*; and Iverson, *Diné*.

44. Waziyatawin A. Wilson, "Reclaiming Our Humanity," 79.

45. Spicer, *Cycles of Conquest*.

46. White, *Roots of Dependency*, 219.

47. Iverson, *Diné*, 139–44.

48. Weisiger, "Changing Women"; and *Dreaming of Sheep in Navajo Country*.

49. Brugge, *Navajo-Hopi Land Dispute*. Other studies of the dispute

include the following: Benedek, *The Wind Won't Know Me*; and Churchill, "Genocide in Arizona," 135–72.

50. Brugge, *Navajo-Hopi Land Dispute*, ix.

51. Faris, *Navajo and Photography*, 18.

52. Regan, "Paper Faces," 124–43.

53. Bsumek, "Navajos as Borrowers."

54. Faris, "Toward an Archaeology of Navajo Anthropology." I appreciate the many conversations I have had with James regarding the archaeology of knowledge about Navajos.

55. Ibid., 14.

56. Cruikshank, "Images of Society," 20–41.

57. Ibid., 435.

58. My assumptions about the state of oral traditions among Navajos were informed by the still-existing disjuncture between a Western education, to which Navajo students are still subject, and its disengagement with Navajo beliefs and values, as well as with Navajo practice in homes. Like many Diné students, I experienced the chasm between Western education and what I was taught at home. My public school education tried hard to teach me to disregard Diné beliefs and practices. Over the years, I came to realize that my family operates within a Diné value system that is not articulated, but lived.

59. Cohen, "Undefining of Oral Tradition," 12.

60. Wheeler, "Indigenous Oral History."

61. Stevenson, "Every Word is a Bundle."

62. See, for example, Cajete, *Look to the Mountains*; Vine Deloria, *Red Earth, White Lies*; Angela C. Wilson, "Walking Into the Future"; Waziyatawin A. Wilson, *Remember This!*

63. Finnegan, "A Note on Oral Tradition and Historical Evidence," 128.

64. Ibid., 127.

65. Vansina, *Oral Tradition as History*, 12.

66. Angela C. Wilson, "Power of the Spoken Word," 103.

67. Florescano, *Memory, Myth, and Time in Mexico*, 177.

68. Stevenson, "Narrative Wisps of the Ochekwi Sipi Past," 122.

69. Florescano, *Memory, Myth, and Time in Mexico*, 177.

70. Ibid., 179.

71. In his review essay on Garrick Bailey and Roberta Glenn Bailey's Navajo history, Peter Iverson provides a list of oral histories and creation narratives published by the Navajo-controlled presses. Publications include Broderick H. Johnson, *Navajo Stories of World War II*; *Stories of Traditional Navajo Life and Culture*; Broderick H. Johnson and Ruth Roessel, *Navajo Livestock Reduction*; Ruth Roessel, *Women in Navajo Society*; Yazzie, *Navajo History*; and Robert A. Roessel, *Pictorial History of the Navajo*. See Iverson, "Continuity and Change in Navajo Culture."

72. Lee, "'I Came Here to Learn How to Be a Leader.'"

73. Pratt, "Some Navajo Relations," 151.

74. Jim, "Moment in My Life."

75. Ibid, 233.

76. See, for example, Tapahonso, *Blue Horses Rush In*; *A Breeze Swept Through*; *Sáanii Dahataał*; Ruth Roessel, *Women in Navajo Society*; Francisco, *Blue Horses for Navajo Women*; Belin, *From the Belly of My Beauty*; Tohe, *No Parole Today*; McCullough-Brabson and Help, *We'll Be in Your Mountains*; Morris, *From the Glittering World*.

77. Tapahonso, *Blue Horses Rush In*, 39–42.

78. Tapahonso, "Shisóí" and "'Ahidzískéii," in ibid., 3, 4, 7, and 8.

79. Witherspoon, *Navajo Kinship and Marriage*, 15.

80. Frank Mitchell, *Navajo Blessingway Singer*; Rose Mitchell, *Tall Woman*; McPherson, *Journey of Navajo Oshley*. Earlier autobiographies include Walter Dyk, *Son of Old Man Hat*; Dyk and Dyk, *Left Handed*; Leighton and Leighton, *Gregorio the Hand-Trembler*; Stewart, *A Voice in Her Tribe*; and Leighton, *Lucky the Navajo Singer*. Although there have been critical analyses of Native American autobiographies and life stories in general, Navajo ones have yet to be scrutinized and examined for the ways in which non-Navajo cultural viewpoints have shaped them.

81. Holiday and McPherson, *A Navajo Legacy*.

82. Smith, *Decolonizing Methodologies*, 39.

83. Ross, "Personalizing Methodology," 61.

84. Stevenson, "Every Word is a Bundle."

85. Sarris, "The Woman Who Loved a Snake," 145.

86. See Denetdale, "Chairmen, Presidents, and Princesses."

87. Linda T. Smith, *Decolonizing Methodologies*, 28.

Chapter 3. A Biographical Account of Manuelito

1. Born of either a Hispanic or white father, Dodge came to prominence because of his understanding of the English language and his business acumen. He has been often described as the bridge between the Navajo and white worlds. See Hoffman and Johnson, "Henry Chee Dodge," in *Navajo Biographies*; and Brugge, "Henry Chee Dodge."

2. Correll, "Manuelito, Navajo *Naat'anni*."

3. Johansen and Grinde, *Encyclopedia of Native American Biography*.

4. McNitt, *Navajo Wars*.

5. O. O. Howard, *Famous Indian Chiefs*; Hoffman and Johnson, *Navajo Biographies*; and Waters, *Brave Are My People*.

6. Trafzer, *Kit Carson Campaign*, 216.

7. Slotkin, *Regeneration through Violence*; Dippie, *Vanishing American*;

Berkhofer, *White Man's Indian*; and Phillip J. Deloria, *Indians in Unexpected Places*.

8. Interview with Bob Manuelito, by Correll and Brugge.

9. Forbes, *Africans and Native Americans*, 22.

10. Weisiger, "Origins of Navajo Pastoralism," 254.

11. Ibid., 257.

12. Young, *Role of the Navajo*, 12–16.

13. Towner, *Defending the Dinétah*.

14. Sando, *Pueblo Nations*, 80.

15. McNitt, *Navajo Wars*, 18.

16. Hendricks and Wilson, *Navajos in 1705*.

17. Ibid., 21.

18. Ibid., 92, 93.

19. McNitt, *Navajo Wars*, 23.

20. Ibid., 23–41. See also, Reeve, "Navajo-Spanish Diplomacy."

21. Weisiger, "Origins of Navajo Pastoralism," 266–67.

22. Ibid., 267.

23. Bob Manuelito, interviewed by Correll and Brugge. My father, Frank Nez, a healer who is knowledgeable about Navajo ceremonies, elaborated on the practice of making medicine from animals, which was then placed in a Navajo person's mouth. Personal correspondence with Frank Nez, February 17, 2005.

24. McNitt, *Navajo Wars*, 120, 121. McNitt notes that information about Manuelito's family comes from testimonies collected for the Navajo Land Claims project by J. Lee Correll. See Eddie Nakai's testimony before the Indian Land Claim Commission in 1961. (*Navajo Tribe v. U.S.*, Docket 229, 2516–18.) Navajo Land Claims papers are housed in the Navajo Nation Library. See also Correll, "Manuelito, Navajo Naat'aani."

25. Cremony, *Life among the Apaches*, 30, 308. Ralph H. Agle makes note of Cremony's observation in his "Federal Control of the Western Apaches."

26. William F. Arny to G. Edwin Dudley, March 2, 1874, New Mexico Supt., 1849–80 Roll 22, 1874, National Archives; and Bender, *New Hope for the Indians*, 112–14.

27. (W. B.) Truax, "Conversation with Manuelito, War Chief of the Navajos; Lorenzo (Hubbell) and Jesus (Arviso) Interpreters. 25 September 1874," Bureau of Ethnology, manuscript no. 3247, National Anthropological Archives, Smithsonian Institution.

28. The Enemy Way is still performed today for soldiers who have returned from wars, including Vietnam and the Persian Gulf. The ceremony is based on the stories of the Hero Twins and their slaying of the monsters. The ceremony is also performed for those who have been in contact with the enemy. It is more popularly known as the squaw dance, which is a derogatory term.

29. Bighorse, *Bighorse the Warrior*, xxiv.

30. Ibid., 3.

31. Brugge, "Vizcarra's Navajo Campaign of 1823."

32. McNitt, *Navajo Wars*, 65.

33. Ibid., 54.

34. Lynn R. Bailey, *Indian Slave Trade*, 84.

35. Van Valkenburgh, "Last Powow of the Navajo."

36. Van Valkenburgh, "Massacre in the Mountains," 18.

37. Ibid., 22.

38. Hoffman and Johnson, "Antonio Cebolla Sandoval," in *Navajo Biographies*, 28–57; Correll, "Antonio Sandoval." See also, chapters, "Cebolleta and the Diné Ana'aii"; "Mexican Rule"; and "The Many Faces of Sandoval," in McNitt, *Navajos Wars*.

39. Brooks, "Violence, Justice, and State Power," 25–38.

40. Ibid., 39.

41. Gregg, *Commerce of the Prairies*. Quoted in Sparks, "Land Incarnate," 143.

42. Sparks, "Land Incarnate," 142.

43. Dodge, "Between the United States Government and the Navajo Indian Tribe."

44. McNitt, *Navajo Wars*, 95.

45. Kearny's Proclamation is in House Executive Document 19, 29th Congress, 2d sess., 21. See also, Trafzer, *Anglo Expansionists and Navajo Raiders*, 6.

46. Trafzer, *Anglo Expansionists and Navajo Raiders*, 9.

47. Ibid., 6; McNitt, *Navajo Wars*, 118; Hughes, *Doniphan's Expedition*, 84, 85.

48. Hoffman and Johnson, "Manuelito," in *Navajo Biographies*, 94.

49. McNitt, *Navajo Wars*, 136, 137.

50. Hoffman and Johnson, "Narbona," in *Navajo Biographies*, 26; McNitt, *Navajo Wars*; Utter, "Death of a Navajo Patriot."

51. Wilkins, *The Navajo Political Experience*, 206, 223–26.

52. McNitt, *Navajo Wars*, 319.

53. Brooks to Asst. Adj. Gen., April 4, 1858. Cited in Correll, *Through White Men's Eyes*, 118, 119.

54. McNitt, *Navajo Wars*, 316.

55. Ibid., 316, 317.

56. Correll, "Navajo History: Manuelito."

57. Ibid., 7.

58. Brooks to Asst. Adj. Gen., May 30 and June 25, 1858. Cited in Correll, *Through White Men's Eyes*, 129, 130, and Correll, "Navajo History: Manuelito, 1833."

59. Brooks to Asst. Adj. Gen., June 16, 1858. Cited in Correll, *Through White Men's Eyes*, 130–32.

60. Brooks to Asst. Adj. Gen., July 15 and 16 postscript, 1858, cited in Correll, *Through White Men's Eyes*, 133. Agent Samuel Yost, who arrived at Fort Defiance, wrote a letter to Collins and gave another explanation for the killing of the black slave. According to Yost, the Navajo man who had killed Jim did the deed out of frustration related to his relationship with "one of his women." Yost to Collins, August 31 and September 3, 1858, cited in Correll, *Through White Men's Eyes*, 148, 149.

61. For an excellent discussion of the origins of race as a classification system, racism, and the evolution of white Americans' sense of superiority over other races, see Horsman, *Race and Manifest Destiny*.

62. Dixon S. Miles, Order No. 3, September 4, 1858, cited in Correll, *Through White Men's Eyes*, 151.

63. Iverson, *Diné*, 46, 47.

64. Ibid., 47.

65. Ibid. See military reports from Shepherd to Wilkins, May 7, 1860, and Nichols to Fauntleroy, July 14 and 21, 1860. Cited in Correll, *Through White Men's Eyes*, 386–92.

66. Gerald Thompson, *Army and the Navajo*, 7–9.

67. Carleton to Thomas, September 6, 1863, cited in Kelly, *Navajo Roundup*, 56–57.

68. Carleton to Carson, September 19, 1863, cited in Kelly, *Navajo Roundup*, 52.

69. Trafzer, *Kit Carson Campaign*, 102.

70. Ibid., 167.

71. Broderick H. Johnson, *Navajo Stories of the Long Walk Period*, 200, 201. Eli Gorman's story is also referenced in Trafzer, *Kit Carson Campaign*, 158–60.

72. Trafzer, *Kit Carson Campaign*, 169–73.

73. Carleton to Lorenzo Thomas, "Report of the Condition of the Navajo Prisoners of War at the Basque Redondo, New Mexico, Santa Fe, N.M.," March 12, 1864, Appendix in Lipps, *Little History of the Navajos*, 122–27.

74. Trafzer, *Kit Carson Campaign*, 198–200.

75. Ibid.

76. Report of Lieut. Col. J. C. Shaw, *Santa Fe (N.M.) Weekly Gazette*, July 29, 1868.

77. Trafzer, *Kit Carson Campaign*, 212.

78. Ibid., 152, 153.

79. Carleton to unnamed addressee, March 21, 1865, cited in Correll, *Through White Men's Eyes*, 92, 93.

80. Carleton, March 21, 1865, Condition of the Indian Tribes, 221, Frank

McNitt Collection, Box 15–25 (17) Bosque Redondo 3, Serial # 10683, New Mexico State Records Center and Archives. Santa Fe, N.M.

81. Bighorse, *Bighorse the Warrior*, 21.

82. Ibid.

83. See ibid.; Broderick Johnson, *Navajo Stories of the Long Walk Period*; Taphonso, *Blue Horses Rush In*; and *Sáani Dahataał*; Morris, *From the Glittering World*: Tohe, *No Parole Today*; Frank Mitchell, *Navajo Blessingway Singer*; Jim, "Moment in My Life"; Willink and Zolbrod, *Weaving a World*; Rose Mitchell, *Tall Woman*; Parsons, *Dzání Yázhí Naazbaa'*.

84. Andrea Smith, "Rape and the War against Native Women," 65.

85. See, for example, Primeaux and Mike, "Blood, Sweat and Tears"; and Cody, "The Return Home." Navajo educator Marilyn Help has a CD of Navajo traditional songs, which includes a song titled "Shii Naa Sha," composed to remember the people's return from Hwéeldi. See McCullough-Brabson and Help, *We'll Be in Your Mountains*.

86. Testimony of Dághá Chíí Bi'kis, January 16, 17, 1951, Land Claims Commission Papers, J. Lee Correll Papers, Navajo Nation Library, Window Rock, Ariz.

87. Gerald Thompson gives an excellent report of the day-to-day operations at Bosque Redondo. See Gerald Thompson, *Army and the Navajo*.

88. Barboncito, "Council Proceedings," in Link, *The Navajo Treaty*, 2.

89. Ibid., 5.

90. Iverson, *Diné*, 66.

91. Lavender, *The Southwest*, 181, 182.

92. Lynn R. Bailey, *Bosque Redondo*, 197.

93. Ibid., 197–99.

94. See Bill Dovovan's review of Martin Link's booklet, "Long Walk Steeped in Myths." See also Jennifer Nez Denetdale's response to Link's assertions, "The Long Walk," and Link's letter to the editor in reply to Denetdale, "The Long Walk and Academic Freedom."

95. Hoffman and Johnson, *Navajo Biographies*, 108.

96. Waters, *Brave Are My People*, 120.

97. William H. Moore, *Chiefs, Agents, and Soldiers*, 272, 273.

98. Babcock, "'A New Mexican Rebecca,'" 428.

99. Interview of Bob Manuelito, by Correll and Brugge.

100. Broder, *Shadows on Glass*, 44.

101. Mamie N. Maxwell to Richard Van Valkenburgh, October 17, 1940, Richard Van Valkenburgh Papers, 1904–1957, MS 831 Series 1, File 45, Arizona Historical Society, Tucson, Ariz. There are several accounts of how Manuelito received the wound in his chest. For example, Gar and Maggy Packard, who published a collection of Wittick's photographs, declare, "In 1849 he [Manuelito] witnessed the senseless killing of his father-in-law by troops under the

command of Colonel John Washington. A few years later, a raiding party of New Mexicans wounded Manuelito with a musket ball that cut a furrow across his chest. He called it his scar of honor." See Packard and Packard, *Southwest 1880*, 26.

102. Broder, *Shadows on Glass*, 44.

103. Gar Packard and Maggy Packard propose that Manuelito desired the silver coins for decoration. See Packard and Packard, *Southwest 1880*, 26.

104. Hoffman and Johnson, "Manuelito," in *Navajo Biographies*, 101.

105. Locke, *Book of the Navajo*, 409.

106. William H. Moore, *Chiefs, Agents, and Soldiers*, 258, 259; and Pavlik, "Short History of Navajo Education."

107. Fuchs and Havighurst, *To Live on This Earth*, 39, 246.

108. Hildegard Thompson, *The Navajos' Long Walk for Education*, 149. See also, Robert A. Roessel, *Navajo Education, 1948–1978*, 39–43.

109. William Nakai, interview by author, October 10, 2005; Nofchissey and Burson, "Go My Son."

110. Clark, keynote address at Fifteenth Annual Navajo Studies Conference, October 2004; personal communication with the author, September 7, 2005.

111. Reproduced from Indian Agent's Letterbook, FD-4A, 1888, J. Lee Correll Papers, Navajo Nation Library, Window Rock, Ariz. The original is deposited in the Arizona Historical Society, Tucson, Ariz. Richard Van Valkenburgh also makes note of this speech and attributed it to Manuelito when he heard of Riordan's resignation. Van Valkenburgh, "The History of the Navajo Nation," chap. 4: "A Period of Dishonor: 1880–1884," MS 831 Papers 1880–1946, Box 4 S2, Folder 111, Arizona Historical Society, Tucson, Ariz.

112. Van Valkenburgh, "History of the Navajo Nation," 86, 87.

113. John H. Bowman to Commissioner, Navajo Agency, September 3, 1884, in U.S. Office of Indian Affairs, *Annual Report*, 135.

114. William H. Moore, *Chiefs, Agents, and Soldiers*, 259.

115. Bob Manuelito, interview by Correll and Brugge.

116. Ibid.

117. Waters, *Brave Are My People*, 121.

118. Durham, "Geronimo!" 56.

119. Duran, "Indigenous Versus Colonial Discourse," 112.

120. Peterson Zah, interview by author, October 13, 2005.

121. Bob Manuelito, interview by Correll and Brugge.

122. Owens, *Mixedblood Messages*, 18.

Chapter 4. The Imperial Gaze

1. James, *What the White Race May Learn*, 212.

2. Laura J. Moore, "Elle Meets the President," 350–74.

3. Navajo women did not fit into stereotypical perceptions of American Indian women, and non-Indian observers often had difficulty attempting to characterize the nature of Navajo women's roles. See, for example, Sparks, "Land Incarnate"; and Denetdale, "Representing Changing Woman."

4. Bighorse, *Bighorse the Warrior*, 53.

5. Locke, *Book of the Navajo*, 392.

6. Ibid. See also Brooks, "Violence, Justice, and State Power," 23–60; and *Captives and Cousins*, 351. John H. Bowman, to Commissioner of Indian Affairs, September 3, 1884, in U.S. Office of Indian Affairs, *Annual Report*, 177–80.

7. Faye Yazzie, interview by author, September 10, 1993; and Mike Allison Sr., interview by author, October 10, 1996.

8. Faris, *Navajo and Photography*, 12.

9. Said, *Orientalism*; Graham-Brown, *Images of Women*; Hartmann, Silvester, and Hayes, *Colonising Camera*; Pinney and Peterson, *Photography's Other Histories*.

10. Lyman, *Vanishing Race*. See also Albers and James, "Travel Photography"; Fleming and Luskey, *North American Indians*; Bush and Mitchell, *Photograph and the American Indian*; Broder, *Shadows on Glass*; and Jim Johnson, *Spirit Capture*.

11. Buscombe, "Photographing the Indian," 29–45.

12. Banta and Hinsley, *From Site to Sight*; and Faris, *Navajo and Photography*.

13. Babcock, "By Way of Introduction," 384.

14. Babcock, "'A New Mexican Rebecca,'" 401.

15. Weigle and Babcock, *Great Southwest*; and Dilworth, *Imagining Indians*.

16. Dilworth, *Imagining Indians*.

17. Green, "Pocahontas Perplex," 182–92. See also, Smits, "'The Squaw Drudge'"; and Smith-Roseberg, "Captured Subjects/Savage Others."

18. Albers and James, "Illusion and Illumination."

19. Day, *Heart of the Circle*.

20. Babcock, "'A New Mexican Rebecca,'" 404, 405.

21. Ibid., 402.

22. Bernardin et al., *Trading Gazes*; Carol J. Williams, *Framing the West*; and Morrissey and Jensen, *Picturing Arizona*.

23. Jacobs, "Maternal Colonialism," 455.

24. Faris, "Photographing the Navajo."

25. See, for example, M'Closkey, "Weaving and Mothering," 115–27; and *Swept Under the Rug*; Willink and Zolbrod, *Weaving a World*. Most scholars place Navajo textiles within a Navajo history framework that focuses on outside forces that created these textiles, although some are paying attention to how Navajo weavers themselves view their art and labor as they produce these rugs. See for example, Hedlund, "Give-and-Take," 53–77; Bonar, *Woven by the Grandmothers*; and Coulter, *Navajo Saddle Blankets*.

26. Robert A. Roessel, *Pictorial History of the Navajo*.

27. Ibid.

28. James, *Indian Blankets and Their Makers*, 112–18.

29. Faris, *Navajo and Photography*, 75.

30. Albers and James, "Illusion and Illumination," 45.

31. Faris, *Navajo and Photography*, 56.

32. Faye Yazzie, interview by author, September 10, 1993.

33. Locke, *Book of the Navajo*, 398.

34. O. O. Howard, *Famous Indian Chiefs*, 148.

35. Bender, *New Hope for the Indians*, 55.

36. Williamson, "Family, Education, Photography," 236–44.

37. Wexler, *Tender Violence*, 9.

38. Ibid., 65, 66.

39. Stoler, "Carnal Knowledge and Imperial Power, 51–101.

40. Ibid., 76, 77.

41. Viola, *Diplomats in Buckskins*.

42. William F. Arny to Edward P. Smith September 28, 1874, New Mexico Supt., National Archives, Office of Indian Affairs, RG 75, J. Lee Correll Papers, Navajo Nation Library, Window Rock, Ariz.

43. Martha A. Sandweiss argues that earlier scholarship on photographs and American Indians have painted simplistic portrayals of native peoples as victims who have little or no control in the photographic endeavors. She asserts that photographic encounters between photographers and native peoples should be seen as collaborative endeavors. See Sandweiss, *Print the Legend*.

44. Faris, *Navajo and Photography*, 68.

45. *Navajo Times*, November 22, 1961, 2.

46. See *Textiles of the North American Southwest*.

47. Personal correspondence with Felicia Pickering, August 1, 2003. I am grateful to the Smithsonian Museum Support Center's staff for taking the time to show me artifacts that once belonged to Juanita and Manuelito.

48. In a review of an exhibit of Native American arts and crafts that featured the American Flag, David Robbins explained that Natives' incorporation of the American flag into their work reflects a shift in the meaning of their handiwork from an "exchange value" to a "use value." Robbins suggests that

native artists attached a "rich if ambiguous interplay of uses and meanings," including the merging of native warrior traditions with American patriotism, natives' "ambiguous though dignified reconciliation" to U.S. power, and the taking of power on multiple levels often associated with the American flag. See Robbins, "American Indian and the American Flag," 28, 57.

49. *Daily New Mexican*, November 16, 18, 20, 1874; and Murphy, *Frontier Crusader*, 227.

50. Dilworth, *Imagining Indians*, 125.

51. Ibid., 125–26.

52. E. H. Plummer to Whom it May concern, April 26, 1894, letter on behalf of Shizie; and E. H. DeVorn, note on behalf of Shizie, September 19, 1906. Letter and note in the possession of author, previously in the possession of Charles Manuelito, Toadlena, N.M.

53. James, *Indians of the Painted Desert Region*.

54. Ibid., 146.

55. James, *Indian Blankets and Their Makers*, vi.

56. Ibid, 149.

57. Ibid.

58. Ibid., 118.

59. Dilworth, *Imagining Indians*, 137.

60. James, *What the White Race May Learn from the Indian*.

61. Ibid., 212.

62. A recent publication about Elle and her work with the Fred Harvey Company focuses on how she was represented as an icon of the Southwest. Interestingly, the author reiterates stereotypes about Navajos and identity, writing, "Although outwardly exhibiting many of the cultural attributes of a Navajo, there is question about her [Elle's] actual ethnic heritage." The author goes on: "If this account is true, it would be ironic that the icon most used by the Harvey Company to depict Navajos was not of Navajo descent." The Euro-American constructions of race, ethnicity, and identity have obscured how other cultures addresses identity. See Kathleen L. Howard, "Weaving a Legend," 129.

63. Lippard, *Partial Recall*; and the *American Indian Culture and Research Journal* 20, no. 3 (1996), in which native photographers and writers present their perspectives on Native Americans and photographs in several articles.

64. O'Neill, *Working the Navajo Way*, 154.

65. Dilworth, *Imagining Indians*, 8.

Chapter 5. Stories of Asdzáá Tł'ógi

1. Ortiz, *Woven Stone*, 20.

2. Witherspoon, *Navajo Kinship and Marriage*, 15.

3. Ibid., 16.

4. Indian Scout Files, J. Lee Correll Papers, Navajo Nation Library, Willow Rock, Ariz. Dághá Chíí is named in the Indian Scout papers as Pete Dugal Chee.

5. It needs to be noted that some of my grandparents, mostly the descendants of Ałk'iníbaa, are also devoted Catholics. The Catholic Church in Tohatchi has a very strong presence in the Tohatchi community. As Nancy Allison has pointed out to me, her parents, Mike Sr. and Anna, were devout Catholics who also looked to Diné teachings to raise their family. In many cases, Christianity and traditional religious practices are not dichotomous, but practiced simultaneously.

6. I have deliberately chosen to rely on published creation narratives, especially those by Navajo writers. Like other native scholars, I find divulging information about the sacred stories and ceremonies from my family, kin relations, and medicine people a violation of ethical and responsible research. I consciously did not inquire about sacred knowledge from my grandparents, and if references were made, I did not include them in my publications. Many members of the Navajo community practice the values found in the traditional stories.

7. I refer to Ethelou Yazzie's version of the Navajo creation narratives. Yazzie writes that there were four worlds. Other Navajos give another version in which there are five worlds. See Yazzie, *Navajo History*.

8. Kellogg, "Tenocha Mexica Women," 125.

9. Haile, *Women versus Men*.

10. Feminist scholars have taken as illustrations of complementarity creation stories such as the one about the argument between First Man and First Woman, their separation after the argument, and then their realization that, in order to survive, they must reconcile and work together. For one version of this argument, see Zolbrod, *Diné Bahane'*, 58–69.

11. Yazzie, *Navajo History*, 47–49.

12. I was fortunate to attend several sessions of storytelling by Earnest Harry Begay. With each session, the audience grew. The two hours allotted flew by as we listened attentively and with great appreciation. Sessions that I attended took place in February 2005.

13. Versions vary on identities of Changing Woman and White Shell Woman. Some say they are one and the same person, whereas others say they are two different women. Ethelou Yazzie says they are the same person, that Changing Woman was first known as White Shell Woman. See Yazzie, *Navajo History*, 49.

14. Witherspoon, *Navajo Kinship and Marriage*, 15, 16.

15. Ibid., 17.

16. Udel, "Revision and Resistance."

17. Yazzie, *Navajo History*, 54.

18. Ibid., 74.

19. Jim, "Moment in My Life," 232, 233.

20. Fairly recently, I did speak to one of my grandmothers, a descendent of Juanita's younger daughter, who told me that our grandmother had been a Mexican slave.

21. Brooks, *Captives and Cousins*, 331, 322.

22. Forbes, *Apache, Navaho, and Spaniard*. Jonathan Haas has raised questions about the prevailing assumption that early Diné caused Pueblos to abandon some of their villages. He points out that in the sixteenth century the forebears of the Diné simply did not have the technology to mount an assault on Pueblos who lived in well-protected villages, often atop mesa. See Haas, "Warfare among the Pueblos."

23. McNitt, *Navajo Wars*; Brugge, *Navajos in the Catholic Church Records*; Brooks, "'This Evil.'"

24. John Bowman to Commissioner of Indian affairs, September 3, 1884, in U.S. Office of Indian Affairs, *Annual Report*, 401.

25. Rael-Gálvez, "Identifying Captivity and Capturing Identity."

26. See, for example, Broderick H. Johnson, *Navajo Stories of the Long Walk Period*.

27. See, for example, Barker, "Indian USA"; Strong, "Transforming Outsiders"; Jaimes, "American Racism"; and Naylor, "Playing Indian?"

28. Franciscan Fathers, *Ethnologic Dictionary of the Navaho Language*, 428.

29. Mike Allison, interview by author, October 10, 1996.

30. Waziyatawin A. Wilson explains the significance of the phrase *long ago* for native people who are part of an oral tradition. See *Remember This!* 31, 32.

31. Broderick H. Johnson, *Navajo Stories of the Long Walk Period*; Bighorse, *Bighorse the Warrior*; and Iverson, *Diné*.

32. Zolbrod, *Diné Bahane'*, 46, 47.

33. Perdue, "Writing the Ethnohistory of Native Women," 73–86; and *Cherokee Women*.

34. Sarris, "The Woman Who Loved a Snake," 143.

35. Richard White, *Roots of Dependency*, 215–20.

36. Navajo leaders to Edward T. Smith, December 1873, J. Lee Correll Papers, Navajo Nation Library, Window Rock, Ariz.

37. William F. Arny, on behalf of Navajo leaders, to Edward T. Smith, February 11 and December 29, 1873, J. Lee Correll Papers, Navajo Nation Library, Window Rock, Ariz.

38. *Washington (D.C.) Evening Star*, December 3 and 4, 1874.

39. Bender, *New Hope for the Indians*, 124.

40. Dougal Chee Bikis, testimony before the Indian Land Claims Com-

mission, *Navajo Tribe vs. United States*, Docket 229, 1951, Serial 10683, Box 15–2517, Frank McNitt Papers, New Mexico State Records Center and Archives, Santa Fe, N.M.

41. Faye Yazzie, interview by author, September 10, 1993.

42. R. B. Morrison to Charles Ewing, December 10, 1874, quoted in Viola, *Diplomats in Buckskins*, 127.

43. For example, see Broderick H. Johnson, *Navajo Stories of the Long Walk Period*.

44. Mintz, *Tasting Food, Tasting Freedom*.

45. hooks, *Yearning*, 42.

46. Hughes, *Doniphan's*, 166–85; Young, *Role of the Navajo*, 32. See also Sparks, "Land Incarnate."

47. Franciscan Fathers, *Ethnologic Dictionary of the Navajo Language*, 424; and Van Valkenburgh, "Navajo Naat'aáni."

48. Locke, *Book of the Navajo*.

49. Joann Kinsel, interview by author, August 28, 1996.

50. Faye Yazzie, interview by author, September 10, 1993.

51. Charles Manuelito, interview by author, August 28, 1993.

52. E. H. Plummer to Whom It May Concern, April 27, 1894, in possession of the author.

53. Note from E. H. DeVorn on behalf of Shizie, September 19, 1906, in possession of the author.

54. Faye Yazzie, interview by author, October 21, 1997.

55. Ibid.

56. Mike Allison Sr., interview by author, October 10, 1996.

57. Ibid.

58. Faye Yazzie, interview by author, September 10, 1993.

59. Kathleen S. Bahr, "Strengths of Apache Grandmothers."

60. Kelley and Francis, *Navajo Sacred Places*, 224.

61. Kelley and Whitely, *Navajoland*.

62. Basso, *Wisdom Sits in Places*, 32, 33.

63. Angela C. Wilson, "Grandmother to Granddaughter," 514.

Chapter 6. Stories in the Land

1. Tsosie, "Changing Women."

2. Turner, "Significance of the Frontier," 199–227.

3. Yellow Bird, "Cowboys and Indians."

4. Merchant, *Death of Nature*; and Kolodny, *Lay of the Land*.

5. Merchant, *Earthcare*.

6. See, for example, McPherson, *Sacred Land*; and Vine Deloria, *God is Red*.

7. LaDuke, *All Our Relations*. See also, Grinde and Johansen, "Navajos and National Sacrifice," 204–17.

8. Andrea Smith, *Conquest*.

9. Basso, *Wisdom Sits in Places*, 4.

10. Watt, *Don't Let the Sun Step Over You*.

11. Momaday, *The Man Made of Words*, 39.

12. Kelley and Francis, *Navajo Sacred Places*.

13. Kelley and Francis, "Abalone Shell Buffalo People."

14. Begay, "Tsé Bíyah 'Anii'áhí," 54–60.

15. Charles Manuelito, interview by author, August 28, 1993.

16. Blu, "'Where Do You Stay At?'"

17. Ibid., 216.

18. O'Neil, "The 'Making' of the Navajo Worker."

19. Trennert, *White Man's Medicine*; and Davies, *Healing Ways*.

20. Trennert, *White Man's Medicine*, 96–100.

21. Ibid., 102.

22. Charles Manuelito, interview by author, 28 August 1993.

23. Rose Nez, interview by author, October 12, 1996.

24. Hagan, *Indian Police and Judges*, 26, 27.

25. See, for example, Blue, *Witch Purge of 1878*.

26. Collman, "Navajo Scouts."

27. Collman includes in his study a tabulation of scouts, including dates of service, age at time of service, dates of death, and dates when pensions were filed.

28. Dougal Chee Bikis, testimony before the Indian Claims Commission, *Navajo Tribe vs. United States of America*, Docket 229, 1951, Serial 10683, Box 15–2517, Frank McNitt Papers, Records Center, Santa Fe, N.M.

29. Charles Manuelito, interview by author, August 18, 1996.

30. Rose Nez, interview by author, October 12, 1996.

31. Ibid.

32. Wheeler, "Talking Back to Columbus."

33. Robert Manuelito, interview by author, October 26, 1997.

34. Tapahonso, *Sáanii Dahataał*, 19.

Selected Bibliography

Primary Sources

Archives and Photograph Collections

Arizona Historical Society, Tucson, Ariz.
    Richard Van Valkenburgh Papers
Autry National Center, Southwest Museum. Los Angeles, Calif.
    George Wharton James Photographs
National Archives. Washington, D.C.
    Indian Census Rolls, 1885–1940. M595. 692 Rolls.
    Indian Census Rolls, 1885–1940, Navajo 1915 (with letters in 1919 and 1923)
        M595, #273, National Archives. Washington, D.C. Microfilm.
    Indian Census Rolls, 1885–1940, Microcopy 595, Records of the Bureau of
        Indian Affairs, Record Group 75, National Archives (Washington,
        D.C.: National Archives and Record Service, 1965).
National Anthropological Archives. Smithsonian Institution. Washington, D.C.
Navajo Nation Library, Window Rock, Ariz.
    Navajo Land Claims Papers, J. Lee Correll Collection
New Mexico State Records Center and Archives. Santa Fe, N.M.
    Frank McNitt Papers
St. Michaels Mission, St. Michaels, Ariz.
    Archives
University of Arizona Library, Special Collections

Interviews and Personal Correspondence

Allison, Mike Sr. Interviews by author. Tape recordings. Tohatchi, N.M., October 10, 1996, and August 29, 1997.

Clark, Ferlin. Keynote address at Fifteenth Annual Navajo Studies Conference, Fort Lewis College, Durango, Colo., October 2004.

———. Personal communication with author. Albuquerque, N.M., September 7, 2005.

Holyan, Arthur. Interviews by author. Flagstaff, Ariz., May 22, 1998, and Grants, N.M., April 9, 2006.

Kinsel, Joan. Interviews by author. Tape recordings. Yah-Ta-Hey, N.M., August 28, 1996, and October 10, 1997.

Manuelito, Charles. Interviews by author. Tape recording. Toadlena, N.M., August 28, 1993, and August 18, 1996.

Manuelito, Robert. Interview by author. Tape recording. Tohatchi, N.M., October 26, 1997.

Nakai, William. Interview by author. Albuquerque, N.M., October 10, 2005.

Naaltsoos Neiyéhí (Bob Manuelito, or Manuelito Number Two). Interview by J. Lee Correll and David Brugge. Tape 18 T1S1. Office of Economic Opportunity Oral History Collection, Navajo Nation Library, Window Rock, Ariz., February 1966.

Nez, Frank. Personal correspondence with author. February 17, 2005.

Nez, Rose. Interview by author. Tape recording. Tohatchi, New Mexico, October 12, 1996.

Pickering, Felicia. Personal correspondence with author. August 1, 2003.

Yazzie, Faye. Interview by authors. Tape recordings. Tohatchi, New Mexico, September 10, 1993, and October 21, 1997.

Zah, Peterson. Interview by author. Phoenix, Ariz., October 13, 2005.

Song Recordings

Cody, Radmilla. "The Return Home." Song in *Seeds of Life: Traditional Songs of the Navajo*. Phoenix, Ariz.: Canyon Records, 2001.

Craig, Vincent, "Chief Manuelito." Song in music recording. N.p.: Muttonman Productions, n.d.

Nofchissey, Arlene, and Carnes Burson, "Go My Son." Song in *Go My Son* tape cassette. *Go My Son*. Phoenix, Ariz.: Canyon Records, 1988.

Primeaux, Verdell, and Johnny Mike. "Blood, Sweat and Tears." In *Hours Before Dawn: Harmonized Peyote Songs of the Navajo American Church*. Phoenix, Ariz.: Canyon Records, 2002.

Newspapers

Albuquerque Journal
Gallup (N.M.) Independent
LA Weekly
Navajo Times
Santa Fe (N.M.) Gazette
Washington (D.C.) Evening Star

Secondary Sources

Acrey, Bill P. *Navajo History: The Land and the People*. 1978. Reprint, Shiprock, N.M.: Department of Curriculum Materials Development, 1994.

Agle, Ralph. H. "Federal Control of the Western Apaches, 1848–1886." *New Mexico Historical Review* 14, no. 4 (1939): 309–65.

Albers, Patricia, and Beatrice Medicine. *The Hidden Half: Studies of Plains Indian Women*. New York: University Press of America, 1983.

Albers, Patricia, and William R. James. "Illusion and Illumination: Visual Images of American Indian Women in the West." In Susan Armitage and Elizabeth Jameson, eds., *The Women's West*. Norman: University of Oklahoma Press, 1987.

———. "Travel Photography: A Methodological Approach." *Annals of Tourism Research* 15, no. 1 (1988): 134–58.

Alexie, Sherman. "Redeemers: Sherman Alexie Talks about His Native American Heritage, the Challenges of Filmmaking, and the Dangers of Tribalism." Interview by Matt Dellinger. *The New Yorker*, April 23, 2003, http://www.newyorker.com/.

———. "American Indian Filmmaker/Writer Talks with Robert Capriccioso." Interview by Robert Capriccioso, March 23, 2003, http://www.identitytheory.com/.

American Indian and Alaska Native Population 2000. Washington, D.C.: U.S. Census Bureau. 2002. Online at http://www.census.gov/prod/2002pubs/c2bro1-15pdf.

Amsden, Charles A. *Navajo Weaving: Its Technique and History*. Salt Lake City: Peregrine Smith, 1975.

Anderson, Benedict. *Imagined Communities: Reflections on the Origin and Spread of Nationalism*. New York: Verso, 1991.

Austin, Martha, and Regina Lynch, eds. *Saad Ahaah Sinil: Dual Language/A Navajo-English Dictionary*. Rough Rock, Ariz.: Rough Rock Demonstration School, n.d.

Axtell, James. "The Ethnohistory of Early America: A Review Essay." *William and Mary Quarterly* 35, no. 1 (January 1978): 110–44.

Babcock, Barbara A. "By Way of Introduction." *Journal of the Southwest* 32 (winter 1990): 383–99.

———."'A New Mexican Rebecca': Imaging Pueblo Woman." *Journal of the Southwest* 32 (winter 1990): 400–37.

Babcock, Barbara A., and Nancy J. Parezo. *Daughters of the Desert: Women Anthropologists and the Native American Southwest, 1880–1980: An Illustrated Catalogue*. Albuquerque: University of New Mexico Press, 1988.

Bahr, Howard M. *Diné Bibliography to the 1990s: A Companion to the Navajo Bibliography of 1969*. Lanham. Md.: Scarecrow Press, 1999.

Bahr, Kathleen S. "The Strengths of Apache Grandmothers: Observations on Commitment, Culture and Caretaking." *Journal of Comparative Family Studies* 15, no. 2 (summer 1994): 233–48.

Bailey, Garrick, and Roberta Glenn Bailey. *A History of the Navajos: The Reservation Years*. Santa Fe, N.M.: School of American Research, 1986.

Bailey, Lynn R. *Indian Slave Trade in the Southwest: A Study of Slavetaking and the Traffic of Indian Captives*. Los Angeles, Calif.: Westernlore Press, 1966.

———. *Bosque Redondo: The Navajo Internment at Fort Sumner, New Mexico, 1863–68*. Tucson: Westernlore Press, 1998.

Banta, Melissa, and Curtis M. Hinsley. *From Site to Sight: Anthropology, Photography, and the Power of Imagery*. Cambridge, Mass.: Peabody Museum Press, 1986.

Barker, Joanne. "Indian USA." *Wicazo Sa Review* 18, no. 1 (spring 2003): 25–79.

Basso, Keith H. *Wisdom Sits in Places: Landscape and Language among the Western Apache*. Albuquerque: University of New Mexico Press, 1996.

Bataille, Gretchen M., and Kathleen Mullen Sands, eds. *American Indian Women: A Guide to Research*. New York: Garland, 1991.

Begay, Richard. "Tsé Bíyah 'Anii'ahí: Chaco Canyon and Its Place in Navajo History." In David Grants Nobel, ed., *In Search of Chaco: New Approaches to an Archaeological Enigma*. Santa Fe, N.M.: School of American Research Press, 2004.

Belin, Esther. *From the Belly of My Beauty: Poems*. Tucson: University of Arizona Press, 1999.

Bender, Norman J. *New Hope for the Indians: The Grant Peace Policy and the Navajos in the 1870s*. Albuquerque: University of New Mexico Press, 1989.

Benedek, Emily. *The Wind Won't Know Me: A History of the Navajo-Hopi Land Dispute*. New York: Vintage Books, 1993.

Berkhofer, Robert F. "The Political Context of a New Indian History." *Pacific Historical Review* 40 (August 1971): 357–82.

————. *The White Man's Indian: Images of the American Indian from Columbus to the Present*. New York: Vintage Books, 1979.

Bernardin, Susan, Melody Graulich, Lisa MacFarlane, and Nicole Tonkovich, eds. *Trading Gazes: Euro-American Photographers and Native North Americans, 1880–1940*. New Brunswick, N.J.: Rutgers University Press, 2003.

Bighorse, Tiana. *Bighorse the Warrior*. Edited by Noel Bennett. Tucson: University of Arizona Press, 1990.

Bird, S. Elizabeth, ed. *Dressing in Feathers: The Construction of the Indian in American Popular Culture*. Boulder, Colo.: Westview Press, 1996.

Blu, Karen I. "'Where Do You Stay At?': Home Place and Community among the Lumbee." In Steven Feld and Keith H. Basso, eds., *Senses of Place*. Santa Fe, N.M.: School of American Research Press, 1996.

Blue, Martha. *The Witch Purge of 1878: Oral and Documentary History in the Early Reservation Years*. Tsaile, Ariz.: Navajo Community College Press, 1988.

Bodo, Murray, ed., *Tales of an Endishodi: Father Berard Haile and the Navajos, 1900–1961*. Albuquerque: University of New Mexico Press, 1998.

Bonar, Eulalie H., ed. *Woven by the Grandmothers: Nineteenth-Century Navajo Textiles from the National Museum of the American Indian*. Washington, D.C.: Smithsonian Institution Press, 1996.

Boyce, Grace. *When the Navajos Had Too Many Sheep*. San Francisco: Indian Historian Press, 1974.

Broder, Patricia Janis. *Shadows on Glass: The Indian World of Ben Wittick*. Savage, Md.: Rowland and Littlefield, 1990.

Brooks, James F. *Captives and Cousins: Slavery, Kinship and Community in the Southwest Borderlands*. Chapel Hill: University of Carolina Press, 2002.

————. "This Evil Extends Especially to the Feminine Sex: Captivity and Identity in New Mexico, 1700–1846." In Elizabeth Jameson and Susan Armitage, eds., *Writing the Range: Race, Class, and Culture in the Women's West*. Norman: University of Oklahoma Press, 1997.

————. "Violence, Justice, and State Power in the New Mexican Borderlands, 1780–1880." In Richard White and John M. Findlay, eds., *Power and Place in the North American West*. Seattle: University of Washington Press, 1999.

Brugge, David M. "Henry Chee Dodge: From the Long Walk to Self-Determination." In L. G. Moses and Raymond Wilson, eds., *Indian Lives: Essays on the Nineteenth and Twentieth Century Native American Leaders*. Albuquerque: University of New Mexico Press, 1985.

————. *Navajo Pottery and Ethnohistory*. Window Rock, Ariz.: Navajo Tribal Museum, Navajoland Publications, 1963.

————. "Navajo Prehistory and History to 1850." In Alfonso Ortiz ed., *Hand-*

book of the North American Indians: Southwest, vol. 10. Washington, D.C.: Smithsonian Press, 1983.

———. *The Navajo-Hopi Land Dispute: An American Tragedy*. Albuquerque: University of New Mexico Press, 1994.

———. *Navajos in the Catholic Church Records of New Mexico, 1694–1875*. Tsaile, Ariz.: Navajo Community College Press, 1985.

———, trans. "Vizcarra's Navajo Campaign of 1823." *Arizona and the West: A Quarterly Journal of History* 6, no. 3 (autumn 1964): 223–44.

Brumbaugh, Lee Phillip. "Shadow Catchers or Shadow Snatchers? Ethical Issue for Photographers of Contemporary Native Americans." *American Indian Culture and Research Journal* 20, no. 3 (1996): 33–50.

Bsumek, Erika Marie. "The Navajos as Borrowers: Stewart Culin and the Genesis of an Ethnographic Theory." *New Mexico Historical Review* 79, no. 3 (summer 2004): 319–51.

Buscombe, Edward. "Photographing the Indian." In Edward Buscombe and Roberta E. Pearson, eds., *Back in the Saddle Again: New Essays*. London: British Film Institute, 1998.

Bush, Alfred L., and Lee Clark Mitchell. *The Photograph and the American Indian*. Princeton: Princeton University Press, 1994.

Cajete, Gregory. *Look to the Mountain: An Ecology of Indigenous Education*. Durango, Colo.: Kivak Press, 1994.

Churchill, Ward. "Genocide in Arizona: The 'Navajo-Hopi Land Dispute' in Perspective." In *Struggle for the Land: Native North American Resistance to Genocide, Ecocide and Colonization*. San Francisco: City Lights, 2002.

Clifton, James, ed. *Being and Becoming Indian: Biographical Studies of Native American Frontiers*. Chicago: Dorsey Press, 1989.

Cohen, David William. "The Undefining of Oral Tradition." *Ethnohistory* 36 (winter 1989): 9–17.

Collman, Robert Christie. "Navajo Scouts, 1873–1895: An Integration of Various Cultural Interpretations of Events." Master's thesis, Franconia College, May 1975.

Conte, Christine. "Changing Woman Meets Madonna: Navajo Women's Networks and Sex-Gender Values in Transition." In Elizabeth Jameson and Susan Armitage, eds., *Writing the Range: Race, Class, and Culture in the Women's West*. Norman: University of Oklahoma Press, 1997.

Cook-Lynn, Elizabeth. *Why I Can't Read Wallace Stegner and Other Essays: A Tribal Voice*. Madison: University of Wisconsin Press, 1996.

Correll, J. Lee. "Antonio Sandoval, Navajo Leader." *Navajo Times*, October and November 1967.

———. "Navajo History: Manuelito." Unpublished manuscript. Navajo Nation Library, Navajo Land Claim Papers, Window Rock, Ariz.

————. "Manuelito, Navajo *Naat'anni*: About 1820 to 1894." *Navajo Times*, September 9, 1965.

————. *Through White Men's Eyes: A Contribution to Navajo History Vol. 2*. Window Rock, Ariz.: Navajo Heritage Center, 1979.

Coulter, Lane, ed., *Navajo Saddle Blankets: Textiles to Ride in the American West*. Santa Fe: Museum of New Mexico Press, 2002.

Cremony, John. *Life among the Apaches*. 1868. Reprint, New York: Indian Head Books, 1991.

Cruikshank, Julie. "Images of Society in Klondike Gold Rush Narratives: Skookum Jim and the Discovery of Gold." *Ethnohistory* 39 (winter 1992): 20–41.

————. "Negotiating with Narrative: Storytelling Festival." *American Anthropologist* 99, no. 1 (1997): 56–69.

————. *The Social Life of Stories: Narrative and Knowledge in the Yukon Territory*. Lincoln: University of Nebraska Press, 1998.

Davies, Wade. *Healing Ways: Navajo Health Care in the Twentieth Century*. Albuquerque: University of New Mexico Press, 2001.

Day, Sarah, ed. *Heart of the Circle: Photographs by Edward S. Curtis of Native American Women*. San Francisco: Pomegranate Artbooks, 1997.

Deloria, Philip J. *Indians in Unexpected Places*. Lawrence: University Press of Kansas, 2004.

Deloria, Vine, Jr. *Custer Died for Your Sins: An Indian Manifesto*. London: Collier-Macmillan, 1969.

————. *God is Red*. New York: Dell, 1983.

————. *Red Earth, White Lies: Native Americans and the Myth of Scientific Fact*. New York: Scribner, 1995.

Denetdale, Jennifer Nez. "Chairmen, Presidents, and Princesses: The Navajo Nation, Gender, and the Politics of Tradition." *Wicazo Sa Review* 21, no. 1 (spring 2006): 9–44.

————. "The Long Walk: A Response to an Amateur Historian." *Navajo Times*, March 8, 2001.

————. "Representing Changing Woman: A Review Essay on Navajo Women." *American Indian Culture and Research Journal* 25, no. 3 (2001): 1–26.

Dilworth, Leah. "Discovering Indians in Fred Harvey's Southwest." In Marta Weigle and Barbara A. Babcock, eds., *The Great Southwest of the Fred Harvey Company and the Santa Fe Railway*. Phoenix, Ariz.: Heard Museum, 1996.

————. *Imagining Indians in the Southwest: Persistent Visions of a Primitive Past*. Washington, D.C.: Smithsonian Institution Press, 1996.

Dippie, Brian. *Custer's Last Stand: The Anatomy of an American Myth*. Missoula: University of Montana Press, 1976.

———. *The Vanishing American: White Attitudes and U.S. Indian Policy.* Middletown, Conn.: Wesleyan University Press, 1982.

Dodge, Chee. "Between the United States Government and the Navajo Indian Tribe Back in 1846." *Albuquerque Journal,* January 1931.

Donovan, Bill. "Long Walk Steeped in Myths." *Gallup (N.M.) Independent,* January 30, 2001.

Duran, Bonnie. "Indigenous Versus Colonial Discourse: Alcohol and American Indian Identity." In S. Elizabeth Bird, ed., *Dressing in Feathers: The Construction of the Indian in American Popular Culture.* Boulder, Colo.: Westview Press, 1996.

Durham, Jimmie. "Geronimo!" In Lucy R. Lippard, ed., *Partial Recall: With Essays on Photographs of Native Americans.* New York: New Press, 1992.

Durkin, Pat. Introduction to Sara Day, ed., *Heart of the Circle: Photographs by Edward S. Curtis of Native American Women.* San Francisco: Pomegranate Artbooks, 1997.

Dyk, Walter. *Son of Old Man Hat: A Navaho Autobiography.* Lincoln: University of Nebraska Press, 1967.

Dyk, Walter, and Ruth Dyk, *Left Handed: A Navajo Autobiography.* New York: Columbia University Press, 1980.

Edmunds, R. David, ed. *American Indian Leaders: Studies in Diversity.* Lincoln: University of Nebraska Press, 1980.

———. "Native Americans, New Voices: American Indian History, 1895–1995." *American Historical Review* 100 (June 1995): 717–40.

Emerson, Gloria. Afterword to Katherine Spencer Halpern and Susan Brown McGreevy, eds., *Washington Matthews: Studies of Navajo Culture, 1880–1894.* Albuquerque: University of New Mexico Press, 1997.

Faris, James C. *Navajo and Photography: A Critical History of the Representation of an American People.* Albuquerque: University of New Mexico Press, 1996.

———. "The Navajo Photography of Edward S. Curtis." *History of Photography* 17 (winter 1993): 377–87.

———. "Photographing the Navajo: Scanning the Abuse." *American Indian Culture and Research Journal* 20 (1996): 65–81

———. "Some Observations on the Ethical Integrity of Washington Matthews in Navajo Research." In Katherine Spencer Halpern and Susan Brown McGreevy, eds., *Washington Matthews: Studies of Navajo Culture, 1880–1894.* Albuquerque: University of New Mexico Press, 1997.

———. "Taking Navajo Truths Seriously: The Consequences of the Accretions of Disbelief." In June-el Piper, ed., *Papers from the Third, Fourth, and Sixth Navajo Studies Conferences.* Window Rock, Ariz.: Navajo Nation Historic Preservation Department, 1993.

———. "Toward an Archaeology of Navajo Anthropology: Commentary on Anthropological Research in Navajo Land." In Regge N. Wiseman, Thomas C. O'Laughlin, and Cordelia T. Snow, eds., *Southwestern Interludes: Papers in Honor of Charlotte J. and Theodore R. Frisbie*, no. 32. Albuquerque: Archaeological Society of New Mexico, 2006.

Faris, James C., and Harry Walters. "Navajo History: Some Implications of Contrasts of Navajo Ceremonial Discourse." *History and Anthropology* 5 (1990): 1–18.

Finnegan, Ruth. "A Note on Oral Tradition and Historical Evidence." In David K. Dunaway and Willa K. Baum, eds., *Oral History: An Interdisciplinary Anthology*. Walnut Creek, Calif.: Alta Mira Press, 1996.

Fixico, Donald L., ed. *Rethinking American Indian History*. Albuquerque: University of New Mexico Press, 1997.

Fleming, Paula Richardson, and Judith Luskey. *Grand Endeavors of American Indian Photography*. Washington, D.C.: Smithsonian Institution Press, 1993.

———. *The North American Indians in Early Photographs*. New York: Dorset Press, 1986.

Fleischer, Matthew. "Navahoax." *LA Weekly*, January 23, 2006, http://www.laweekly.com/index.php?option=com_lawcontent&task=view&id=12468&Item.d=47.

Florescano, Enrique. *Memory, Myth, and Time in Mexico: From the Aztecs to Independence*. Trans. Albert G. Bork and Kathryn R. Bork. Austin: University of Texas Press, 1994.

Fogelson, Raymond D. "The Ethnohistory of Events and Nonevents." *Ethnohistory* 36 (spring 1989): 133–47.

Forbes, Jack. *Africans and Native Americans: The Language of Race and the Evolution of Red-Black Peoples*. Urbana: University of Illinois Press, 1993.

———. *Apache, Navajo, and Spaniard*. 1960. Reprint, Norman: University of Oklahoma Press, 1994.

Franciscan Fathers. *An Ethnologic Dictionary of the Navaho Language*. St. Michaels, Ariz.: Franciscan Fathers, 1910.

Francisco, Nia. *Blue Horses for Navajo Women*. New York: Greenfield Review Press, 1988.

Frazier, Lessie Jo. "Genre, Methodology and Feminist Practice." *Critique of Anthropology* 13, no. 4 (1993): 363–78.

Frisbie, Charlotte Johnson. *Kinaaldá: A Study of the Navaho Girl's Puberty Ceremony*. 1967. Reprint, Salt Lake City: University of Utah Press, 1993.

———. "Traditional Navajo Women: Ethnographic and Life History Portrayals." *American Indian Quarterly* 6 (spring/summer 1982): 11–33.

Fuchs, Estelle, and Robert J. Havighurst. *To Live on This Earth: American Indian Education*. Albuquerque: University of New Mexico Press, 1972.

Gonzales, Angela. "The (Re) Articulation of American Indian Identity: Maintaining Boundaries and Regulating Access to Ethnically Tied Resources." *American Indian Culture and Research Journal* 22 (1998): 199–225.

Gordon, Deborah. "Among Women: Gender and Ethnographic Authority of the Southwest, 1930–1980." In Nancy Parezo, ed., *Hidden Scholars: Women Anthropologists and the Native American Southwest*. Albuquerque: University of New Mexico Press, 1993.

Graham-Brown, Sarah. *Images of Women: The Portrayal of Women in Photography of the Middle East, 1860–1950*. London: Quartet Books, 1988.

Graves, Laura. *Thomas Varker Keam, Indian Trader*. Norman: University of Oklahoma Press, 1998.

Green Rayna. "Review Essay: Native American Women." *Signs: Journal of Women in Culture and Society* 6 (winter 1980): 248–67.

———. "The Pocahontas Perplex: The Image of Indian Women in American Cultures." In Susan Lobo and Steve Talbot, eds., *Native American Voices: A Reader*. New York: Longman, 1998.

Gregg, Josiah. *Commerce of the Prairies*, 2 vols. 1844. Reprint, Ann Arbor, Mich.: University Microfilms, 1966.

Grinde, Donald, and Bruce Johansen. "The Navajos and National Sacrifice." In A. Gabriel Meléndez, M. Jane Young, Patricia Moore, and Patrick Pynes, eds., *The Multicultural Southwest: A Reader*. Tucson: University of Arizona Press, 2001.

Haas, Jonathan. "Warfare among the Pueblos: Myth, History, and Ethnography." *Ethnohistory* 44 (spring 1997): 235–61.

Hagan, William T. *Indian Police and Judges: Experiments in Acculturation and Control*. Lincoln: University of Nebraska Press, 1966.

———. "The New Indian History." In Donald L. Fixico, ed., *Rethinking American Indian History*. Albuquerque: University of New Mexico Press, 1997.

Haile, Berard. *Origin Legend of the Navaho Enemyway*. Yale University Publication in Anthropology, no. 17. London: H. Milford, Oxford University Press, 1938.

———. *Starlore among the Navaho*. Santa Fe, N.M.: Museum of Navajo Ceremonial Art, 1947.

Haile, Berard, recorder. *Women versus Men: A Conflict of Navajo Emergence/ The Curly to Aheedliinii Version*. Edited by Karl W. Luckert. Lincoln: University of Nebraska Press, 1981.

Hales, Peter B. *William Henry Jackson and the Transformation of the American Landscape*. Philadelphia: Temple University Press, 1988.

Hall, Thomas D. "Global View of Local History." In *Teaching and Writing Local and Reservation: The Navajos*. Occasional Papers in Curriculum Series 19. Chicago: Newberry Library, 1995.

———. *Social Change in the Southwest, 1350–1880*. Lawrence: University of Kansas Press, 1989.

Halpern, Katherine Spencer, and Susan Brown McGreevy, eds. *Washington Matthews: Studies of Navajo Culture, 1880–1894*. Albuquerque: University of New Mexico Press, 1997.

Hamamsy, Laila Shukry. "The Role of Women in a Changing Navajo Society." *American Anthropologist* 59 (1957): 101–11.

Hartman, Wolfram, Jeremy Silvester, and Patricia Hayes, eds. *The Colonising Camera: Photographs in the Making of Namibian History*. Athens: Ohio University Press, 1999.

Hedlund, Ann Lane. "Give-and-Take: Navajo Grandmothers and the Role of Craftswoman." In Majorie M. Schweitzer, ed., *American Indian Grandmothers: Traditions and Transitions*. Albuquerque: University of New Mexico Press, 1999.

———. "'More Survival than an Art': Comparing Late Nineteenth- and Late Twentieth-Century Lifeways and Weaving." In Eulalie H. Bonar, ed., *Woven by the Grandmothers: Nineteenth-Century Navajo Textiles from the National Museum of the American Indian*. Washington, D.C.: Smithsonian Institution Press, 1996.

Hendricks, Rick, and John P. Wilson. *The Navajos in 1705: Roque Madrid's Campaign Journal*. Albuquerque: University of New Mexico Press, 1996.

Hill, Jonathan D., ed. *History, Power, and Identity: Ethnogenesis in the Americas, 1492–1992*. Iowa City: University of Iowa Press, 1996.

———. *Rethinking History and Myth: Indigenous South American Perspectives on the Past*. Urbana: University of Illinois Press, 1988.

Hill, Rick. "High-Speed Film Captures the Vanishing Americans in Living Color." *American Indian Culture and Research Journal* 20, no. 3 (1996): 111–28.

Hinsley, Curtis M. *The Smithsonian and the American Indian: Making a Moral Anthropology in Victorian America*. Washington, D.C.: Smithsonian Institution Press, 1981.

Hoffman, Virginia, and Broderick H. Johnson. *Navajo Biographies*. Rough Rock, Ariz.: Navajo Curriculum Center, 1970.

Holiday, John, and Robert S. McPherson. *A Navajo Legacy: The Life and Teachings of John Holiday*. Norman: University of Oklahoma Press, 2005.

Holman, Nigel. "Photography as Social and Economic Exchange: Understanding the Challenges Posed by Photography." *American Indian Culture and Research Journal* 20, no. 3(1996): 93–110.

hooks, bell. *Yearning: Race, Gender, and Cultural Politics*. Boston: South End Press, 1990.

Horsman, Reginald. *Race and Manifest Destiny: The Origins of American Racial Anglo-Saxonism*. Cambridge, Mass.: Harvard University Press, 1981.

Howard, Kathleen L. "Weaving a Legend: Elle of Ganado Promotes the Indian Southwest." *New Mexico Historical Review* 74, no. 2 (April 1999): 127–53.

Howard, O. O. *Famous Indians Chiefs I Have Known*. New York: Century, 1908.

Hoxie, Frederick E. "Ethnohistory for a Tribal World." *Ethnohistory* 44 (fall 1997): 595–615.

Hughes, John T. *Doniphan's Expedition: Continuing Account of the Conquest of New Mexico*. Cincinnati, Ohio: James, 1848.

Hymes, Dell. *In Vain I Tried to Tell You: Essays in Native American Ethnopoetics*. Philadelphia: University of Pennsylvania Press, 1981.

Iverson, Peter. "Continuity and Change in Navajo Culture: A Review Essay." *New Mexico Historical Review* (April 1987): 191–200.

———. *Diné: A History of the Navajo People*. Albuquerque: University of New Mexico Press, 2002.

———. *The Navajo Nation*. Westport, Conn.: Greenwood Press, 1981.

Jacknis, Ira. "Alfred Kroeber and the Photographic Representation of California Indians." *American Indian Culture and Research Journal* 20, no. 3 (1996): 15–32.

Jacobs, Margaret D. "Maternal Colonialism: White Women and Indigenous Child Removal in the American West and Australia, 1880–1940." *Western Historical Quarterly* 36, no. 1 (winter 2005): 453–76.

Jaimes, M. Annette. "American Racism: The Impact on American-Indian Identity and Survival." In Steven Gregory and Roger Sanjek, eds., *Race*. New Brunswick, N.J.: Rutgers University Press, 1994.

James, George Wharton. *Indian Blankets and Their Makers*. Chicago: A.C. McClurg, 1914.

———. *The Indians of the Painted Desert Region: Hopi, Navahoes, Willapais, Havasuapis*. Boston: Little, Brown, 1903.

———. *What the White Race May Learn from the Indian*. Chicago: Forbes, 1908.

Jim, Rex Lee. "A Moment in My Life." In Arnold Krupat and Brian Swann, eds., *Here First: Autobiographical Essays by Native American Writers*. New York: Modern Library, 2000.

Johansen, Bruce E., and Donald A. Grinde Jr., eds. *Encyclopedia of Native American Biography: Six Hundred Life Stories of Important People from Powhatan to Wilma Mankiller*. New York: Henry Holt, 1997.

Johnson, Broderick H., ed. *Navajo Stories of the Long Walk Period*. Tsaile, Ariz.: Navajo Community College Press, 1973.

———. *Navajo Stories of World War II*. Tsaile, Ariz.: Navajo Community College Press, 1977.

———. *Stories of Traditional Navajo Life and Culture*. Tsaile, Ariz.: Navajo Community College Press, 1977.

Johnson, Broderick H., and Ruth Roessel, eds., *Navajo Livestock Reduction: A National Disgrace*. Tsaile, Ariz.: Navajo Community College Press, 1974.

Johnson, Jim, ed. *Spirit Capture: Photographs from the National Museum of the American Indian*. Washington, D.C.: Smithsonian Institution Press, 1998.

Josephy, Alvin M. *The Patriot Chiefs: A Chronicle of American Indian Leadership*. New York: Viking Press, 1961.

Kammer, Jerry. *The Second Long Walk: The Navajo-Hopi Land Dispute*. Albuquerque: University of New Mexico Press, 1980.

Kehoe, Alice B. "The Shackles of Tradition." In Patricia Albers and Beatrice Medicine, eds., *The Hidden Half*. New York: University Press of America, 1983.

Kelley, Klara B., and Harris Francis. "Abalone Shell Buffalo People: Navajo Narrated Routes and Pre-Columbian Archaeological Sites." *New Mexico Historical Review* 78, no. 1 (winter 2003): 29–58.

———. *Navajo Sacred Places*. Bloomington: Indiana University Press, 1994.

Kelley, Klara B., and Peter M. Whiteley. *Navajoland: Family Settlement and Land Use*. Tsaile, Ariz.: Navajo Community College, 1989.

Kellogg, Susan. "Tenocha Mexica Women, 1500–1700." In Susan Schroeder, Stephanie Wood, and Robert Haskett, eds., *Indian Women in Early Mexico*. Norman: University of Oklahoma Press, 1997.

Kelly, Lawrence. *Navajo Roundup: Selected Correspondence of Kit Carson's Expedition against the Navajo, 1863–1865*. Boulder, Colo.: Pruett Publishing, 1970.

Klein, Kerwin Lee. *Frontiers of Historical Imagination: Narrating the European Conquest of Native America, 1890–1990*. Berkeley: University of California Press, 1999.

Kolodny, Annette. *The Lay of the Land: Metaphor as Experience and History in American Life and Letters*. Chapel Hill: University of North Carolina Press, 1975.

Krupat, Arnold, ed., *New Voices in Native American Literary Criticism*. Washington: Smithsonian Institution Press, 1993.

LaDuke, Winona. *All Our Relations: Native Struggles for Land and Life*. Cambridge, Mass.: South End Press, 1999.

Lamphere, Louise. "Gladys Reichard among the Navajo." In Nancy Parezo, ed., *Hidden Scholars: Women Anthropologists and the Native American Southwest*. Albuquerque: University of New Mexico Press, 1993.

Lavender, David. *The Southwest*. New York: Harper and Row, 1980.

Lee, Tiffany S. "'I Came Here to Learn How to Be a Leader': An Intersection of Critical Pedagogy and Indigenous Education." *InterActions: UCLA Journal of Education and Information Studies* 2, no. 2 (2006), http://repositories.cdlib.org/gseis/interactions/vol2/iss1/art3.

Leighton, Alexander. *Lucky the Navajo Singer*. Edited by Joyce J. Griffen. Albuquerque: University of New Mexico Press, 1992.

Leighton, Alexander H., and Dorothea C. Leighton. *Gregorio the Hand-Trembler: A Psychobiological Personality Study of a Navaho Indian.* Papers of the Peabody Museum of American Archaeology and Ethnology, vol. 40. Cambridge, Mass.: Harvard University Press, 1949.

Leonardo, Micaela di, ed. *Gender at the Crossroads of Knowledge: Feminist Anthropology in the Postmodern Era.* Berkeley: University of California Press, 1991.

Limerick, Patricia Nelson. *The Legacy of Conquest: The Unbroken Past of the American West.* New York: W.W. Norton, 1987.

Link, Martin. "The Long Walk and Academic Freedom." *Navajo Times,* April 5, 2001, A-4.

———, ed. *The Navajo Treaty—1868: Treaty between the United States of America and the Navajo Tribe of Indians/With a Record of the Discussions that Led to Its Signing.* Las Vegas, Nev.: K.C. Publications, 1968.

Lippard, Lucy R., ed. *Partial Recall: With Essays on Photographs of Native North Americans.* New York: New Press, 1992.

Lipps, Oscar H. *A Little History of the Navajos.* Albuquerque: Avanyu, 1989.

Locke, Raymond Friday. *The Book of the Navajo.* Los Angeles: Mankind Press, 1992.

Long, Paul V. *Big Eyes: The Southwestern Photographs of Simeon Schwemberger, 1902–1980.* Essay by Michele M. Penhall. Albuquerque: University of New Mexico Press, 1992.

Lyman, Christopher M. *The Vanishing Race and Other Illusions: Photographs of Indians by Edward S. Curtis.* Washington, D.C.: Smithsonian Institution Press, 1982.

Lyon, William H. "Gladys Reichard at the Frontiers of Navajo Culture." *American Indian Quarterly* 8 (spring 1989): 137–163.

———. "The Navajo Histories: The Surveys of the Navajo Past." *New Mexico Historical Review* (July 1993): 247–68.

———. "The Navajos in the American Historical Imagination, 1868–1900." *Ethnohistory* 45 (spring 1998): 237–75.

———. "The Navajos in the Anglo-American Historical Imagination, 1807–1870." *Ethnohistory* 43 (summer 1996): 483–509.

Malinowski, Sharon, ed., *Notable Native Americans.* New York: Gale Research, 1995.

Markowitz, Harvey. *American Indian Biographies.* Pasadena, Calif.: Salem Press, 1999.

Marr, Carolyn J. "Marking Oneself: Use of Photographs by Native Americans of the Southern Northwest Coast." *American Indian Culture and Research Journal* 20, no. 3 (1996):51–64.

Matthews, Washington. "The Cubature of the Skull." *Anthropological Society of Washington, Transactions* 3 (1885): 171–72.

————. "On Measuring the Cubic Capacity of Skulls." *Memoirs of the National Academy of Sciences* 3, pt. 2, (1886): 107–16.

Matthews, Washington, collector and trans. *Navaho Legends*. 1897. Reprint, Salt Lake City: University of Utah Press, 2002.

M'Closkey, Kathy. "Art or Craft: The Paradox of the Pangnirtung Weave Shop." In Christine Miller, Patricia Chuchryk, Brenda Manyfingers, Cheryl Deering, and Marie Smallface Marule, eds., *Women of the First Nations: Power, Wisdom and Strength*. Winnipeg: University of Manitoba Press, 1996.

————. "Marketing Multiple Myths: The Hidden History of Navajo Weaving." *Journal of the Southwest* 36 (autumn 1994): 185–220.

————. "'Part-Time for Pin Money': The Legacy of Navajo Women's Craft Productions." In Kimberly M. Grimes and B. Lynne Milgram, eds., *Artisans and Cooperatives: Developing Alternative Trade for the Global Economy*. Tucson: University of Arizona Press, 2000.

————. *Swept Under the Rug: The Hidden History of Navajo Weaving*, University of Arizona Southwest Center Series. Albuquerque: University of New Mexico Press, 2002.

————. "Weaving and Mothering: Reframing Navajo Weaving as Recursive Manifestations of K'e." In Suzan Ilcan and Lynne Phillips, eds., *Transgressing Borders: Critical Perspectives on Gender, Household, and Culture*. Westport, Conn.: Bergin and Garvey, 1998.

McCullough-Brabson, Ellen, and Marilyn Help. *We'll Be in Your Mountains, We'll Be in Your Songs: A Navajo Woman Sings*. Albuquerque: University of New Mexico Press, 2001.

McNitt, Frank. *Indian Traders*. Norman: University of Oklahoma Press, 1962.

————. *Navajo Wars: Military Campaigns, Slave Raids and Reprisals*. Albuquerque: University of New Mexico Press, 1990.

McPherson, Robert S. *The Journey of Navajo Oshley: An Autobiography and Life History*. Logan: Utah State University Press, 2000.

————. *Sacred Land, Sacred View: Navajo Perceptions of the Four Corners Region*. Provo, Utah: Brigham Young University, Charles Redd Center for Western Studies, 1992.

Merchant, Carolyn. *The Death of Nature: Women, Ecology, and the Scientific Revolution*. San Francisco: Harper and Row, 1980.

————. *Earthcare: Women and the Environment*. New York: Routledge, 1996.

Mintz, Sidney W. *Tasting Food, Tasting Freedom: Excursions into Eating, Culture, and the Past*. Boston: Beacon Press, 1996.

Mitchell, Frank. *Navajo Blessingway Singer: The Autobiography of Frank Mitchell, 1881–1967*. Edited by Charlotte J. Frisbie and David P. McAllester. Albuquerque: University of New Mexico Press, 1978.

Mitchell, Marie. *The Navajo Peace Treaty–1868.* New York: Mason and Lip-
    scomb, 1973.

Mitchell, Rose. *Tall Woman: The Life Story of Rose Mitchell, A Navajo Woman,
    c. 1874–1977.* Edited by Charlotte J. Frisbie. Albuquerque: University of
    New Mexico Press, 2001.

Mohanty, Chandra. "Under Western Eyes: Feminist Scholarship and Colonial
    Discourses." *Feminist Review* 30 (1988): 61–88.

Momaday, N. Scott. *The Man Made of Words: Essays, Stories, Passages.* New
    York: St. Martin's Press, 1997.

Moore, Laura Jane. "Elle Meets the President: Weaving Navajo Culture and
    Commerce in the Southwestern Tourist Industry." In Sandra K. Schackel,
    ed., *Western Women's Lives: Continuity and Change in the Twentieth Cen-
    tury.* Albuquerque: University of New Mexico Pres, 2003.

Moore, William Haas. *Chiefs, Agents, and Soldiers: Conflict on the Navajo
    Frontier, 1868–1882.* Albuquerque: University of New Mexico Press, 1994.

Morgan, Lewis H. *Ancient Society: Or, Research in the Lines of Human Prog-
    ress from Savagery through Barbarism to Civilization.* New York: H. Holt,
    1907.

Morris, Irvin. *From the Glittering World: A Navajo Story.* Norman: University
    of Oklahoma Press, 1997.

Morrissey, Katherine G., and Kirsten M. Jensen, eds. *Picturing Arizona: The
    Photographic Record of the 1930s.* Tucson: University of Arizona Press,
    2005.

Morrow, Phyllis, and William Schneider, eds., *When Our Words Return: Writ-
    ing, Hearing, and Remembering Oral Traditions of Alaska and the Yukon.*
    Logan: Utah State University Press, 1995.

Moses, L. G., and Raymond Wilson, eds. *Indian Lives: Essays on Nineteenth
    and Twentieth Century Native American Leaders.* Albuquerque: Univer-
    sity of New Mexico Press, 1985.

Murphy, Lawrence R. *Frontier Crusader—William F. M. Arny.* Tucson: Uni-
    versity of Arizona Press, 1972.

Nabokov, Peter. "Native Views of History." In Bruce G. Trigger and Wilcomb
    E. Washburn, eds., *The Cambridge History of the Native Peoples of the
    Americas*, North America Volume 1, Part 1. New York: Cambridge Uni-
    versity Press, 1996.

Nagel, Joane. "American Indian Ethnic Renewal: Politics and Resurgence of
    Identity." *American Sociological Review* 60 (1995): 947–65.

Nasdijj, *The Blood Runs Like a River through My Dreams: A Memoir.* Boston:
    Houghton Mifflin, 2000.

———. *The Boy and Dog Are Sleeping.* New York: Ballantine Books, 2003.

———. *Geronimo's Bones: A Memoir of My Brother and Me.* New York: Bal-
    lantine Books, 2004.

Naylor, Celia. "Playing Indian? The Selection of Radmilla Cody as Miss Navajo Nation 1997–98." In Sharon P. Holland and Tiya Miles, eds., *Crossing Waters, Crossing Worlds: The African Diaspora in Indian Country*. Durham: N.C.: Duke University Press, 2006.

Oakes, Maude, ed. *Where the Two Came to Their Father: A Navaho War Ceremonial Given by Jeff King Bollingen*, Series 1. 1943. Reprint Princeton: Princeton University Press, 1969.

O'Bryan, Aileen. *Navaho Indian Myths*. 1956. Reprint, New York: Dover, 1993.

O'Neill, Colleen. "The 'Making' of the Navajo Worker: Navajo Households, the Bureau of Indian Affairs, and Off-Reservation Wage Work, 1948–1960." *New Mexico Historical Review* 74, no. 4 (October 1999): 375–403.

———. "Rethinking Modernity and the Discourse of Development in American Indian History: An Introduction." In Brian Hosmer and Colleen O'Neill, eds., *Native Pathways: American Indian Culture and Economic Development in the Twentieth Century*. Boulder: University Press of Colorado, 2005.

———. *Working the Navajo Way: Labor and Culture in the Twentieth Century*. Lawrence: University Press of Kansas, 2005.

Ortiz, Simon J. *Beyond the Reach of Time and Change: Native American Reflections on the Frank A. Rinehart Photograph Collection*. Tucson: University of Arizona Press, 2004.

———. *Woven Stone*. Tucson: University of Arizona Press, 1992.

Owens, Louis. *Mixedblood Messages: Literature, Film, Family, Place*. Norman: University of Oklahoma Press, 1998.

Packard, Gar, and Maggy Packard. *Southwest 1880 with Ben Wittick: Pioneer Photographer of Indian and Frontier Life*. Santa Fe: Packard Publications, 1970.

Parezo, Nancy J., ed. *Hidden Scholars: Women Anthropologists and the Native American Southwest*. Albuquerque: University of New Mexico Press, 1993.

Parman, Donald L. *The Navajos and the New Deal*. New Haven, Conn.: Yale University Press, 1976.

Parsons, Evangeline. *Dzání Yázhí Naazbaa': Little Woman Warrior Who Came Home*. Flagstaff, Ariz.: Salina Bookshelf, 2005.

Pavlik, Steve. "A Short History of Navajo Education, Part I." *Journal of Navajo Education* 2 (winter 1985): 25–34.

Perdue, Diana F., and Kathleen L. Howard. "Making Art, Making Money: The Fred Harvey Company and the Indian Artisan." In Marta Weigle and Barbara A. Babcock, eds., *The Great Southwest of the Fred Harvey Company and the Santa Fe Railway*. Phoenix, Ariz.: Heard Museum, 1996.

Perdue, Theda. *Cherokee Women: Gender and Culture Change, 1700–1835*. Lincoln: University of Nebraska Press, 1998.

———. "Women, Men and American Indian Policy: The Cherokee Response to 'Civilization.'" In Nancy Shoemaker, ed., *Negotiators of Change: Historical Perspectives on Native Women*. New York: Routledge, 1995.

———. "Writing the Ethnohistory of Native Women." In Donald L. Fixico, ed., *Rethinking American Indian History*. Albuquerque: University of New Mexico Press, 1997.

Pinney, Christopher, and Nicolas Peterson, eds. *Photography's Other Histories*. Durham, N.C.: Duke University Press, 2003.

Powers, Willow Roberts. "Images across Boundaries: History, Use, and Ethics of Photographs of American Indians." *American Indian Culture and Research Journal* 20, no. 3 (1996): 129–36.

Pratt, Kenneth J. "Some Navajo Relations to the Past." In June-el Piper, ed., *Papers from the Third, Fourth, and Sixth Navajo Studies Conference*. Window Rock, Ariz.: Navajo Nation Historic Preservation Department, 1993.

Rael-Gálvez, Estévan. "Identifying Captivity and Capturing Identity: Narratives of American Indian Slavery/Colorado and New Mexico, 1776–1934." Ph.D. diss., University of Michigan, 2002.

———. "Testifying to the Present Tense of American Indian Slavery: Reading and Writing From Representation to Recovery." Paper presented School of American Research seminar, Santa Fe, N.M., April 2004.

Rappaport, Joanne. *The Politics of Memory: Native Historical Interpretation in the Colombian Andes*. New York: Cambridge University Press, 1990.

Reeve, Frank. "Early Navajo Geography." *New Mexico Historical Review* 31 (October 1956): 290–309.

———. "The Navaho-Spanish Peace: 1720s–1770s." *New Mexico Historical Review* 34 (January 1959): 9–40.

———. "Navajo-Spanish Diplomacy, 1770–1790." *New Mexico Historical Review* 35 (July 1960): 200–35.

———. "Seventeenth Century Navaho-Spanish Relations." *New Mexico Historical Review* 32 (January 1957): 36–52.

Regan, Margaret. "Paper Faces: Photographs of Navajos and Hopis." In Katherine G. Morrissey and Kirsten M. Jensen, eds., *Picturing Arizona: The Photographic Record of the 1930s*. Tucson: University of Arizona Press, 2005.

Reichard, Gladys A. *Dezba: Woman of the Desert*. 1931. Reprint, Glorieta, N.M.: Rio Grande Press, 1971.

———. *Navaho Grammar*. New York: Augustin, 1951.

———. *Navaho Religion: A Study of Symbolism*. New York: Pantheon Books, 1963.

———. *Navajo Shepherd and Weaver*. New York: J.J. Augustin, 1936.

———. *Prayer: The Compulsive Word*. New York: J.J. Augustin, 1944.

———. *Social Life of the Navajo Indians*. Columbia University Contributions to Anthropology, vol. 7 (1928).

————. *Spider Woman: A Story of Navajo Weavers and Chanters.* 1934. Reprint, Glorieta, N.M.: Rio Grande Press, 1968.

Robbins, David. "The American Indian and the American Flag." *American Indian Art Magazine* 2, no. 1 (winter 1976): 28, 57.

Roessel, Monty. "Navajo Photography." *American Indian Culture and Research Journal* 20, no. 3 (1996): 83–92.

Roessel, Robert A., Jr. *Navajo Education, 1948–1978: Its Progress and Its Problems. Navajo History*, vol. 3, part A. Rough Rock, Ariz.: Navajo Curriculum Center, Rough Rock Demonstration School, 1979.

————. *Pictorial History of the Navajo from 1860 to 1910.* Rough Rock, Ariz: Navajo Curriculum Center, Rough Rock Demonstration School, 1980.

Roessel, Ruth. *Women in Navajo Society.* Rough Rock, Ariz.: Navajo Resource Center, 1981.

Rosaldo, Renato. "Imperialist Nostalgia." *Representations* 26 (spring 1989): 107–22.

Ross, Luana. "Personalizing Methodology: Narratives of Imprisoned Native Women." In Inéz Hernández-Avila, ed., *Reading Native American Women: Critical/Creative Representations.* Lanham, Md.: Alta Mira Press, 2005.

Said, Edward S. *Culture and Imperialism.* New York: Vintage Books, 1994.

————. *Orientalism.* New York: Vintage Books, 1979.

Sando, Joe S. *Pueblo Nations: Eight Centuries of Pueblo Indian History.* Santa Fe, N.M.: ClearLight, 1992.

Sandweiss, Martha A. *Print the Legend: Photography and the American West.* New Haven, Conn.: Yale University Press, 2002.

Sarris, Greg. "The Woman Who Loved a Snake: Orality in Mabel McKay's Stories." In John L. Purdy and James Ruppert, eds., *Nothing But the Truth: An Anthology of Native American Literature.* Upper Saddle River, N.J.: Prentice-Hall, 2001.

Schlissel, Lillian, Vicki L. Ruiz, and Janice Monk, eds. *Western Women: Their Land, Their Lives.* Albuquerque: University of New Mexico Press, 1988.

Scott, Joan Wallach. *Gender and the Politics of History.* New York: Columbia University Press, 1988.

Shepardson, Mary. "The Status of Navajo Women." *American Indian Quarterly* 6 (spring/summer 1982): 149–69.

Sheridan, Thomas E., and Nancy Parezo. *Paths of Life: American Indians of the Southwest and Northern Mexico.* Tucson: University of Arizona Press, 1996.

Slotkin, Richard. *Regeneration through Violence: The Mythology of the American Frontier, 1600–1860.* Middletown, Conn.: Wesleyan University Press, 1978.

Smith, Andrea. *Conquest: Sexual Violence and American Indian Genocide.* Cambridge, Mass.: South End Press, 2005.

————. "Rape and the War against Native Women." In Inés Hernández-Avila, ed., *Reading Native American Women: Critical/Creative Representations*. New York: Alta Mira Press, 2005.

Smith, Linda Tuhiwai. *Decolonizing Methodologies: Research and Indigenous Peoples*. New York: St. Martin's Press, 1999.

Smith-Rosenberg, Carroll. "Captured Subjects/Savage Others: Violently Engendering the New American." *Gender and History* 5 (summer 1993): 177–95.

Smits, David D. "'The Squaw Drudge': A Prime Index of Savagism." *Ethnohistory* 29, no. 4 (1982): 281–306.

Sontag, Susan. *On Photography*. New York: Farrar, Straus and Giroux, 1977.

Sparks, Carol Douglas. "Anglo-American Perceptions of the Navajo: 1807–1857." Ph.D. diss., Northern Arizona University, 1990.

————. "The Land Incarnate: Navajo Women and the Dialogue of Colonialism, 1821–1870." In Nancy Shoemaker, ed., *Negotiators of Change: Historical Perspectives on Native Women*. New York: Routledge, 1995.

Spencer, Katherine Halpern, and Susan Brown McGreevy, eds. *Washington Matthews: Studies of Navajo Culture, 1880–1894*. Albuquerque: University of New Mexico Press, 1997.

Spicer, Edward H. *Cycles of Conquest: The Impact of Spain, Mexico, and the United States on the Indians of the Southwest, 1533–1960*. Tucson: University of Arizona Press, 1962.

Stevenson, Winona Lu-Ann. "Calling Badger and the Symbols of the Spirit Languages: The Cree Origins of the Syllabic System." *Oral History Forum* 19–20 (1999–2000): 19–24.

————. "Decolonizing Tribal Histories." Ph.D. diss., University of California, Berkeley, 2000.

————. "Every Word Is a Bundle: Cree Intellectual Traditions and History." Paper presented at the Western History Association meetings, Sacramento, Calif., October 15, 1998.

————. "Narrative Wisps of the Ochekwi Sipi Past: A Journey in Recovering Collective Memories." *Oral History Forum* 19–20 (1999–2000): 113–25.

Stewart, Irene. *A Voice in Her Tribe: A Navajo Woman's Own Story*. Socorro, N.M.: Ballena Press, 1980.

Stoler, Ann Laura. "Carnal Knowledge and Imperial Power: Gender, Race, and Morality in Colonial Asia." In Micaela di Leonardo, ed., *Gender at the Crossroads of Knowledge: Feminist Anthropology in the Postmodern Era*. Berkeley: University of California Press, 1991.

Strong, Pauline Turner. "Transforming Outsiders: Captivity, Adoption, and Slavery Reconsidered." In Philip J. Deloria and Neal Salisbury, eds., *A Companion to American Indian History*. Malden, Mass.: Blackwell, 2004.

Sundberg, Lawrence D. *Dinétah: An Early History of the Navajo People*. Santa Fe, N.M.: Sunstone Press, 1995.

Swann, Brian, ed. *Coming to Light: Contemporary Translations of Native Literature of Native Americans*. New York: Random House, 1994.

———. *Native American Songs and Prose: An Anthology*. New York: Dover, 1994.

———. *Smoothing the Ground: Essays on Native American Oral Literature*. Berkeley: University of California Press, 1983.

Tapahonso, Luci. *Blue Horses Rush In: Poems and Stories*. Tucson: University of Arizona Press, 1997.

———. *A Breeze Swept Through*. Albuquerque: West End Press, 1987.

———. *Sáanii Dahataał: The Women Are Singing*. Tucson: University of Arizona Press, 1993.

Terrell, John Upton. *The Navajos: The Past and Present of a Great People*. New York: Weybright and Talley, 1970.

Textiles of the North American Southwest. http://smithsonianeducation.org/lidealabs/textiles/english/cataloh/eo16494.htm.

Thompson, Gerald. *The Army and the Navajo*. Tucson: University of Arizona Press, 1976.

Thompson, Hildegard. *The Navajos' Long Walk for Education: A History of Navajo Education*. Tsaile, Ariz.: Navajo Community Press, 1975.

Tohe, Laura. *No Parole Today*. Albuquerque, N.M.: West End Press, 1999.

Towner, Ronald. *Defending the Dinétah: Pueblitos in the Ancestral Navajo Heartland*. Salt Lake City: University of Utah Press, 2003.

Trafzer, Clifford E. *Anglo Expansionists and Navajo Raiders: A Conflict of Interest*. Historical Monograph No. 3. Tsaile, Ariz.: Navajo Community College Press, 1978.

———. *The Kit Carson Campaign: The Last Great Navajo War*. Norman: University of Oklahoma Press, 1982.

Trask, Haunani-Kay. *From a Native Daughter: Colonialism and Sovereignty in Hawai'i*. Honolulu: University of Hawai'i Press, 1999.

Trennert, Robert A. *White Man's Medicine: Government Doctors and the Navajo, 1863–1955*. Albuquerque: University of New Mexico Press, 1998.

Trouillot, Michel-Rolph. *Silencing the Past: Power and the Production of History*. Boston: Beacon Press, 1995.

Tsosie, Rebecca. "Changing Women: The Crosscurrents of American Indian Feminine Identity." In Vicki L. Ruiz and Ellen Carol DuBois, eds., *Unequal Sisters: A Multicultural Reader in U.S. Women's History*. New York: Routledge, 2000.

Turner, Frederick Jackson. "The Significance of the Frontier in American History." *Annual Report of the American Association for the Year 1893*. Washington, D.C.: Government Printing Office, 1894.

Udel, Lisa J. "Revision and Resistance: The Politics of Native Women's Motherword." *Frontiers* 22, no. 3 (June 2001): 43–64.

Underhill, Ruth Murray. *Here Come the Navaho! A History of the Largest Tribe in the United States.* Lawrence, Kans.: U.S. Department of the Interior, 1953.

———. *The Navajos.* Norman: University of Oklahoma Press, 1965.

U.S. Office of Indian Affairs. *Annual Report of the Commissioner of Indian Affairs for the Year 1884.* Washington, D.C.: Government Printing Office, 1884.

Utter, Jack. "The Death of a Navajo Patriot—And his Ties to Federal Recognition, Treaty Rights, the Trust Relationship, and the San Juan Water Settlement." Unpublished paper in author's possession, August 3, 2004.

Vansina, Jan. *Oral Tradition as History.* Madison: University of Wisconsin Press, 1985.

Van Valkenburgh, Richard. *Dine Bikeyah.* Window Rock, Ariz.: Department of the Interior, Offices of Indian Affairs, Navajo Service, 1941.

———. "The History of the Navajo Nation." MS 831 Box 4, S2, File 111, Richard Van Valkenburgh Papers, 1880–1946, Arizona Historical Society, Tucson, Ariz.

———. "Last Powow of the Navajo." *Desert Magazine,* November 1946, 4–7.

———. "Massacre in the Mountains," *Desert Magazine,* February 1943, 18–22.

———. "Navajo Naat'aáni." *The Kiva* 13, no. 2 (January 1948): 13–23.

———. *A Short History of the Navajo People, Navajo Indians III.* New York: Garland, 1974.

Viola, Herman J. *Diplomats in Buckskins: A History of Indian Delegations in Washington City.* 1981. Reprint, Bluffton, S.C.: Rivilo Books, 1995.

Wall, Leon, and William Morgan. *Navajo-English Dictionary.* 1958. Reprint, New York: Hippocrene Books, 1994.

Warrior, Robert Allen. *Tribal Secrets: Recovering American Indian Intellectual Traditions.* Minneapolis: University of Minnesota Press, 1995.

Washburn, Wilcomb. "The Writing of American Indian History: A Status Report." *Pacific Historical Review* 40 (August 1971): 261–81.

Waters, Frank. *Brave Are My People: Indian Heroes Not Forgotten.* Santa Fe, N.M.: Clear Light, 1993.

Watt, Eva Tulene. *Don't Let the Sun Step Over You: A White Mountain Apache Family Life, 1860–1975.* With assistance from Keith H. Basso. Tucson: University of Arizona Press, 2004.

Weber, David J. *Foreigners in Their Native Land: Historical Roots of the Mexican Americans.* Albuquerque: University of New Mexico Press, 1973.

———. *The Mexican Frontier, 1821–1846: The American Southwest under Mexico.* Albuquerque: University of New Mexico Press, 1982.

———. *New Spain's Northern Frontier: Essays on Spain in the American West, 1540–1821.* Albuquerque: University of New Mexico Press, 1979.

Weigle, Marta, and Barbara A. Babcock, eds. *The Great Southwest of the Fred Harvey Company and the Santa Fe Railway*. Phoenix, Ariz.: Heard Museum, 1996.

Weisiger, Marsha. "Changing Women: Navajo Women and Livestock Reduction." Paper presented at the Western History Association conference, Scottsdale, Arizona, October 2005.

———. *Dreaming of Sheep in Navajo Country*. Seattle: University of Washington Press, forthcoming.

———. "The Origins of Navajo Pastoralism." *Journal of the Southwest* 46, no. 2 (summer 2004): 253–82.

Wexler, Laura. *Tender Violence: Domestic Visions in an Age of U.S. Imperialism*. Chapel Hill: University of North Carolina Press, 2000.

Wheeler, Winona. "Indigenous Oral History in the Academy—A Report on Works in Progress." Lecture given at the Native Historians' College, Scottsdale, Arizona, October 13, 2005.

———. "Talking Back to Columbus: Indigenous Oral History in the Academy." Lecture given at Arizona State University, October 12, 2005.

Whitaker, Kathleen. *Common Threads: Pueblo and Navajo Textiles in the Southwest Museum*. Los Angeles: Southwest Museum, 1998.

———. *Southwest Textiles: Weavings of the Navajo and Pueblo*. Seattle: University of Washington Press, 2002.

White, Hayden. *Tropics of Discourse: Essays in Cultural Criticism*. Baltimore: Johns Hopkins University Press, 1978.

White, Richard. *It's Your Misfortune and None of My Own: A New History of the American West*. Norman: University of Oklahoma Press, 1992.

———. *Roots of Dependency: Subsistence, Environment and Social Change among the Choctaws, Pawnees, and the Navajos*. Lincoln: University of Nebraska Press, 1983.

Wilkins, David E. *The Navajo Political Experience*. Tsaile, Ariz.: Diné College Press, 1999.

Wilkinson, Charles. *Fire on the Plateau: Conflict and Endurance in the American Southwest*. Washington, D.C.: Island Press, 2004.

Williams, Carol J. *Framing the West: Race, Gender, and the Photographic Frontier in the Pacific Northwest*. New York: Oxford University Press, 2003.

Williams, Lester L. *C. N. Cotton and His Navajo Blankets*. Albuquerque, N.M., Avanyu, 1989.

Williamson, Judith. "Family, Education, Photography." In Nicholas B. Dirks, Geoff Eley, and Sherry B. Ortner, eds., *Culture/Power/History: A Reader in Contemporary Social Theory*. Princeton, N.J.: Princeton University Press, 1994.

Willink, Roseann Sandoval, and Paul Zolbrod. *Weaving a World: Textiles and the Navajo Way of Seeing*. Santa Fe: Museum of New Mexico Press, 1996.

Wilson, Angela Cavender. "American Indian History or Non-Indian Percep-
    tions of American Indian History?" In Devon A. Mihesuah, ed., *Natives
    and Academics: Researching and Writing about American Indians*. Lincoln:
    University of Nebraska Press, 1998.

———. "Grandmother to Granddaughter: Generations of Oral History in
    a Dakota Family." In Devon A. Mihesuah, ed., *Natives and Academics:
    Researching and Writing about American Indians*. Lincoln: University of
    Nebraska Press, 1998.

———. "Power of the Spoken Word: Native Oral Traditions in American
    Indian History." In Donald L. Fixico, ed., *Rethinking American Indian
    History*. Albuquerque: University of New Mexico Press, 1997.

———. "Walking Into the Future: Dakota Oral Tradition and the Shaping
    of Historical Consciousness." *Oral History Forum* 19–20 (1999–2000):
    25–36.

Wilson, Garth A. *Conversational Navajo Dictionary: English to Navajo*. Bland-
    ing, Utah: Conversational Navajo Publications, 1989.

Wilson, Waziyatawin Angela. "Reclaiming Our Humanity." In Devon Mihe-
    suah and Angela Cavender Wilson, eds., *Indigenizing the Academy: Trans-
    forming Scholarship and Empowering Communities*. Lincoln: University
    of Nebraska Press, 2004.

———. *Remember This! Dakota Decolonization and the Eli Taylor Narratives*.
    Lincoln: University of Nebraska Press, 2005.

Witherspoon, Gary. *Navajo Kinship and Marriage*. Chicago: University of
    Chicago Press, 1975.

Wolf, Eric. *Europe and the People without History*. Berkeley: University of
    California Press, 1982.

Womack, Craig S. *Red on Red: Native American Literary Separatism*. Minne-
    apolis: University of Minnesota Press, 1999.

Yazzie, Ethelou. *Navajo History*. Chinle, Ariz.: Navajo Curriculum Center,
    Rough Rock Demonstration School, 1971.

Yellow Bird, Michael. "Cowboys and Indians: Toys of Genocide, Icons of
    American Colonialism." *Wicazo Sa Review* 19, no. 2 (fall 2004): 33–48.

Young, Robert. *The Role of the Navajo in the Southwest Drama*. Gallup, N.M.:
    Gallup Independent and the *Navajo Tribune*, 1968.

Zolbrod, Paul. *Diné Bahane': The Navajo Creation Story*. Albuquerque: Uni-
    versity of New Mexico Press, 1984.

———. *Reading the Voice: Native American Oral Poetry on the Page*. Salt Lake
    City: University of Utah Press, 1995.

———. "Squirrel Reddens His Cheeks: Cognition, Recognition, and Poetic
    Production in the Ancient Navajo Stories." *Journal of the Southwest* 46,
    no. 4 (winter 2004): 679–704.

Figure Credits

Arizona Historical Society/Tucson

Figure 7. Manuelito and Juanita, 1881. (Photograph by Ben Wittick; neg. no. 30333)

Autry National Center, Southwest Museum, Los Angeles; George Wharton James Collection

Figure 9. Dághá Ch'íí Bik'is and his wife, Ałk'iníbaa, 1902. (Photograph by George Wharton James; N.42550 LS.745)

Figure 10. Dághá Ch'íí doo be Asdzáá, Dłíhaazbaa', and George Manuelito, 1902. (Photograph by George Wharton James; neg. no. PS.10153, N.42553, LS.727)

Figure 11. The Manuelito family, 1902. (Photograph by George Wharton James; neg. no. P.10153, N.42549)

Figure 12. "Manuelito's widow," Juanita, 1902. (Photograph by George Wharton James; neg. no. P.10159)

Family photographs

Figure 13. Dághá Chíí and his granddaughter, Marie Dennison (Benally), ca. 1938.

Figure 14. Juanita's granddaughter, Dłíhaazbaa', ca. 1939.

Figure 16. Billboard near Gallup, New Mexico, 1996. (Photograph by Gwen Saul)

Figure 17. Arthur and Theresa Holyan, 1997. (Photograph by Cate Gilles)

Figure 18. Charles and Esther Manuelito, 1997. (Photograph by Cate Gilles)

Figure 19. Rose Nez, Joan Kinsel, and Jennifer Nez Denetdale, 1997. (Photograph by Cate Gilles)

Figure 20. Faye Yazzie, 1997. (Photograph by Cate Gilles)

Figure 21. Juanita's dress in the Southwest Museum, 1998.

Figure 22. Mike Sr. and Anna Allison, 2002. (Photograph by Nancy Allison)

Figure 23. Nelson and Helena Bitsilly, 2006. (Photograph by Alex Nez)

Library of Congress, Prints and Photographs Division

Figure 8. Asdzáá Tł'ógi with her family, 1902. (Photograph by George Wharton James; neg. no. LC-USZ62-8962)

National Anthropological Archives, Smithsonian Institution

Figure 2. Juanita, or Asdzáá Tł'ógi, 1868. (Neg. no. 55,770)

Figure 3. Manuelito, Juanita, and their son, 1868. (Neg. no. 55,769)

Figure 4. Juanita (Asdzáá Tł'ógi), Washington, D.C., 1874. (Photograph by Charles Bell; neg. no. GN 02391)

Figure 5. Juanita with William F. Arny, 1874. (Neg. no. GN 02405)

Figure 6. The Navajo delegation, Washington, D.C., 1874. (Inv. 01007800)

National Archives

Figure 15. Naltsoos Neiyéhí with his daughter and grandson. (Photo no. 75-N-NAV-N09-206)

New Mexico State Records Center and Archives, Santa Fe, New Mexico

Figure 1. Group that includes Manuelito (sitting) and wife, ca. 1868. (McNitt Photograph Collection, image no. 5849)

Index

About the Author

Jennifer Nez Denetdale is Diné of the Navajo Nation and of the Tł'ógi (Zia) and 'Áshiihí (Salt) clans. Originally from Tohatchi, New Mexico, she earned her Ph.D. in history from Northern Arizona University in 1999. An associate professor of history at the University of New Mexico, Denetdale will join the faculty of the Department of History at Northern Arizona University in the fall of 2008.

Her book for young adults, *The Long Walk: The Forced Navajo Exile*, was published by Chelsea House in 2008. She has also published articles in the *American Indian Culture and Research Journal*, the *Journal of Social Archaeology, Wicazo Sa Review*, and *New Mexico Historical Review*. She is currently working on a history of Navajo women.